"It is rare to find a work that blends epistemological, hermeneutical and historiographic sophistication with mature handling of the extensive primary and secondary literature, but this is such a work. Padilla's introduction to questions of the authorship and genre of Acts and the character of its speeches is a superbly informed and trustworthy guide."

Craig Keener, F. M. and Ada Thompson Professor of Biblical Studies, Asbury Theological Seminary

"This study of the book of Acts presents Luke not only as author but also as exemplary historian, storyteller and theologian. Luke's three-stranded cord of authorial discourse is on conspicuous display in his composition of Peter's, Stephen's, Philip's and Paul's speeches. Where other textbooks often focus on the narratives in Acts (e.g., Pentecost) and the practices of the early church, Padilla highlights the speeches in Acts and their continuing significance, going beyond the call of New Testament duty by dialoguing with postliberal theologians and asking whether they can do justice to the speeches in Acts and in particular their truth claims. The result is an introductory text that not only illumines the book of Acts, but also encourages Christians today to 'act out the acts of the apostles' (John Donne), to speak out their speech acts."

Kevin J. Vanhoozer, research professor of systematic theology, Trinity Evangelical Divinity School

"Osvaldo Padilla has put students and professors in his debt with this lucid and wide-ranging 'advanced introduction' to Acts. He shows a fine grasp of Acts itself and the extensive scholarly discussion over the last two hundred years. He identifies the key points at issue in the debates and provides accessible and well-thought-out assessments that guide readers clearly through the forest of opinions. He addresses issues that particularly concern readers who hold a 'high view' of Scripture and want to relate historical claims to faith. His concluding chapter, engaging with the justification of truth claims as expounded in post-liberalism, is fresh and provocative, showing a thoughtful and nuanced understanding of the claims that Acts makes as part of Christian Scripture. A valuable and helpful book."

Steve Walton, St. Mary's University, Twickenham, London

The Acts of
the Apostles

Interpretation, History and Theology

Osvaldo Padilla

APOLLOS (an imprint of Inter-Varsity Press)
36 Causton Street, London SW1P 4ST, England
Email: ivp@ivpbooks.com
Website: www.ivpbooks.com

First published 2016

British Library Cataloguing-in-Publication Data
A catalogue record for this book is available from the British Library

ISBN: 978-1-78359-427-6

Typeset in the United States of America

Inter-Varsity Press publishes Christian books that are true to the Bible and that communicate the gospel, develop discipleship and strengthen the church for its mission in the world.

IVP originated within the Inter-Varsity Fellowship, now the Universities and Colleges Christian Fellowship, a student movement connecting Christian Unions in universities and colleges throughout Great Britain, and a member movement of the International Fellowship of Evangelical Students. Website: www.uccf.org.uk. That historic association is maintained, and all senior IVP staff and committee members subscribe to the UCCF Basis of Faith.

Para Kristen: Con todo mi amor

CONTENTS

Acknowledgments 9

Abbreviations 11

Introduction 13

1 Who Wrote Acts? 21

    Who Was Luke? 22

    How Important Is the Identity of the Author to Interpret Acts? 31

    Conclusion 36

2 The Genre of Acts 39

    A Brief History of Genre Theory 43

    Proposals on the Genre of Acts 52

    Conclusion—Acts as Historical Monograph: How Does It Help? 72

3 How Luke Writes History 75

    Luke the Theological Historian 76

    Luke the Storyteller 88

    Luke the Historian 107

    Conclusion 120

4 The Speeches in Acts (Part One): The Speeches in
Their Ancient Context 123

    The Reporting of Speeches in Ancient History 124

    Luke as a Conservative Reporter of Speeches 138

    Conclusion: Believing the Speeches 146

5 The Speeches in Acts (Part Two): The Theology of the Speeches 151

    The Speech of Peter at Pentecost (Acts 2:1-41) 152

    The Speech of Stephen (Acts 7:1-53) 161

    The Speech at the Home of Cornelius (Acts 10:34-48) 168

    The Speech at Athens (Acts 17:16-31) 177

    The Speech Before Agrippa (Acts 26:1-32) 189

    Summary and Conclusions 195

**6 The Justification of Truth-Claims in Acts: A Conversation
with Postliberalism**   199

Postliberalism: A Sketch   202

Postliberalism and the Question of Truth-Claims   210

The Justification of Truth-Claims in Acts   224

Conclusions   236

Bibliography   245

Author Index   259

Subject Index   261

Scripture Index   262

ACKNOWLEDGMENTS

The work at hand is the result of approximately ten years of interest, reading, research and prayer over the Acts of the Apostles. As such, there are many to mention who at one point or another have encouraged, supported (financially and otherwise), corrected and guided.

My colleagues at Beeson Divinity School of Samford University have allowed me often to interrupt their own research as I sought their guidance in one area or another. I am particularly grateful to Frank Thielman, Paul House and Mark Gignilliat. Associate Dean David Hogg has been a model of pastoral care and friendship. His support and guidance have been invaluable. Dean Timothy George has constantly supported my work and offered wise counsel. I am also grateful to two research assistants, Fred Senko and Nic Seaborn, for their help with the bibliography. I am also very grateful to Mr. Yannick Christos-Wanab, for his friendship and for compiling the index.

This work could not have been brought to completion without a generous sabbatical leave from Beeson Divinity School. Samford University granted a faculty research grant that allowed us to spend six months in Cambridge, England. While at Cambridge I had the privilege of researching at Tyndale House and the numerous libraries of Cambridge University. In addition to the unequaled resources found at Tyndale House, there have been encouraging and stimulating conversations. I thank Steve Walton, Monique Cuany and Greg Lanier. My dear friend, Joseph Dodson, read and commented on all of chapter four. Kevin Vanhoozer read the entirety of chapter six, providing detailed comments. I am grateful to Kevin—who is the type of theologian I wish to emulate—for helping a New Testament scholar make sense of the theological landscape. I thank the folks at IVP, particularly David Congdon for his professionalism and efficiency. Any mistakes are of course my own!

I thank my gracious God, without whom the ability to do any of this research would be impossible.

The book is dedicated to the person who is closest to me: my wife, Kristen. She has patiently heard and read each chapter of this book, offering suggestions from her keen intelligence. She has been supportive in every possible way. Our son, Philip, and I are the constant recipients of rare love. *Este libro es para ti.*

ABBREVIATIONS

AJP   *American Journal of Philology*

ALGHJ   Arbeiten zur Literatur und Geschichte des hellenistischen
             Judentums

AnBib   Analecta biblica

ANTC   Abingdon New Testament Commentary

ASNU   Acta seminarii neotestamentici upsaliensis

BBR   *Bulletin for Biblical Research*

BDAG   W. Bauer, F. W. Danker, W. F. Arndt and F. W. Gingrich. *Greek
             English Lexicon of the New Testament and Other Early Christian
             Literature*. 3rd ed. Chicago: University of Chicago Press, 1999.

BegChr   F. J. F. Jackson and Kirsopp Lake. *The Beginnings of Christianity:
             The Acts of the Apostles*. New York: Macmillan, 1933.

BETL   Bibliotheca ephemeridum theologicarum lovaniensium

BZNW   Beihefte zur Zeitschrift für die neutestamentliche Wissenschaft

CBQ   *Catholic Biblical Quarterly*

CBR   *Currents in Biblical Research*

CD   Karl Barth, *Church Dogmatics*, ed. G. W. Bromiley and T. F.
             Torrance, study edition, 31 vols. London: T&T Clark, 2010.

CNT   Commentaire du Nouveau Testament

FGH   *Die Fragmente der griechischen Historiker*. Edited by F. Jacoby.
             Leiden: Brill, 1954–1964.

ICC   International Critical Commentary

JBL   *Journal of Biblical Literature*

JSNT   *Journal for the Study of the New Testament*

JTS   *Journal of Theological Studies*

KEK   H. A. W. Meyer, Kritisch-exegetischer Kommentar über das
           Neue Testament

LCL   Loeb Classical Library

LEC   Library of Early Christianity

LNTS   Library of New Testament Studies

LSJ   H. G. Liddell, R. Scott and H. S. Jones. *A Greek-English Lexicon.*
           9th ed. Oxford: Oxford University Press, 1940.

MM   James H. Moulton and George Milligan. *The Vocabulary of the
           Greek New Testament.* London, 1930. Repr. Peabody, MA:
           Hendrickson, 1997.

NICNT   New International Commentary of the New Testament

NovT   *Novum Testamentum*

NovTSup   Novum Testamentum Supplements

NSBT   New Studies in Biblical Theology

NTS   *New Testament Studies*

OCD   *Oxford Classical Dictionary.* Edited by S. Hornblower and A.
           Spawforth. 3rd ed. Oxford: Oxford University Press, 1996.

PNTC   Pillar New Testament Commentary

RPP   *Religion Past and Present.* Edited by Hans Dieter Betz, Don S.
           Browning, Bernd Janowski and Eberhard Jüngel. Leiden: Brill,
           2008.

SC   Sources chrétiennes. Paris: CERF, 1943–.

SFC   Selections from the Fathers of the Church

SNTSMS   Society for New Testament Studies Monograph Series

SQE   *Synopsis Quattuor Evangeliorum. Locis parallelis evangeliorum
           apocryphorum et patrum adhibitis.* Edited by Kurt Aland. 13th ed.
           Stuttgart: Deutsche Bibelgesellschaft, 1988.

TLG   *Thesaurus linguae graecae.* http://stephanus.tlg.uci.edu.

WUNT   Wissenschaftliche Untersuchungen zum Neuen Testament

INTRODUCTION

This work is an attempt to do for a new generation of Acts students what Howard Marshall's *Luke: Historian and Theologian* did for a previous generation.[1] As such, it is an "advanced" introduction (paradox noted) in which a number of prolegomena to Acts are presented (e.g., authorship, genre, etc.) as well as subjects that go beyond introductory necessities. Whether the work has equaled Professor Marshall's excellence I cannot say; the attempt at least has been made.

This type of work is needed in the way that it is here conceived for various reasons. Let me mention two. First, there is the matter of philosophical hermeneutics with its turn to the community and with its emphasis (sometimes healthy) on subjectivity, which has affected virtually all areas of the humanities, including biblical studies and theology. In this environment, the argument (for example) for the authorship of Luke-Acts is not completed by just arriving at a particular individual (Luke the companion of Paul or someone else). The question must also be posed: What difference does it make to propose an author at all, if ultimately, so the argument goes, he or she is of little or no relevance for a valid interpretation? So, even though we lack the space to engage on a defense of chastened authorial intention for the validity of an interpretation (after all, this is not a hermeneutics book!), we must at least give a brief response for why the authorship of Acts matters at all.

---

[1] I. Howard Marshall, *Luke: Historian and Theologian*, 3rd ed. (Downers Grove, IL: InterVarsity Press, 1998).

The same can be said of other areas. Genre, for example, is viewed differently today than it was even twenty years ago. You say that the genre of Acts is history: So what? What follows as interpretative gain from this generic labeling is different today than it was in the past, in large part because our conception of what history is has changed. The list could go on. Thus, in addition to suggesting answers to some basic questions of Acts, we must also go a bit deeper and, briefly, engage these broader philosophical and theological questions. Otherwise, the student simply will not be prepared responsibly to interact with contemporary discussions.

The second reason for writing a book like this is specific to Acts: namely, there are new proposals to old subjects as well as new subjects being proposed. If we concentrate on the former, consider the relatively recent proposal that Acts is best understood as an example of the ancient novel. The acceptance of this genre has massive repercussions for virtually all areas of Acts. Or think of the interpretative gains that can be acquired when we explore the suggestion that the speeches in Acts are best interpreted when they are studied within their specific narrative blocks.

Instead of mentioning further reasons somewhat briefly and abstractly, a description of the contents of the book is now in order to provide a map to the reader as well as a more concrete description of what we are trying to accomplish.

Chapter one investigates the question of the author of Acts. I put forth three main proposals. First, the tradition that the author was a man named Luke, who moreover was a companion of Paul, more than likely goes back to the first part of the second century, if not earlier. This tradition should be preserved. Second, Irenaeus of Lyons is a crucial witness to the identification of Luke as the author of Acts. I argue that Irenaeus's conclusion is essentially derived from traditions that he received; but given the flow of argument in *Against Heresies*, he also uses Scripture for decisive, biblical support. Last, I question the contemporary attitude that says that, because Acts was accepted as canonical by the early church, we today should not be overly concerned with the matter of authorship. I find this attitude ironic, since the early church *was* concerned about the authors of the New Testament books. For the church understood that since the New Testament was the written testimony about Jesus, its authors had to be apostles and their companions—that is, eyewitnesses or companions of eyewitnesses. This is so because the New Testament testifies to the Word that became flesh, and therefore truthful testimony at the historical level is essential.

Chapter two asks what kind of book Acts is, and thus is an investigation of its genre.[2] I provide a sketch of genre theory, culminating with Claire Clivaz's understanding of genre as a "category of reception," which she applies to Luke-Acts.[3] While receptive to some aspects of this proposal, I suggest that in order to avoid the excesses of the effacement of the author current in much modern philosophical hermeneutics, we should think of the genre of Acts firstly as a "category of *ancient* reception." The sketch is followed by a survey of contemporary proposals for the genre of Acts. My own conclusion is that in view of external and internal features, Acts is best understood as an example of the ancient historical monograph. This genre, although Greek in origin, had been appropriated by Jewish writers of the Second Temple period (e.g., 2 Maccabees), lending credibility to the proposal that a Jewish author like Luke would have possessed sufficient mastery to compose Acts in it. The repercussions of selecting this genre are numerous. The one that I emphasize in this chapter is the genre of history and its relationship to the world. While the novel (a genre with which a number of authors today are infatuated as being concretized in Acts) is parasitic of the real world—that is, it may use a real city (e.g., London) with a real person (e.g., Winston Churchill) at the right time (1940s)—it nevertheless does not claim correspondence to that world. Thus it is necessary for novelists to state in the initial pages of the book the old statement about "coincidence." A historian, on the other hand, *affirms* that the way he or she is describing events is as they actually happened. Acts as history means that Luke is claiming correspondence between the events he describes in the book and things as they truly happened in the world outside the book. That

---

[2] I am sorry to say that Sean A. Adams, *The Genre of Acts and Collected Biography*, SNTSMS 156 (Cambridge: Cambridge University Press, 2013), reached me too late for sustained interaction with this chapter. The book looks promising and perhaps may cause some rethinking of this chapter!

[3] Claire Clivaz, *L'Ange et la Sueur de Sang (Lc 22, 43-44). Ou Comment on Pourrait Bien Encore Écrire L'Histoire* (Leuven: Peeters, 2010).

puts pressure on the reader: she must not read Acts as symbolic, or as parabolic, or as figural (even though Acts may contain those features). No, Acts should be approached as history, even though this does not in *itself* guarantee that the contents are accurate.[4]

Chapter two thus argues that we should understand Acts as history. But history as we understand it today is often quite different from the way it was understood in Luke's day. Thus in chapter three we ask the question: What kind of history is Acts? Exegesis of Luke's preface and other sections of Acts are brought into conversation with Greco-Roman and contemporary historiography. The results are the following.

First, Acts, even by ancient standards, is an extraordinary fusion of the historical with the theological. Luke, especially in his preface, uses "scientific" language that would have communicated to the ancient reader that what he was about to write was a careful, objective account based on his being an eyewitness as well as interviewing eyewitnesses. The ancient term for this venerable approach was *autopsia*. And yet, in the same preface, Luke uses theologically loaded words and phrases such as "fulfilled" and "servants of the word." Such a fusion of the historical and theological would have been strange to a Greek audience; but not to one with a Jewish understanding of history.

Second, Luke employs numerous narrative procedures in his unfolding of the history of the early church. These include compressing, epitomizing, telescoping, irony and so on. In fact, there is so much artistic shaping and stylization that—from a modern perspective—it would appear that Luke has come dangerously close to that zone where history is left behind and fiction begins. This at least is what F. C. Baur and his disciples concluded. For them Luke's theological *Tendenz* was such that he manipulated data and invented things in order to make his argument more persuasive. Baur was followed by many, especially in Germany and the United States. Could Luke the historian be rehabilitated?

This leads to a detour in which we examine the modern "professionalization of history." Beginning in Germany in the nineteenth century and

---

[4]See chapter four, where we argue that Luke is in fact an accurate historian.

then making its way to France and the United States, there was an attempt to position history under the branches of the sciences. As such, history was to be entirely objective and austere in presentation. This resulted in the disapproval of the aesthetic (read: narrative features) in the writing of history. How could Luke, with his suffusing of the theological and narrative in Acts, survive as a credible historian in such an environment? It came to be, therefore, that Acts was viewed as a flawed piece of history or outright fiction. Nevertheless, with the advent of postmodernity, "professional" history itself has been subjected to relentless questioning. The result has been an admission of the subjective, without (at least in some circles) denial for the possibility of truth in historical research, and the recognition of the aesthetic as a legitimate—indeed welcoming—aspect of historical writing. In some ways, contemporary history is a return to the ancient way of writing history.

And so we come back to Acts. It is my view that the historiographic reforms of postmodernity have allowed us to comprehend better how premodern history was done. This opens the doors for us who live in the twenty-first century to grasp how Acts could be a historical document even though it is written in a different way from a modern book of history.

With the conviction that Acts is a work of history, we proceed in chapter four to a more precise question: Granted that Acts belongs to the *genre* of history, is it *genuine* history? Is it true? What a big question! It was necessary to narrow things. And so we focus on the historicity of one of the most salient features of Acts—namely, the speeches. The first section of the chapter is an attempt to grasp how speeches were understood in Greco-Roman history vis-à-vis truth. We discover that things were very different in this regard from today: there was no intention to provide a transcript of what the speaker said; there was even a lack of the modern quotation marks to separate the voice of the narrator from that of a speaking character. More than likely ancient authors fell within a spectrum from those who invented speeches to those who provided a creative summary of what the speakers said.

Where was Luke in this spectrum? I argue that, based on the length and lack of artificiality of the speeches in Acts, Luke was a conservative reporter of speeches. The chapter closes with a brief discussion of our stance toward the authenticity of the speeches. Do we believe that the speeches are true because we can prove their reliability? Or do we believe their veracity because, being part of Holy Scripture, they must in some sense be true?

In chapter five we move from the historical nature of the speeches to the theology Luke was communicating through them. For it is clear that the speeches, attached to their respective narrative settings, are one of the clearest places to apprehend Luke's theology. We examine here the main speeches in Acts: Pentecost, Stephen, Cornelius, Areopagus and Agrippa.

Chapter six is the climax of the book. It is an attempt to fuse the historical with the theological by exploring the evidence for the messianic truth-claims of Acts in conversation with the theological movement known as postliberalism.

From the description of the contents above it will be clear that this book does not have a single thesis that is advanced and defended chapter after chapter. There are, however, two animating convictions that hold the work together. One of these convictions was present at the beginning of the work. However, it lacked comprehensive exegetical rigor over the entirety of Acts. In other words, now that I have worked over many sections of Acts, I feel that it can be defended with more rigor. The other conviction did not exist. By the time I was concluding the final chapter, however, not only had it been conceived and born, but it also had become very strong. What are these two convictions?

First, I am persuaded that Luke wants to be taken as—and actually is—a serious historian, who in the Acts of the Apostles has given us a wholly dependable portrait of the early church. In composing the Acts of the Apostles Luke did not want to be understood as a novelist or epic writer but as a historian, and a careful one too. With respect to this particular book, I argue that he accomplishes this by the use of, positively, particular terminology and, negatively, by his refusal to engage in the type of rhetorical excesses that were dominant in the period in which he wrote. Luke was a sober historian. I am equally convinced that Luke was a serious historian *of his age*. Hence his belief that what he was narrating was no less than a movement of God in the world; his extensive stylization;

and his use of speeches, while acceptable in a Jewish setting, might leave those nourished in the modernist approach to history confused—if not in disbelief.

This first animating conviction—namely, that Luke is a serious, dependable historian of his age—I work out from various angles in chapters one through four.

The second animating conviction of the work is theological. And it is this: while history—understood as the events that actually happened—is a sine qua non for Luke's theology, nevertheless it is not in itself the final word. The mighty works of God that are described in Acts cannot be understood unless they are explicated by God himself. Without the divine explication the miracle of speaking in tongues in Acts 2, or the healing of the paralytic in Acts 3, for example, can be interpreted in numerous ways, including the charge of charlatanry: "They are filled with new wine" (Acts 2:13). For the miracle to be understood in its christological particularity, it is necessary that God himself explain it. And this explanation is the apostolic testimony, which is based on the teaching of the risen Jesus and the Old Testament (as explained by Christ himself) and inscripturated in the New Testament. One often finds this divine explication in the speeches of Acts (chapter five).

The conviction that Acts, while firmly grounded in historical events, cannot ultimately be understood if those events are sundered from their divine explication finds its sharpest expression in the final chapter of this book. The chapter is an exploration of how Acts defends its primary truth-claim—that is, that Jesus of Nazareth is the messiah. And so it is in some sense a chapter on apologetics. In order to refine our thoughts in this matter, we bring the text of Acts into conversation with postliberal theology, a movement that has been wrestling for some decades with the question of the appropriateness of apologetics. The question is this: How do Acts and postliberal theologians, respectively, defend before the public the truth-claim that Jesus Christ is the crucified and raised Messiah who will judge the living and the dead?

The answer from Acts is that corroboration for the messianic status of Jesus is found in the resurrection. How do we know that Jesus is the

Messiah? Because he was raised from the dead as promised in the Scriptures. The resurrection, moreover, is presented as based on historical testimony. We see this in the constant statement by the apostles that *they were eyewitnesses of the raised Christ*. They saw him alive, and ate and spoke with him (Lk 24; Acts 1:2-3). Postliberals, as we shall see, because of the type of epistemology they embrace and the pneumatological weakness in their account of Scripture, do not (cannot?) operate with the apologetic scheme present in Acts.

While we conclude that postliberalism, in view of Acts, is deficient in its approach to apologetics, it nevertheless does make a contribution in how the evidence of the resurrection is to be grasped vis-à-vis history. We will naturally go into more detail in chapter six, but the general statement can be made here: the resurrection of Jesus as witnessed and explained by the apostles is the historical evidence for the evangelical truth-claim about Jesus; yet, this historical evidence, because it is mediated by the Scriptures and the Holy Spirit, is itself revelatory. On the one hand, if the resurrection of Jesus is false, if it did not happen as the apostles testified, then our faith is "vain" and futile (1 Cor 15:12-16). The testimony of Acts is that the resurrection is a historical event. And yet, this historical event cannot be understood apart from Scripture. It cannot be reconstructed and given the meaning that *we* think it should have. To be a Christian understanding of the resurrection of Christ, it *must be mediated by the Scriptures, which come from the Spirit and are (by the same Spirit) interpreted by the apostles*. Thus it goes beyond history as such. Therefore the resurrection, which is the corroborative evidence in Acts for the messianic claim about Jesus, is both historical event and transcendent revelation. These two ends must be held together without sacrificing the inevitable tension.

one

WHO WROTE ACTS?

WHO IS THE AUTHOR OF the Acts of the Apostles? The traditional response, going back firmly to Irenaeus of Lyons, is that the author was an individual by the name of Luke, writer of the Gospel that bears his name, who was also a companion of the apostles and Paul. This is a view that was not significantly contested until the period of the so-called Tübingen school (nineteenth century). Attacks on the traditional view were taken up again with renewed interest around the middle of the twentieth century by individuals such as Philipp Vielhauer. He argued that the theology of Paul as found in his genuine epistles is strikingly different from that presented in the speeches of Acts.[1] It was impossible, therefore, to continue holding to the traditional view of Luke as a traveling companion of Paul. Since that period, much of Acts scholarship has rejected the traditional view.[2] In addition, the current climate of suspicion toward the motives of the church fathers has made the traditional view of the author of Acts even more difficult to hold.[3] Should we thus completely abandon this view as one untenable, given our progress in historical and biblical studies? Or is

---

[1] See Philipp Vielhauer's classic article, "On the 'Paulinism' of Acts," in *Studies in Luke-Acts*, ed. Leander E. Keck and J. Louis Martyn (Nashville: Abingdon, 1966), 33-50.

[2] A contemporary representative is Daniel Marguerat in his recently composed commentary: "Does the Lucan work confirm this traditional attribution? No. The author of Acts cannot be a historical companion of Paul. . . . But above all, the notable difference between the Lucan portrait of Paul and the thought of the apostle displayed in his epistles makes the hypothesis of accompaniment difficult" (*Les Actes des Apôtres 1-12* [Genève: Labor et Fides, 2007], 19; my translation).

[3] See, e.g., Bart Ehrman, *Lost Christianities: The Battle for Scripture and the Faiths We Never Knew* (Oxford: Oxford University Press, 2003).

there still something to be said for the traditional view? Indeed, does it even matter who wrote the Acts of the Apostles?[4]

Our task in this chapter, then, is to examine the evidence for the authorship of Acts and then ask what impact our conclusion may have for interpretation.

WHO WAS LUKE?

It is quite possible that our earliest extant evidence for an individual named Luke, who, moreover, was connected with the writing of parts of the New Testament, comes from the early Bodmer papyrus 75. At the end of P[75] we find the following title: εὐαγγέλιον κατὰ Λουκᾶν. P[75] was thought by its editors to range between 175 and 225 CE in date.[5] It is the earliest copy of the Gospel of Luke that we possess. Furthermore, it has been argued that P[75] evinces a form that is very close to the Alexandrian family as found in Codex Vaticanus.[6] Since P[75] already connects Luke to the Gospel, then we can cautiously suggest that the linkage between the two may go back earlier into the second century. How far back? This is a question that we will address shortly.

Writing circa 180 CE, Irenaeus, bishop of Lyons, provides some very helpful information on the authorship of the Gospels. Concerning that of the third Gospel and Acts, he makes the following statement: "Luke also, the companion [ἀκόλουθος; sectator] of Paul, set down in writing the gospel preached by him" (Against Heresies 3.1.1). Further on he states: "That this Luke was inseparable from Paul, and his fellow-laborer in the Gospel, he himself makes clear, not boasting, but as bound to do so by the truth itself." To provide proof of this, Irenaeus then cites a number of passages from what we call today the "we" sections of the Acts of the Apostles (e.g., Acts 16:10-16; 20:6, etc.). He then states: "Being present in all these events,

---

[4]Among those who view the Acts of the Apostles as a canonical document, it is becoming almost completely de rigueur to say that since the book is canonical, we really should not be concerned about its authorship. But this is a fallacy. The canonical status of Acts does not logically preclude a careful search for its author. And in any case, why *did* Acts become part of the canon in the first place? This view seems to me to hold a romantic view of the canon. We will come back to this at the end of the chapter.

[5]Victor Martin and Rodolphe Kasser, eds., *Papyrus Bodmer XIV-XV: Évangiles de Luc et Jean*, vol. 1, *Papyrus Bodmer XIV: Évangile de Luc chap. 3-24* (Cologny-Geneva: Bibliotheca Bodmeriana, 1961).

[6]See Bruce M. Metzger and Bart D. Ehrman, *The Text of the New Testament: Its Transmission, Corruption, and Restoration*, 4th ed. (Oxford: Oxford University Press, 2005), 58-59.

Luke carefully set them down in writing" (*Against Heresies* 3.14.1). In other words, as the "we" passages demonstrate, Luke was a close companion of Paul and therefore an eyewitness of many of the events in the life of the apostle. But if the "we" passages are not sufficient, Irenaeus then adds support from Paul's own letters: "That he was not only a follower, but also a fellow-laborer of the apostles, and above all of Paul, Paul himself made clear in the epistles."[7] There follow quotations from 2 Timothy 4:9-10 and Colossians 4:14. From Irenaeus we can thus glean the following information about Luke: (1) He authored the third Gospel; (2) he was a companion of the apostles and Paul; (3) he authored the Acts of the Apostles; (4) he is mentioned by Paul in two of his epistles.

Information on the person of Luke and the authorship of the Gospels and Acts is also found in the so-called Anti-Marcionite preface. There is debate on the exact date of this preface, although it is probably contemporaneous with Irenaeus, if not earlier. Here the connection between a person called Luke and the third Gospel and Acts continues; we also receive some further biographic information on the shadowy figure of Luke. The text reads:

> Luke is an Antiochean Syrian, a doctor by trade; he was a disciple of the apostles, and later, having followed [παρακολουθήσας; Latin, *secutus*] Paul until his death [μαρτυρίου] and having served the Lord single-mindedly, without wife or children, he passed at the age of eighty-four, full of the Holy Spirit. . . . And afterwards the same Luke wrote the Acts of the Apostles.[8]

This is the first document outside the New Testament that tells us of Luke's origin and profession as well as his death. This is a tradition that is then found in subsequent authors.[9]

The final early document to be cited linking Luke-Acts with the individual Luke is the Muratorian Fragment. This document more than likely dates from the last quarter of the second century and probably originated

---

[7]Greek and Latin text from the critical edition by Adelin Rousseau and Louis Doutreleau in *Sources Chrétiennes*; my translation.

[8]Greek and Latin text from *SQE*, 549; my translation.

[9]E.g., Eusebius, *Ecclesiastical History* 4.6-7; Jerome, *On Illustrious Men* 7; *Prologue of the Four Gospels* 1.11-14; *Preface to Luke* 1.269-271.

in Rome.[10] It thus stems from the same period of the three other documents we have noted above. Although we are missing the beginning and end of the document, fortunately the section on the third Gospel and Acts survives. It reads thus:

> The third book of the Gospel is that according to Luke. Luke, the well-known physician, after the ascension of Christ, when Paul had taken with him as one zealous for the law, composed it in his own name, according to the general belief. . . . Moreover, the acts of all the apostles were written in one book. For "most excellent Theophilus" Luke compiled the individual events that took place in his presence.[11]

To sum up, from this early tradition we can build a stable outline of how Luke was perceived: (1) He was a follower of all the apostles but especially Paul; (2) he was a physician; and (3) he wrote the Gospel of Luke and the Acts of the Apostles. The question that we must ask here is: On what basis were the name "Luke" and the descriptors about him noted above attached to the author of the third Gospel and the Acts of the Apostles? Asked differently, is the patristic tradition generally a result of data about the author that is *independent* of the New Testament text; or is it no more than *inferences* from Luke-Acts and other parts of the New Testament? Or is it perhaps a combination of both?

Concentrating on Irenaeus and the early second century, Andrew Gregory, in his meticulously researched Oxford dissertation, concludes that the notices about Luke are the result of Irenaeus's reading of the New Testament, not external tradition that may have reached him from an earlier period.[12] Gregory acknowledges that, with P[75] stemming from the third or late second century, and the careful hand of the copyist, it may be possible to move backward and conclude that behind the papyrus there is

---

[10]See the discussion in Geoffrey Hahneman, *The Muratorian Fragment and the Development of the Canon* (Oxford: Clarendon, 1992), 27-30.

[11]Translation from Bruce Metzger, *The Canon of the New Testament* (Oxford: Clarendon, 1987), 305-7.

[12]Andrew Gregory, *The Reception of Luke and Acts in the Period Before Irenaeus: Looking for Luke in the Second Century*, WUNT 2.169 (Tübingen: Mohr Siebeck, 2003). His conclusion in this respect was already anticipated (as Gregory acknowledges) by Henry Joel Cadbury, "The Identity of the Editor of Luke and Acts: The Tradition," in *The Beginnings of Christianity*, part 1, vol. 2, *The Acts of the Apostles. Prolegomena II. Criticism*, ed. F. J. Foakes Jackson and Kirsopp Lake (London: Macmillan, 1922), 209-64.

an old tradition that goes back to the earlier second century. Despite this possibility, Gregory opts for a very conservative conclusion: "Unfortunately we cannot be certain either how skilled (and therefore potentially accurate) were the earliest copyists of the Gospels or the extent to which they may have altered their texts in the light of increasing theological precision in the development of Christian doctrine."[13] He thus dismisses the possibility of knowing with certainty that the joining of the name of Luke to the third Gospel is *prior* to Irenaeus. Moving to the patristic testimony, Gregory is convinced that the earliest evidence joining Luke with the third Gospel and Acts is that which comes from the pen of Irenaeus. Furthermore, Irenaeus's arguments are not based on information external to the New Testament but rather are entirely the result of his inferences from Acts and Paul's letters.[14]

It may be the case that the earliest notices about the authorship of Luke-Acts stem from Irenaeus and that, furthermore, they are the result of the bishop's detective type of New Testament interpretation for the sake of apologetics. There are at least two issues, however, that Gregory (and others) has not adequately addressed. These are (1) just how, out of so many available persons in primitive Christianity, did the individual "Luke" come to be associated with Luke-Acts; and (2) can Greco-Roman practices on the cataloguing of books (scrolls) shed any light on the names attached to the Gospels, in our particular case Luke-Acts?

Concerning the first question, the evidence is that at some point the third Gospel and Acts were believed to have been written by *Luke*. Why *this* particular individual? For Irenaeus, to be sure, could have deduced from exegesis that the author of Acts was a traveling companion of Paul. But Paul had many companions. Why not associate Luke-Acts with, say, Barnabas, or Silas, or, perhaps more logical given their labor together, Timothy?[15] Why, instead, was the two-volume work associated with Luke, a figure not very prominent in the pages of the New Testament?

---

[13]Gregory, *Reception of Luke and Acts*, 29.
[14]Ibid., 53.
[15]Silas was both a traveling companion of Paul and had the ability to compose, as 1 Pet 5:12 shows.

Henry Joel Cadbury's answer appears to me to be wholly unsatis-
factory. He suggests that "perhaps Luke's selection was due to a process
of elimination."[16] Even if we were to go in this direction, that would certainly leave more than one individual as the potential author—and more
likely persons too. In any case, if it were mere guesswork, why would
there be such a strong unanimity across diverse geographic regions in the
second and third centuries to the effect that the author was Luke? Here
the words of Martin Hengel concerning the four Gospels are to the point:
"It can therefore also by no means be assumed that at some time . . . before
Irenaeus . . . there had been a kind of general 'council' of a number of
churches in a province at which the four hitherto anonymous writings
gained recognition, were given their titles, and were then brought together as a 'four-Gospel canon.' Such an idea would be completely
anachronistic."[17] Cadbury and Gregory's hypothesis is weak in what it
leaves unexplained.

A more convincing thesis, one that attempts to explain the linkage between the individual Luke and Luke-Acts, is that of Claus-Jürgen
Thornton.[18] He argues that the statements concerning the authorship of
the Gospels in Irenaeus's third book stem from preexistent traditional material. To buttress this, Thornton suggests that the different order of the
Gospels given in *Against Heresies* 3.1.1, as well as the difference in verb
tenses between Matthew, Luke and John on the one hand and Mark on the
other, suggest a written tradition from which Irenaeus drew.[19] Where
could this traditional material come from? Thornton argues that, given the
preeminence of the Roman congregation in the second century as well as
the list of bishops of Rome that Irenaeus provides in book 3, the tradition
probably came from the library of the Roman church.[20] He thus reaches
the following conclusion:

---

[16]Cadbury, "Tradition," 261. Recall that Gregory's conclusion on this matter is almost identical to Cadbury's.
In fact, he appeals to Cadbury for an explanation of the problem being discussed.

[17]Martin Hengel, *The Four Gospels and the One Gospel of Jesus Christ: An Investigation of the Collection and Origin of the Canonical Gospels*, trans. John Bowden (Harrisburg, PA: Trinity Press International, 2000), 53.

[18]Claus-Jürgen Thornton, *Der Zeuge des Zeugen: Lukas als Historiker der Paulusreisen*, WUNT 1.56 (Tübingen: Mohr Siebeck, 1991). Surprisingly, Gregory does not interact with Thornton's work.

[19]Ibid., 12-20.

[20]Ibid., 40-67.

It has been shown that a series of statements concerning Luke was not first "invented" by Irenaeus. The appellation "Paul's companion" comes at least from the first third of the second century. The identification of this Luke with the fellow-laborer and physician of Paul is possibly already assumed by Marcion; also, Irenaeus already probably had available the designation "disciple of the apostles."[21]

Not all of Thornton's arguments are equally convincing.[22] On the whole, however, they show that it is probable that the notices about the author of the third Gospel and Acts in Irenaeus represent a previously formed tradition, perhaps from the early part of the second century.

One of the curious omissions in research on the possible authors of the Gospels is the lack of work on ancient practices concerning authors and the title of their works. That is, what was the Greco-Roman custom with regard to the naming of written works? The supposition that the Gospels were anonymous from their inception is entrenched in New Testament scholarship. But does it have support from Greco-Roman conventions? Surprisingly, this is a question that has not often been asked. The work of Martin Hengel has sought to fill this gap. Drawing on numerous examples, Hengel shows that the convention was to put the name of the author in the genitive case followed by the title of the work.[23] To have a work circulating anonymously would have been the exception. Hengel argues that the same can be expected of the Gospels, with the difference that, as the extant text-critical evidence shows, the title of the work with the assumed author's name was put in a prepositional phrase using κατά, "according to." Hengel suggests that the reason for this is that the real "author" of the gospel is Jesus Christ, and the Evangelists simply bear witness to that gospel.[24] In addition, Hengel argues from Justin that the Gospels were read in the context of worship. This is an important observation, since it was crucial

---

[21]Ibid., 60; my translation.

[22]As, for example, when he says that the statement in *Against Heresies* 3.14.1 about Luke being a physician does not forward the thought in the section and thus it probably already comes from an existing passage (ibid., 68).

[23]Hengel, *Four Gospels*, 48.

[24]Ibid., 49. He further notes, correctly, that a double genitive phrase such as "Gospel of Mark of Jesus Christ" would have been strange to Greek ears.

for the early church that material read in worship come from eyewitnesses of Jesus or their companions. And this would make the issue of names very important. Hengel therefore concludes that the tradition of the Gospel writers found in Irenaeus is an old tradition, predating even Justin.[25] Hengel also calls attention to the uniformity of the titles of the Gospels, which goes against the argument of anonymity. He states:

> There is no trace of such anonymity. Not only the complete uniformity of the titles from Alexandria to Lyons and from Antioch to Carthage before the end of the second century and their "historical sequence" (Matthew), Mark, Luke, John, but also manifold references in the later second century itself, whether to the Gospels as authoritative scripture or to its authors, show their great date, indeed in my view their original character.[26]

Let us summarize the data and offer arguments for our own view of the author of Acts. The traditional view is that Luke, the companion of the apostles and Paul, wrote Luke-Acts. This belief is encountered in clear exposition in the work of Irenaeus of Lyons, who is dependent on previous tradition. This argument has been challenged, most recently by Gregory. When asked how we can explain the association of the third Gospel and Acts with the obscure figure of Luke, Gregory responds that this conclusion was probably arrived at first by Irenaeus through a process of inductive exegesis and elimination. Once "Luke" was landed on, Irenaeus cleverly used the "we" sections of Acts and Paul's letters to buttress the argument that Luke was a companion and follower of Paul. The tradition, then, which links Acts with the individual Luke who was also a companion of Paul is entirely the result of the independent investigation of Irenaeus. Future notices on the author of Luke-Acts (e.g., Eusebius, Tertullian, etc.) are all dependent on Irenaeus.

Despite the apparent force of the arguments presented above, I believe there are good reasons to hold to the traditional (i.e., patristic) view of the author of Acts. I make the following observations and arguments in support of this view.

---

[25] Ibid., 52-53.
[26] Ibid., 54.

First, as has been noted above, there is a very uniform tradition in the second century concerning the author of Luke-Acts. In the second-century Anti-Marcionite preface the individual Luke is presented as the author of the third Gospel and the Acts of the Apostles. In Irenaeus's *Against Heresies* Luke is the author of the third Gospel and Acts. In *Against Heresies* 3.1.1 Irenaeus is showing that the Gospels originated with apostles (Matthew and John) or close companions of the apostles (Mark and Luke). Hence, of Mark it is said that he was "the disciple and interpreter of Peter." Luke is then also linked to an apostle: he was the companion and follower of Paul and the author of the Acts of the Apostles.

Second, it should be noted that the above argument was not original to Irenaeus. It is already found in Papias with respect to Mark.[27] The same can be said of Justin, writing around 150: "For in the memoirs of the apostles *and their successors*, it is written that his perspiration poured out like drops of blood as he prayed."[28] This tradition, then, of associating apostles with Gospel writers is an ancient one, certainly not original with Irenaeus. Following Thornton and Hengel, we would argue that it probably goes back to the archives of the Roman church and may indicate that the Gospels—either from their origin or very early after their production—circulated with the names of the Evangelists. Since this tradition (as encountered in Irenaeus and the Muratorian Fragment) speaks of Luke as the writer of the Acts of the Apostles, it could be said that from the first half of the second century and probably the end of the first, the third Gospel and Acts were associated with Luke, who was viewed as a companion of the apostle Paul.

Third, it is important to tackle with more force the proposal of Cadbury and Gregory—namely, that Irenaeus's conclusion that Luke was a companion of Paul is totally derived from exegesis of Acts and Pauline letters, and not at all from independent tradition. Prima facie, it is true that in *Against Heresies* 3.14.1 Irenaeus appeals to the "we" sections of Acts and Paul's letters; but it should be noted that this is not the only context in

[27] Eusebius, *Ecclesiastical History* 3.39.14-16.

[28] Justin Martyr, *Dialogue with Trypho* 103.8. Translation from Thomas B. Falls in the SFC series. For further support that Justin is here referring to the Gospels (probably the four), see Graham Stanton, *Jesus and Gospel* (Cambridge: Cambridge University Press, 2004), 75-76.

which Irenaeus asserts that Luke was a companion of Paul or the apostles. In 1.23.1, the first time he mentions Luke, he immediately adds about him: "the disciple and follower of the apostles." In 3.1.1 he states: "Luke also, the companion of Paul. . . ." Again, in 3.10.1, he describes Luke as "the follower and disciple of the apostles." In none of these passages does Irenaeus appeal to Scripture. It is thus misleading to say that Irenaeus *explicitly* draws his information about Luke *only* from the "we" passages and Paul's letters. In fact, all of these short notices appended to the name of Luke have the ring of tradition in view of their length and uniformity. It is also crucial to note that short, descriptive notices are not only appended to Luke but also to the rest of the Gospel authors (e.g., *Against Heresies* 2.1.5; 3.1.1; 3.3.4; 3.9.1; 3.10.1, 5; 3.11.1). *If one wants to argue that in the case of Luke even the short, descriptive notices are the result of Irenaeus's exegesis, then one would also presumably have to argue that the short notices attached to Matthew, Mark and John are also the result of Irenaeus's exegesis, not tradition.* This is unlikely, since there are not similar conditions to "construct" a person like Matthew, Mark and John as there are for Luke with the "we" passages. This leads to the question of why in 3.14.1 Irenaeus goes to Acts and Paul to give support for his view concerning the author of Acts.

The answer, I believe, is found in the preface to book 3. Here Irenaeus tells his reader that in the previous books he has (1) attempted to expose the Valentinian heresies, and (2) by means of argument, to refute them. He goes on: "But in this third book, we shall add proofs from the Scriptures." In this way the reader would have a complete arsenal to undo the heretics. Irenaeus has certainly executed this plan very well. Thus, while in book 2 he combats the heresies by means of logical, hermeneutical and historical arguments (Scripture therefore being quoted sparsely), in book 3 scriptural quotations are by contrast copious.[29] In chapters 13–14 of book 3 Irenaeus is combating the Marcionite statements that Paul was the exclusive bearer of the truth. As he stated in the preface, Irenaeus will now refute false teaching *by means of Scripture*. Thus, when he reaches chapter 14, he

---

[29]See the similar comments by Rousseau in *Irénée de Lyon: Contre les Hérésies* in the SC series no. 210, 171-72. See also now John Behr, *Irenaeus of Lyons: Identifying Christianity* (Oxford: Oxford University Press, 2013), 125-44.

debunks the argument by showing through the "we" passages and Paul's letters (i.e., Scripture) that Luke was in fact inseparable from Paul and thus would also know the mysteries revealed to the apostle.

In view of the above, I propose the following. The author of Luke-Acts was Luke, the companion and coworker of Paul. Irenaeus, writing circa 180, is the clearest patristic witness to this. He possessed preexistent, old tradition linking Luke to Paul and the apostles. This tradition may go back to the time of the composition of Acts, since, as Hengel has shown, most works of the Greco-Roman period were not anonymous. Irenaeus provided *confirmation* from Scripture for this tradition by his own exegesis in 3.14.1, as he had promised in the preface to the book. It is also possible that the use of the "we" passages and Paul's letters to show that Luke was a companion of Paul is *itself* a traditional argument repeated by Irenaeus, in a similar way as the short notices appended to the names of the Evangelists are also traditional. More than likely, however, given the length and subtlety of the scriptural argument, the use of the "we" passages and Pauline letters is Irenaeus's own contribution. I conclude that in Irenaeus we have a combination of tradition and exegesis. The short notices that Luke was a companion and follower of Paul and the other apostles stem from tradition. The *confirmation* of this by use of Scripture comes from Irenaeus, thus fulfilling his promise in the preface to book 3 that proof would be adduced from Scripture.

HOW IMPORTANT IS THE IDENTITY OF THE AUTHOR TO INTERPRET ACTS?

This is a question that students in Gospels and Acts courses are asking with more frequency. Having been told that these New Testament documents are anonymous (and were so from the beginning!), and with the contemporary suspicion of the church fathers as individuals whose agenda was one of power and control and not the truth, students feel that the only way forward is to respond to the question above negatively or agnostically. The "expert" answer often provided by scholars is: "The Gospels and Acts are anonymous, and therefore knowing the identity of the authors is irrelevant for interpretation." This response becomes almost a mantra that students then parrot without further thought.

Does knowing the identity of the author of Acts matter in interpretation? A large part of the answer depends on what we mean by interpretation. This is not a book on hermeneutics, and so extensive treatment of the matter of interpretation must be excluded. Nevertheless, a few observations are important in order to make progress on the question being asked in this section.

There are a number of reasons why the matter of the identity of the author of Acts is viewed as largely irrelevant for interpretation. I will concentrate on two.[30] First, we must take into account the impact of philosophical hermeneutics. The monumental works of Hans-Georg Gadamer and (to a lesser extent) Paul Ricoeur have shifted the locus of meaning from the intention of the author to the *Sache* ("matter") or "world" of the text. For Gadamer in particular, the focus is not understanding what *someone* was communicating in the past (for that is unattainable), but rather to come to *self-understanding* by means of dialogue with the *Sache* of the text.[31] In the words of Gadamer, understanding a text "does not mean primarily to reason one's way back into the past, but to have a present involvement in what is said. It is not really a relationship between persons, between the reader and the author . . . but about sharing in what the text shares with us. The meaning of what is said is . . . quite independent of whether the traditionary text gives us a picture of the author."[32]

---

[30]Besides the two reasons given here, we may point to the impact of postliberal theology on scriptural and canonical studies. Given the cultural-linguistic turn of some of the leaders of postliberalism (e.g., George Lindbeck and Hans Frei) and the view of epistemology emerging from it (and stemming from it), it may not be surprising to encounter the view that meaning is entirely textual, the contribution of the author being minimized or completely eclipsed (no pun intended on Frei!). Consider the following statement from Hans Frei with respect to what he calls "realistic narratives": "By speaking of the narrative shape of these accounts [Genesis and the Gospels], I suggest that what they are about and how they make sense are functions of the depiction or narrative rendering of the events constituting them—including their being rendered, at least partially, by the device of chronological sequence" (*The Eclipse of Biblical Narrative: A Study in Eighteenth and Nineteenth Century Hermeneutics* [New Haven, CT: Yale University Press, 1974], 13.) This statement sounds strikingly similar to what one would find in New Criticism. See also ibid., 280. Lynn M. Poland agrees: "For Frei, the crucial point to be stressed is that the narrative form does not 'illustrate' its meaning, but 'constitutes' it. The 'meaning' of the story is located nowhere but in the narrative sequence itself" (*Literary Criticism and Biblical Hermeneutics: A Critique of Formalist Approaches* [Chico, CA: Scholars Press, 1985], 122). We will return to Frei and this question in chapter six.

[31]See Kevin J. Vanhoozer, "Discourse on Matter: Hermeneutics and the 'Miracle' of Understanding," in *Hermeneutics at the Crossroads*, ed. Kevin J. Vanhoozer, James K. A. Smith and Bruce Ellis Benson (Bloomington: Indiana University Press, 2006), 3-34.

[32]Hans-Georg Gadamer, *Truth and Method*, 2nd rev. ed., trans. Joel Weinsheimer and Donald G. Marshall

It is because of this understanding of meaning that a recent writer can seem to want to have it both ways when she says that Acts "is most obviously pernicious because of its anti-Judaism," only to add in an endnote: "In speaking of Acts as anti-Jewish, I note at the outset that I am focusing on the rhetoric of the text, and the effects of that rhetoric, rather than the issue of authorial intention."[33] Much of modern philosophical hermeneutics has attempted to efface the author.

A second reason why the identity of the author of Acts has been sidelined is the effect in biblical studies of what can broadly be called narrative criticism.[34] This method focuses on the final form of the text, paying attention to entities such as setting, characters and plot (among many others), from which interplay meaning is discovered.[35] In many ways narrative criticism has been a breath of fresh air to biblical scholars who grew frustrated with the hypothetical nature and sheer subjectivity of the historical-critical method. With narrative criticism we could finally concentrate on the text without having first to reconstruct the historical setting. But as with any method, narrative criticism carries some ideological baggage that sometimes has passed unperceived or has simply been willfully ignored by practitioners. In particular, narrative criticism receives its theoretical underpinnings from New Criticism or American Formalism.[36] New Criticism reacted to a theory of literary meaning that asserted that it was impossible to understand a text if the circumstances of the author when he or she wrote were unknown. As such, the text was effectively displaced and the locus of interpretation became the author—but not as apprehended *through* the text, but rather *apart* from the mediation of the text. The New Critics' response to this was, in the words of Moore, "to conceptualize the

---

(New York: Continuum, 2003), 391-92. I owe this quotation to Nicholas Wolterstorff, "Resuscitating the Author," in *Hermeneutics at the Crossroads*, 35-50.

[33] Shelly Matthews, *Perfect Martyr: The Stoning of Stephen and the Construction of Christian Identity* (New York: Oxford University Press, 2010), 9, 142.

[34] For what follows, see the work of Stephen D. Moore, *Literary Criticism and the Gospels: The Theoretical Challenge* (New Haven, CT: Yale University Press, 1989). Note Moore's observation that the approach called "narrative criticism," although drawing from literary theory, is essentially in its practice a development exclusive to biblical studies (3-13).

[35] For a useful introduction, see Mark Allan Powell, *What Is Narrative Criticism?* (Minneapolis: Fortress, 1990).

[36] Moore, *Literary Criticism*, 9.

poem (shorthand for the literary work of art) as an autonomous, internally unified organism, the bearer of a meaning that must be validated first and foremost by the context of the work itself."[37] This, in truth, was a salutary response to a misunderstanding of author-intended meaning. Nevertheless, biblical scholars, in adopting the New Critic correction, went too far in the direction of a text's autonomy. As a result, one of the axioms of literary criticism as it came to be used in biblical studies is that the interpreter should bracket out historical questions. The focus of interpretation should not at all be the real, flesh-and-blood author or the real audience, but rather the implied author, the world of the text and the implied reader.[38] When imported into biblical studies under the name of "narrative criticism," a number of scholars were delighted to cast off the burden of history in order to focus on the aesthetics of narrative.

F. Scott Spencer has argued, however, that much narrative criticism of Acts has blended well literary *and* historical concerns.[39] This is somewhat misleading. What Spencer means by "historical" here is the attempt to read the text of Acts within its ancient context—literary, social, political and so on. But note that this type of "historical" reading must be done of *any* literature of the ancient world, whether it be poetry, fiction or history. It stems from the common-sense observation that in order to understand an ancient text (whatever the genre) we must be attuned to the contemporary mores encoded and thus unannounced in the text. We do not say that this approach is illegitimate in the study of historical narrative.[40] Some helpful contributions can and have certainly come from it, not least in the field of Acts. However, it should be clear that these studies are not historical in the robust sense of the term. That is, *there is no attempt to engage the question of the correspondence between the narrative and the external state of affairs that the author promises to have searched accurately* (ἀκριβῶς, Lk 1:3). This trend is the result of a narrative-critical approach that tells us that to engage in

---

[37]Ibid.

[38]"The implied author" meaning, that is, the author as we come to know him or her exclusively through the text.

[39]F. Scott Spencer, "Acts and Modern Literary Approaches," in *The Book of Acts in Its First Century Setting*, ed. Andrew D. Clarke and Bruce W. Winter (Grand Rapids: Eerdmans, 1993), 381-414, esp. 391-405.

[40]I myself have used this approach in *The Speeches of Outsiders in Acts: Poetics, Theology and Historiography*, SNTSMS 144 (Cambridge: Cambridge University Press, 2008), 8-14.

literary study of biblical narrative logically excludes historical study (in its robust sense of historical accuracy) and vice versa.[41] It is one thing to say that the goal of one's study is to focus on the inner literary and theological logic of Acts. This is well and good and should continue to be done. But it is altogether a different thing to say that if one approaches Acts through narrative criticism, historical questions *must* be suspended. This ignores the *historiographic genre* of Acts and thus allows the method to swallow the text. Francis Watson puts it well in speaking of the Gospels:

> But the danger of an indiscriminate rejection of every attempt to look "behind the text" is that the sphere of the historical will simply be abandoned, while the newly-discovered narratives are taken elsewhere. That might perhaps be appropriate if we knew these texts to be fictional. But if they are—in some sense, however attenuated or problematic—works of historiography, then it is clear that they intend to point to that which is external to them, a particular past which lies behind them and which they seek to mediate to their readers. The implied reader of these texts understands them not as an enclosed fictional world but as an imaginative rendering of prior reality.[42]

Let us be clear. We are not suggesting that a historical approach should be the *only* approach to Acts. What we are saying is that the historiographic genre of Acts makes demands on the reader, demands about historical truth-claims that a purist narrative-critical method cannot meet. Thus, alongside narrative readings there should be those that, while attentive to the narrative features of Acts, also are concerned with the reality behind the text of Acts. And this brings us right back to the question of authorship.

If we pursue an interpretation of Acts that is concerned with the fit between the text and the external reality it purports to describe—that is, if it matters for our Christian faith whether the events described in Acts

---

[41]Behind this approach, as we have noted, are philosophical commitments that would suggest that to ask the historicity question is to fall into modernist positivism. But this is not so. See Anthony Thiselton, *New Horizons in Hermeneutics: The Theory and Practice of Transforming Biblical Reading* (Grand Rapids: Zondervan, 1992), 26, who helpfully states: "But within a particular sub-category of examples, historical narrative is more than 'history-like.' It does not miss the point in these instances to ask what occurred or what the author thought occurred, as if this were only a 'modern' question."

[42]Francis Watson, *Text and Truth: Redefining Biblical Theology* (Grand Rapids: Eerdmans, 1997), 34.

happened or not—then the identity of the author is indeed important. The reason for this is the crucial category of *eyewitness*. For in ancient historiography it was the author who had unmediated experience—either by having seen the events himself or interviewing those who had—of the events he writes, who had the superior claim to historical faithfulness.[43] It matters, therefore, whether Luke was, as Irenaeus contends, a follower of the apostles and Paul. And, in fact, Luke himself is keen to highlight both his interaction with the eyewitnesses (αὐτόπται) in Luke 1:1-4 and his own participation in a significant number of the events he describes in connection with Paul's ministry. For the latter he inscribes himself in the text by the use of the first-person pronoun plural "we."[44] It should be clear that we are not saying that viewing Luke as an eyewitness *proves* the historical reliability of Acts. This would be naive, for there are such things as lying eyewitnesses. However, being an eyewitness does strengthen the possibility of historical reliability. And for this, and other reasons, it is important to be concerned with the identity of the author of Acts.

CONCLUSION

The purpose of this chapter has been twofold. First, we inquired about the authorship of Acts. We noted that although Acts has reached us as an anonymous document, that should not in principle detain us from attempting to ascertain (as best we could), through historical research, the identity of the author. As far as documents external to Scripture, we focused our attention on Irenaeus of Lyons, a pivotal figure of the patristic period. Irenaeus (along with other contemporary documents) affirmed that the

---

[43]This was constantly emphasized by ancient historians. See Thucydides 1.1, 21-22; Polybius 4.2; 12.25, 27; Josephus, *Jewish War* 1.1-2; *Against Apion* 1.55; Lucian, *How to Write History* 29. This is one of the reasons why many historians wanted to limit themselves to events of recent memory rather than the mythical past. Hence Thucydides's statement in 1.21-22, which is probably aimed at Herodotus for his going to the mythical past. On the importance of the category of eyewitness for historical writings, see the important works of Samuel Byrskog, *Story as History—History as Story: The Gospel Tradition in the Context of Ancient Oral Historiography*, WUNT 1.123 (Tübingen: Mohr Siebeck, 2000); and Richard Bauckham, *Jesus and the Eyewitnesses: The Gospels as Eyewitness Testimony* (Grand Rapids: Eerdmans, 2006). We will develop this point in chapters two and three.

[44]There is debate on the exact nature of the "we" passages of Acts. See chapters two and three for further discussion. For the moment, it is sufficient to indicate that we hold these passages as evidence of Luke's participation in the events with the pronoun *we*. See David Aune, *The New Testament in Its Literary Environment*, LEC 8 (Philadelphia: Westminster, 1987), 122-24.

author of Luke-Acts was an individual by the name of Luke, who was a companion of the apostles and Paul. We argued that it was plausible that this information reflected preset, oral tradition that stemmed from the early second century, if not (at least as far as the name) from the original documents themselves. In addition, we noted that Irenaeus provided corroboration for this tradition by his own exegesis of Acts and Paul's letters. We concluded that the widespread patristic tradition that the author of Acts was Luke the companion of Paul was very plausible.

Having done this analysis on the question of the author of Acts, we asked whether in fact knowing who he was mattered for interpretation. Influenced, whether consciously or not, by streams of philosophical hermeneutics and narrative criticism, we observed that for many scholars the identity of the author of Acts is viewed as irrelevant. We argued that for those for whose interpretation of Acts the issue of historicity *is* relevant, knowing the identity of the author was very important. We noted that if the patristic tradition as well as the prologue and "we" passages pointed in the direction of an author who had had direct experience of the events described in his works, then there was a greater possibility of claim to historical reliability than if the author had indirect acquaintance with the described events, or none at all. This does not prove the historical accuracy of Acts, which is a matter of performance.

In this chapter we have made a number of comments about Acts as an example of a work of historiography. We have thus pulled the curtain slightly on our opinion of the book's genre. But is this the most plausible genre? What do we make of the current insistence of Acts as an ancient historical novel or as a foundational epic? In the chapter that follows we investigate in more depth the crucial question of the genre of Acts.

two

The Genre of Acts

I HAD ASKED WHAT I THOUGHT was a rather basic question to the Greek class of about twenty students. In response, the students stared blankly at me for a few seconds. And so, with a serious professorial look and somber tone, I said: "If nobody can answer this simple question, I will fail the entire class." The looks turned into frowns and widened eyes. There was an uncomfortable silence for a moment. Then, slowly, a smile began to form on the edge of my lips. First one student, then another, laughed in relief, and in a matter of seconds the entire class was laughing heartily, comprehending my attempt at being humorous.

This small incident in my class may serve as an illustration of how breakdowns in communication happen. On the part of the speaker, certain signals are given (in my case, a serious look and a somber tone) that raise particular expectations on the part of the hearers. The students were led to believe that my comment about failing the class was entirely serious. When I finally smiled, a different signal was given that led them to reformulate their previous conclusion. They then understood that the whole thing was meant to be comical. In fact, they should have known better from the beginning, since the class policy about grading (as outlined in the syllabus) clearly stated that evaluation would be based solely on written work. In other words, there was a context to help in evaluating the veracity of my comment. Despite this, for a few seconds the students and I were—as it were—playing a different game.

Now, if it is easy for there to be misunderstanding when the speaker is present—with all the aids of facial expressions, hand gestures and tone available—imagine how much easier it is to misinterpret when the medium of communication is the written page. In this case all the reader has are ink signs on paper. The speaker is in a sense absent and thus unable to clarify her ideas to the reader. In order to communicate effectively, therefore, writers follow certain conventions that generate in readers a set of expectations for what is to come, thus lighting an interpretational path for the readers to follow.

The terms that I have been using—*signals, games, expectations, conventions* —all lead to the concept of *genre*, an important tool in communication. Perhaps "important" is something of an understatement, for E. D. Hirsch, in his classic work *Validity in Interpretation*, can make the following statement: "All understanding of verbal meaning is necessarily genre-bound."[1] This would imply that if an audience is not competent in the genre in which a message is given, then miscommunication is bound to occur. Genre is thus essential. According to John Frow, "genre . . . defines a set of expectations which guide our engagement with texts."[2] A metaphor that has been used to explain the concept of genre is that of a "contract." Heather Dubrow explains this helpfully:

> The way genre establishes a relationship between author and reader might fruitfully be termed a generic contract. Through such signals as the title, the metre, and the incorporation of familiar topoi into his opening lines, the poet sets up such a contract with us. He in effect agrees that he will follow at least some of the patterns and conventions we associate with the genre . . . in which he is writing, and we in turn agree that we will pay close attention to certain aspects of his work while realizing that others, because of the nature of the genres, are likely to be far less important.[3]

As Dubrow states above, the "terms" of the contract are explained by *signals*. In his classic work on genre, Alastair Fowler speaks of "generic signals," which help to orientate the readers in their reading journey. He notes the following three signals as being of particular significance: allusions, titles

---

[1] E. D. Hirsch, *Validity in Interpretation* (New Haven, CT: Yale University Press, 1967), 76.
[2] John Frow, *Genre* (London: Routledge, 2005), 104.
[3] Heather Dubrow, *Genre* (London: Methuen, 1982), 31.

and opening topics. He comments on the last of these signals: "The generic markers that cluster at the beginning of a work have a strategic role in guiding the reader. They help to establish, as soon as possible, an appropriate mental 'set' that allows the work's generic codes to be read."[4] As we shall see later in this chapter, the prologue of Luke is essential in determining the genre of Acts.

Recently I read a very entertaining novel that focused on the obstacles to the American publication of Dante's *Divine Comedy*.[5] The novel is set, with exquisite detail, in 1865 Boston. The protagonists are the great American littérateurs and Harvard professors Henry Wadsworth Longfellow, Oliver Wendell Holmes and James Russell Lowell. As these men work on the first English translation in the United States of the great Italian poet, a number of murders happen in Boston. What is disconcerting about the murders is that they are modeled after the descriptions of tortures in Dante's *Inferno*, the very section of the *Divine Comedy* that the three professors are translating at that moment. Since no one in the Boston police knows this "coincidence," it falls to the three to become detectives and use the clues from the *Divine Comedy* in order to capture the murderer.

Now, I knew that this book was a novel for a number of reasons. First, I found it in that section of the bookstore labeled "Fiction." But perhaps the book, as often happens, had been misplaced. Perhaps it should have been in the section labeled "History." But there was a second reason I knew with certainty that the work was fictional. At the bottom of the back cover of the book, the label "fiction" was written. Third, the front matter of the book makes the following statement: "*The Dante Club* is a work of fiction. . . . Apart from the historical figures any resemblance between these fictional characters and actual persons, living or dead, is purely coincidental." But imagine for a moment that all indicators—bookstore section, back cover, front matter—were absent and that, given the fact that Longfellow and companions did exist in a Boston and Cambridge as described by the author, I had taken the book as a *history* text. I would

---

[4]Alastair Fowler, *Kinds of Literature: An Introduction to the Theory of Genres and Modes* (Oxford: Oxford University Press, 1982), 88.
[5]Matthew Pearl, *The Dante Club* (New York: Random House, 2003).

have then concluded that there were such things as "the Dante Murders" in Boston in 1865 (which of course never happened) and that three of America's greatest writers had for some time become detectives and had solved some of the most grotesque murders in this history of the United States. There would have been a massive misinterpretation on my part! And at the base of this equivocated reading would have been a failure to grasp the genre of the work.

What can occur in the reading of contemporary literature can also happen in the reading of the Bible. For the Scriptures, although the word of God, are written by humans: and humans cannot effectively communicate if their words do not participate in a genre. We often witness what happens in the study of Scripture when there is a mishandling of genre: wisdom statements such as those found in the book of Proverbs are taken as unconditional promises; features of apocalyptic literature (e.g., the book of Revelation) such as symbols and numbers are taken in a crude, literalistic manner; statements in epistolary literature (occasional documents) such as those of Paul are taken indiscriminately as timeless truths without noting the importance of the original context in the process of interpretation. More examples in other genres could be given. The consequence is a misreading of Scripture that results in bad theology and often in the erosion of the faith of many sincere believers.

If genre, then, is such an integral aspect of interpretation, it is critical that we investigate the genre of Acts. This is especially needed in view of the fact that there have recently been many proposals concerning the genre of Acts. At the moment, suggestions range from Acts as a foundational epic in the manner of Virgil's *Aeneid* to it as an example of ancient history—and many other genres in between. The decision we reach concerning the genre of Acts thus has significant repercussions for the way we approach the book.

But before turning to the different proposals about Acts's genre, it would be useful to explore the concept of genre a little deeper. This is necessary because genre theory has been developing at a fast pace in the past two decades or so. I will suggest below that there have been both negative and positive developments in our understanding of genre. Understanding the strengths and weaknesses of recent theories can provide a strong base from which to evaluate the different proposals for the genre of Acts. After looking at genre from a contemporary perspective at a theoretical level, we will present and assess current proposals for the genre of Acts. We will conclude the chapter with our own suggestion for the genre of Acts and the implications for interpretation.

A Brief History of Genre Theory

Three authors from the Greco-Roman period have exercised considerable influence in the history of genre-theory interpretation. These are Aristotle, Horace and Quintilian.[6] As often happens in the history of ideas, it is with the Greeks that we find initial conceptualizing. Therefore our concentration will be on Aristotle.

With respect to genre, although one finds some discussion in Plato (e.g., *Republic* 2-3, 10), it is generally agreed that the first robust arguments are found in Aristotle's *Poetics*.[7] In speaking of poetry, Aristotle mentions four "kinds" or "forms" (εἶδος). These are epic, tragedy, comedy and dithyrambic (1447a). These differ from one another in their imitation of nature in three ways: means of imitation, object of imitation and manner of imitation.[8] Aristotle makes a number observations about genre, of which the following three are important to keep in mind as we move forward. These observations, although not defended with the rigor of Aristotle, can also be found in Horace and Quintilian. First, insofar as genres are related to art, they are imitative or representational of real life—that is, they are *mimetic*.[9] Second, and following from the first point, there exists an appropriate, natural fit between a piece of literature and the characteristics of the genre in which it is communicated. As Dubrow notes, this principle of decorum was essential in ancient genre theory.[10] One final aspect of genre theory that can be gleaned from classical literature is the concept of genre purity. In the

---

[6]Dubrow, *Genre*, 46-52.

[7]For helpful discussions on ancient genre theory, see *Classical Literary Criticism*, ed. D. A. Russell and M. Winterbottom (Oxford: Oxford University Press, 1989), and Richard A. Burridge, *What Are the Gospels? A Comparison with Graeco-Roman Biography*, 2nd ed. (Grand Rapids: Eerdmans, 2004), 26-27.

[8]See Frow, *Genre*, 56-57.

[9]Aristotle, *Poetics* 1447a-1448b. The origins of Poetry, says Aristotle, come from nature (φυσικαί).

[10]Dubrow, *Genre*, 48. See also Burridge, *What Are the Gospels?*, 27. Burridge helpfully cites *Poetics* 1459b-1460a.

words of René Wellek and Austin Warren: "Classical theory not only believes that genre differs from genre . . . but also that they must be kept apart,
not allowed to mix."[11] Generally speaking, then, Greco-Roman literary
theory viewed genre not as arbitrary (i.e., there is no *natural* reason why
epic should be written in verse rather than prose), but as a fit dictated by
nature. Genre, therefore, theoretically speaking, was viewed as prescriptive,
static and pure. Concerning these aspects vis-à-vis the artist, Dubrow
notes: "The role of the artist is not to express his individuality through
exciting deviations from the art of the past . . . but rather to come as close
as possible to that perfect and natural form."[12]

The theory of genre from the Dark through the Middle Ages developed
very little, if at all.[13] It is in the Romantic movement of the eighteenth and
nineteenth centuries that we see the beginning of drastic changes in the
theory of genre, especially in Germany. Two developments in particular
are worth noting. First, there was a rejection of that facet of classical theory
that stated that genres were natural, universal givens that remained unchanging throughout time. In contrast, Romantics called attention to the
historical *situatedness* of genre. Genres change, they argued, and therefore
one cannot judge the quality of a contemporary work by the genre rules of
the classical period.[14] A second development, advanced in particular by
Friedrich Schlegel, was the devaluing of master, generic categories. Rather
(and as can perhaps be expected given the emphasis on individuality by
the Romantics), every literary work could be seen in the following way:
"Every poem is a genre unto itself."[15] As David Duff has indicated, the momentum created by the Romantics with respect to genre theory has continued into the present.[16] Indeed, beginning in the twentieth century, considerable changes in the theory of genre have emerged. These changes are
sometimes impassioned protests against the classical view of genre. They
include the following.

[11]René Wellek and Austin Warren, *Theory of Literature* (London: Penguin, 1949), 233-34.
[12]Dubrow, *Genre*, 48.
[13]But see ibid., 51-52.
[14]David Duff, *Modern Genre Theory*, ed. and introduced by David Duff (London: Longman, 2000), 3-4.
[15]Ibid., 4-5.
[16]Ibid., 3.

Revolt against prescriptivism. As we saw above, in ancient theory the relationship between literature and genres was viewed as stemming from nature. This led to a view of genre as primarily prescriptive. That is, genre was about exact rules that an author was required to follow to be faithful to the dictates of nature. To deviate from those rules (e.g., purpose of work, medium of presentation, tone, style, etc.) meant the risk of falling into generic oblivion. Perhaps worse, breaking the supposed natural templates of genres may have led to severe criticism by contemporaries and posterity. This extreme form of genre prescriptivism has come under attack. Although some of the initial protests went too far,[17] there is justification in critiquing a perspective of genre that views its principal contribution as dictating immutable rules that an author must follow to receive a favorable reception. On the other hand, one must be careful not to go to the other extreme by viewing the prescriptive aspect of genre as one that inevitably asphyxiates the creativity and artistic spark of an author. This has been a tendency since Romanticism; it has culminated in the modern period of literary theory, including some strands of postmodernity. As Duff states: "If the death of the author has been a familiar refrain of modern literary theory, so too has the dissolution of genres. . . . To the modern ear, the word genre . . . carries unmistakable associations of authority and pedantry."[18]

It is more defensible—theoretically and practically—to argue for a middle ground. Thus, while we recognize that the decision to write in a particular genre involves accepting certain conventions, those conventions should not be viewed as a communicative straitjacket. Rather, the conventions themselves are essential to communication, for genreless communication is an impossibility.[19] Those who view this prescriptive aspect of genre as destructive to originality have probably misunderstood the nature

---

[17]One thinks of Benedetto Croce's tirade: "The greatest triumph of the intellectualist error lies in the theory of artistic and literary kinds, which still has vogue in literary treatises and disturbs the critics and the historians of art" (*Aesthetic as Science of Expression and General Linguistic,* trans. Douglas Ainslie, 2nd ed. [London: Peter Owen, 1953], 35). I owe this quotation to Duff's helpful anthology, *Modern Genre Theory,* 25-28.

[18]Duff, *Modern Genre Theory,* 1.

[19]See Burridge, *What Are the Gospels?,* 26-52. Frow, *Genre,* 10, is also helpful here: "Generic structure both enables and restricts meaning, and is a basic condition for meaning to take place. . . . That is why genre matters: it is central to human meaning-making and to the social struggle over meanings."

and goal of genre. First, it is incorrect to say that boundaries (which are part of genre) and creativity are mutually exclusive. Second, the boundaries of genre are flexible. If this were not the case, it would be impossible for new genres to emerge or for existing genres to adapt to the exigencies of new eras (on which, see below). We should thus view genre as providing a *creative boundary* that makes effective communication between author and reader possible.

The flexibility of genre. We saw that for many centuries it was asserted that genres were both pure and unchanging throughout history. Let us focus on the issue of purity. As we have seen, the classical view is that there are clear, distinct boundaries between one genre and another. Thus there is no overlap between the genre features of, say, comedy and history. In this view there are no mixtures of features between genres.

In fact, the majority of scholars now agree that this theory does not emerge in practice, even in the Greco-Roman period, where we can see blending of generic features occurring. It is better to view the boundaries between genres as blurred. Fowler follows the helpful analogy of Blair when he states: "Literary compositions run into each other, precisely like colours: in their strong tints they are easily distinguished; but are susceptible of so much variety, and take on so many different forms, that we never can say where one species ends and another begins."[20] This view of genre may upset our ability to provide clear and hard classifications. But if it is remembered that the main purpose of genre is not that of labeling but meaning-making, then the interpreter may not be as upset with the blurry edges of genre. On the positive side, an abandonment of classical theory with respect to purity guards against reductionist conclusions as to what work is in and what is out in a particular genre. Since the focus of this work is the book of Acts, it will now be useful to develop this point by employing examples from the Greco-Roman period, that is—the period when Acts was written.

In the case of history—the genre traditionally most associated with Acts—it is true that the best-known authors of Greco-Roman historiography

---

[20]Fowler, *Kinds of Literature*, 37.

focused on the fate of the state as the subject of their works (e.g., Thucydides, Xenophon, Tacitus). This was a core generic feature for these authors. But does this mean that a work that, although having similar historiographic features in other areas, yet differed in subject (say, a focus on the customs of a particular ethnic group), could not have been conceived as belonging to the genre of history? Or, given the general sidelining of the supernatural as a direct cause for change in the state in Greco-Roman historiography, does this mean that a work that featured a deity (or deities) as a clear moving force could not have belonged to historiography? A purist understanding of genre flexibility would answer in the affirmative. But is this defensible in view of the ancient evidence?

A very important article by John Marincola has, in my opinion, dismantled this view.[21] Marincola offers a number of reasons for why the view has been entrenched that in the Greco-Roman period only works that dealt with political and military events were viewed as proper historiography. Two of his reasons are worth mentioning. First, he indicates that there has been an overreliance on the "great" historians (e.g., Thucydides, Polybius, Tacitus, etc.) due to an "over-representation" in surviving works.[22] This has led to an undervaluing of other evidence that suggests that other works were perceived as historiography that did *not* have the military deeds of the state as their subject. Concerning these works Marincola states: "There are, of course, political and military deeds, but there are also cultural events and activities; the religious life of a state and its people; the customs of a people, whether or not these are part of a formal religion."[23]

A second reason for the truncating view of what works could belong to ancient historiography has to do with the results of the monumental work of Felix Jacoby.[24] Jacoby, with a tremendous amount of confidence, postulated a system in which the only true history was "contemporary history" (*Zeitgeschichte*), its apogee being the work of Thucydides. Other pieces that

---

[21] John Marincola, "Genre, Convention, and Innovation in Greco-Roman Historiography," in *The Limits of Historiography: Genre and Narrative in Ancient Historical Texts*, ed. Christina Shuttleworth Kraus (Leiden: Brill, 1999), 281-324.

[22] For this observation Marincola draws on G. Schepens.

[23] Marincola, "Genre, Convention, and Innovation," 307.

[24] This refers to the multivolume *Die Fragmente der griechischen Historiker*.

did not share the features of contemporary history as exemplified in Thucydides were implicitly relegated to something lower than history by being labeled with terms such as mythography, ethnography and so on. What led Jacoby to this classification? Although there are many complex reasons, Marincola helpfully suggests that Jacoby's understanding of *genre* was a major factor. He speaks of Jacoby's "generally static notion of genre." Marincola correctly diagnoses Jacoby's failure to grasp the place of innovation in generic development: "Whereas exact imitation was merely mechanical and/or decorative, the better writers were able to take something familiar and place it in a new context or frame not seen before. *It is this openness to this aspect of historiography that seems to me most lacking in Jacoby's schema.*"[25]

A nuanced understanding of the flexible nature of genre is essential for proper discussion and grasping of the genre of Acts. Understanding that each particular genre has external and internal traits (on which, see below), but that these traits, although generally resembling each other, *are not identical* in the respective examples of the genre, may go a long way in stabilizing the discussion and providing a defensible proposal for the genre of Acts.

The mention above of what constitutes a valid subject for historiography may have triggered in the perceptive reader the recognition of a gap. The reader may be saying: "Wait a minute. You speak of the potential, proper subject of the genre of historiography as if this were something that could be universally agreed upon. But what if I come from a culture where our view of history is different from the Greek one? What if for my culture, due to philosophical and religious reasons, history *does* include the work of God in shaping civilizations? Who has the right to decide what proper history is and what it is not?" The perceptive reader has identified the final development of genre theory to be discussed.

Genre as a category of reception. Postmodern literary theory, as is well known, has endeavored to shift the locus of interpretation to the pole of the reader or reading community. Whereas previously the attempt to

---

[25]Marincola, "Genre, Convention, and Innovation," 299-300; emphasis added.

validate a particular interpretation of a work rested on the reader's ability to understand the intention of the author (as this intention was found apart from the text or in the text), the current tendency, especially in North America, is to focus on the reading community. That is, validation of a work's meaning (assuming that this could ever be retrieved) rests on group consciousness.[26] Many postmodern critics, therefore, "emphasize the reader's reactions to the text to the exclusion of the writer who created it."[27] It should come as no surprise that this has affected contemporary understanding of genre. We can put the contemporary tendency like this: the genre of a work is a category imputed on the text by the readers. In other words, it is the readers who have the final word on the type of genre that a work is.

This view can seem particularly attractive when we are dealing with ancient texts. First, the author is obviously not around to be asked what genre he was writing in. Second, even though titles of works survive and thus are helpful in determining the perception of ancient readers with regard to the genre of a particular work, generic labels were not affixed to ancient works. We are thus dependent on the decisions of reading communities or institutions for the determination of the genre of a piece of literature. To put it bluntly, the genre of a work is what we decide it is.

This understanding of genre has recently been applied to a study of Luke-Acts by Swiss scholar Claire Clivaz.[28] We will have a chance to interact with her work in more depth in the following pages. For the moment the goal is to describe her approach to the genre of Luke-Acts as a category of reception.

Clivaz places herself in what she considers the third stage of genre history—namely, the metacritical stage, which begins at the end of the twentieth century.[29] The following are two of the traits of the metacritical

---

[26]Perhaps the most popular work in this respect is Stanley Fish, *Is There a Text in This Class? The Authority of Interpretive Communities* (Cambridge, MA: Harvard University Press, 1982).

[27]Dubrow, *Genre*, 109. For a masterful analysis and critique of this view, see Kevin J. Vanhoozer, *Is There a Meaning in This Text? The Bible, the Reader, and the Morality of Literary Knowledge* (Grand Rapids: Zondervan, 1998).

[28]Claire Clivaz, *L'Ange et la Sueur de Sang (Lc 22, 43-44). Ou Comment on Pourrait Bien Encore Écrire L'Histoire* (Leuven: Peeters, 2010).

[29]Ibid., 25.

stage. First, the lines between historical and fictional writings have been blurred: history already incorporates a number of fictive elements that challenge a sharp separation between it and fictional works such as the novel. Conversely, fictional works themselves contain historical features.[30] Second, genre is viewed as a category of reception.[31] Clivaz explains: "I consider . . . that literary genre is a category of *reception* continually present: every historical analysis lives from the effect of genre learned in school." This leads to the conclusion that we need to learn to work with an evolutionary notion of genre, because "a text can change its literary genre following its context of reception."[32]

The postmodern suggestion that genre classification is a matter of the decision of reading communities has some appeal. This appeal is all the stronger with respect to ancient literature. In addition to what we mentioned previously, there is a paucity of extant material, which makes comparisons difficult. Also, the chronological gap ensures that the features of genres have changed dramatically, and this forces us to move with trepidation into the foreign country that is the past. It thus often happens that in practice the genre that sticks to a particular piece is that which readers or institutions or communities assign to it. There are also benefits to viewing genre as a category of reception. First, its open-endness enforces humility on our interpretations. Second, it fosters dialogue and thus refinement in our examination of genres.

However, there are some problems with the view that genre is primarily a category of reception. Recall Clivaz's statement: "A text can change its literary genre following its context of reception." It is one thing to say that our *perception* of a work's genre may change depending on the context of reception; it is quite another to say that a work's genre *actually* changes depending on when and where it is received. The latter affirmation would be an eradication of the author—and thus lead to complete indeterminacy in the manner of Jacques Derrida. In fact, the view that a work's genre is determined entirely by its reception is based on the so-called death of the

---

[30]Ibid., 9-13. Clivaz sees the work of Erich Auerbach (*Mimesis*) as foundational to this new orientation.
[31]Ibid., 24-33.
[32]Ibid., 55.

author, which is often part of postmodern philosophical hermeneutics. We had occasion to interact briefly with the works of Ricoeur and Gadamer in the previous chapter, where their emphasis on the role of the reader in the constitution of meaning was flagged. While Gadamer seemed to go a little too far in the meaning-making activity of the reader, Ricoeur posited a more credible account in which the role of the writer as the author of meaning was not eclipsed.[33] We believe that a nuanced approach to author-intended meaning thus remains the most defensible view. Thus in speaking of an ancient book such as Acts, we can say that it falls on *us* as readers to propose a genre, since the work itself does not announce its genre unequivocally. However, our proposal must be tested against the generic markers of the work, *which were put in the text by an author who wrote at a specific time in history*. To say that genre is solely a category of reception may open the door for the legitimacy of entirely anachronistic readings. Genre, in fact, functions as a fence against such anachronistic readings, for "literary genres have, as communicative practices, a social and historical location. That is, literary genres themselves have determinate historical contexts."[34]

For our present study I suggest that the postmodern angle of genre as a category of reception is very helpful—but not, as Clivaz stated, as reception "continually present." Rather, to understand what Luke is communicating in Acts it is necessary to concentrate on the *primitive* reception, which occurred, depending on the date that we assign to the publication of Acts, sometime between 60 and 100 CE.[35] This is another way of asking who the implied readers of Acts are: "If we want to hear Luke's distinctive socio-cultural voice within the interlocking worlds of ancient Mediterranean discourse, we have to identify not only what game he is playing, but which team he plays for."[36] I will suggest that, for various reasons, the "team" he is playing for has been profoundly shaped by the Old Testament and

---

[33]We will come back to Ricoeur in chapter three.

[34]Vanhoozer, *Is There a Meaning*, 339.

[35]Recently there have been restatements of the older view of John Knox—that is, that Acts is to be dated into the second century. See, for example, Joseph Tyson, *Marcion and Luke-Acts: A Defining Struggle* (Columbia: University of South Carolina Press, 2006). We find a date for Acts in the second century as unconvincing.

[36]Loveday Alexander, *Acts in Its Ancient Literary Context: A Classicist Looks at the Acts of the Apostles*, LNTS 298 (London: T&T Clark, 2005), 15.

Jewish tradition. We do well, then, to try to hear his voice within this context of reception.

Conclusion. This section has been necessarily heavy on matters of theory. It will be helpful to summarize our conclusions as we move forward. First, we indicated that in order to understand a work properly it is crucial to have a handle on the genre in which the author is writing. Misunderstanding of genre leads to complete breakdowns in communication. Second, and drawing from modern literary theory, we suggested that the main purpose of genre is not primarily to provide neat classifications. Rather, genre serves to give guidance on how readers should approach a literary work. Third, we showed that genre is flexible. That is, examples of a particular genre do not all share exactly the same generic features: "The temptation to think of genre as defined by *one* particular feature, or even a couple, should be avoided because any one feature can appear in a number of different sorts of works. Therefore, one should look for many features; it is the combination of them which constitutes the genre."[37] We thus need to examine a cluster of features in the areas of form and content in order to reach a conclusion on the genre of a work. Last, we discussed the matter of genre reception. We argued that—especially for ancient works—reading communities must assign a particular genre to a work when that work does not unequivocally reveal its genre. However, we stated that *justification* for a particular genre must rest on the generic features of that work (placed by the author) *as read by the audience contemporary with the ancient author.*[38] In the case of Acts, we believe that audience to have been Christians who were deeply influenced by the Old Testament and possibly Second Temple Jewish literature. Before turning to our particular proposal, it is necessary to canvass other suggestions for the genre of Acts.

PROPOSALS ON THE GENRE OF ACTS

The different suggestions are presented below from the most recent proposals to those that have been part of Acts scholarship for a longer period.

---

[37]Burridge, *What Are the Gospels?*, 41.

[38]The assumption here is that the ancient audience, due to its chronological and ideological proximity to the author, was well equipped to grasp the generic signs placed in the work by the author. The other assumption is that an author would write in a genre familiar to his audience precisely because he wants to be understood by that audience.

Acts as epic. Two authors in particular have made the case for the genre of Acts as an epic in the tradition of Homer and Virgil. The first to be mentioned is Marianne Palmer Bonz in her Harvard dissertation published as *The Past as Legacy: Luke-Acts and Ancient Epic.*[39] She argues that we should view Luke-Acts as a foundational epic, modeled after the *Aeneid*. The Christians addressed by Luke-Acts (mostly Gentiles, according to Bonz) were looking for a way to strengthen their identity.[40] Using the *Aeneid* as a literary model was a great fit for Luke-Acts, as the Roman epic was written to validate the legacy of the Romans by positing their origins to go back to the ancient past. In her words:

> Just as Virgil had created his foundational epic for the Roman people by appropriating and transforming Homer, so also did Luke create his foundational epic for the early Christian community primarily by appropriating and transforming the sacred traditions of Israel's past as narrated in the Bible of the diasporan Jewish communities, the Septuagint.[41]

Thus in the shaping of his narrative Luke uses a bipartite plot structure as well as prophetic-fulfillment motifs to demonstrate that the present of his readers is the eschatological fulfillment of the Scriptures.[42] This is a striking imitation of the *Aeneid*, argues Bonz, thereby showing that Luke-Acts should be equally considered an epic.

The strongest point of Bonz's book is her argument that one of the main purposes of Luke-Acts is the fortification of the readers' identity. This is a position that has been gaining strength in the past decade.[43] There are, however, what I believe to be insurmountable obstacles to her proposal that Luke-Acts is an epic. First, there is the problem of the availability of the *Aeneid* in Greek for Luke's period. For, Bonz suggests, the version of the *Aeneid* available for Luke was a written prose version translated into

---

[39]Marianne Palmer Bonz, *The Past as Legacy: Luke-Acts and Ancient Epic* (Minneapolis: Fortress, 2000).

[40]Bonz believes that Luke-Acts was written between 90 and 100 CE (ibid., 92).

[41]Ibid., 26.

[42]Ibid., 87-128.

[43]This argument has been presented in a persuasive fashion by Daniel Marguerat, *The First Christian Historian: Writing the "Acts of the Apostles,"* trans. Ken McKinney, Gregory Laughery and Richard Bauckham, SNTSMS 121 (Cambridge: Cambridge University Press, 2002), 32-34; idem, *Les Actes des Apôtres 1-12* (Genève: Labor et Fides, 2007), 24. Cf. also Osvaldo Padilla, *The Speeches of Outsiders in Acts: Poetics, Theology and Historiography*, SNTSMS 144 (Cambridge: Cambridge University Press, 2008), 235-36.

Greek by Polybius the freedman, not the extant Latin form.[44] Yet, there is considerable debate concerning the circulation of the *Aeneid* in this Greek version in the first century CE.[45] Second, Bonz's argument that *both* Luke and Acts should be viewed as epic does not sufficiently grapple with the debate of the possibility (one may legitimately say *probability*) of the different genres of the two volumes. The Gospel of Luke is almost certainly an ancient *bios*; Acts is probably something different. By suggesting that the double work is an epic, Bonz flattens out the differences between Luke and Acts. Third, there are problems with Bonz's understanding of genre. Although there are many internal and external differences between the *Aeneid* and Luke-Acts, perhaps the most striking is the difference in medium: the *Aeneid* (at least the Latin version that survives!) is written in Latin hexameter verse while Luke-Acts is clearly prose. Although we certainly do not want to fall into the trap of basing a genre on only one feature, nevertheless the writing of epic in verse was such a fundamental feature (e.g., Homer) that assigning a work written in prose to the epic genre immediately raises red flags. It is highly unlikely that ancient readers would have recognized Luke-Acts as an epic. Fourth, the majority of the parallels that Bonz adduces between the *Aeneid* and Luke-Acts are superficial; she comes very close to parallelomania. Last, we must call attention to Bonz's discussion of the historical claims of Luke-Acts.

Bonz, as she indicates toward the end of her presentation, realizes that the categorization of Luke-Acts as epic represents a serious blow to the credibility of the double work's historical portrait of early Christianity.[46] She attempts to soften the blow by blurring the lines between the genres of epic and history as understood in the ancient world. She thus states: "Homeric epic would qualify as historiography . . . because it conveys the truth about the past—even if that truth is expressed in mythological language."[47] Evidently following Rosalind Thomas, Bonz believes this to be the case because the bard depended on the muses, who were viewed as

---

[44]Bonz, *Past as Legacy*, 24-25.
[45]See the review of Bonz's work by Gregory Sterling in *CBQ* 63 (2001): 334-35.
[46]See especially Bonz, *Past as Legacy*, 183-89.
[47]Ibid., 15.

the guarantors of truth. Thus epic should be viewed as making truth-claims in the same manner that history makes truth-claims.

I am quite surprised that Bonz would affirm that for the ancient audience epic would have been viewed as making truth-claims in the manner of historiography because the former was inspired by the muses. The muses were not in fact "guarantors of truth." The *Theogony* of Hesiod, one of the best-known works of the ancient world, has the muses stating at the beginning: "We know how to say many lies like the truth, and, whenever we wish, we know how to tell the truth" (1.27-28).[48] Removing Bonz's view of the muses as guarantors of truth brings us back to the issue of truth-claims. While it is true that both epic and history refer to the past, we must ask *how* they refer to the past. History refers to the past by making a truth-claim. The author is saying: "My presentation of the past is accurate. I am describing things as they were."[49] One of the ways a historian does this is by the citation of sources that can be checked. Hence, historians often write of the recent past, when evidence is more ready at hand. Epic poets, on the other hand, write of archaic periods, where the distance from the present is so far that they cannot be checked—of course they are not making truth-claims to the effect that their representation of the past is a fit with that past. Hence they can spin tales as they please.

Bonz also fails to ask the question of the status of epic vis-à-vis history in the thought of the Greco-Roman period, and here the evidence is straightforward. Consider Aristotle: "It is also evident from what has been said that it is not the poet's function to relate actual events [τὰ γενόμενα], but the *kinds* of things that might occur and are possible in terms of probability or necessity."[50] Lucian, criticizing historians for excessive liberty with the facts, states:

> Again, such writers seem unaware that history has aims and rules different from poetry and poems. In the case of the latter, liberty is absolute and there is one law—the will of the poet. Inspired and possessed by the Muses as he

---

[48]See also the discussion in Paul Veyne, *Did the Greeks Believe in their Myths?* (Chicago: University of Chicago Press, 1988), 23, 136-37, and his citations of Strabo, *Geography* 1.2.9.

[49]This of course can be subverted for the purposes of parody, as we see in Lucian's *True History*.

[50]Aristotle, *Poetics* 1450-51.

is, even if he wants to harness winged horses to a chariot, even if he sets others to run over water or the tops of flowers, nobody gets annoyed.[51]

Thus Bonz's excessive blurring of the boundaries between epic poetry and history goes against the Greco-Roman tradition of Luke's period. Her arguments therefore fail to carry convincing force.

While Bonz compared Luke-Acts with Virgil's *Aeneid*, Dennis MacDonald compares it with the Homeric epics.[52] MacDonald correctly emphasizes the supreme status of Homer as the literary voice of the Hellenic world. Consequently, it is not surprising that he was the most studied and imitated of all authors.[53] As a matter of accessibility and imitation, therefore, it would not be strange if Luke imitated Homer. This is especially so as MacDonald considers Luke to have been highly educated.[54] Luke's audience, even if not the educated elite, would also have known Homer, as the poet's work was disseminated in festivals, art, coins and pottery, to name some media.[55] MacDonald goes on to compare a number of passages from Acts with some important episodes from the *Iliad*.[56] He concludes that Luke certainly imitated Homer in his composition.

MacDonald's work is intriguing and creative; it will surely open some interesting avenues for future research into Luke-Acts. Nevertheless, there are crippling weaknesses in both his method as well as his parallels, with the result that supposed imitations of Homer are at best strained and at worst sheer parallelomania. As Karl Olav Sandnes has subjected MacDonald's work to detailed and persuasive criticism, we shall only focus on two issues specifically related to genre.[57]

First, for as much attention as MacDonald gives to Homeric imitation in Acts, he does not say how this affects the genre of the work. The closest

---

[51]Lucian, *How to Write History* 8. See also idem, *A Conversation with Hesiod* 5; Herodotus 2.118, 120.

[52]Dennis MacDonald, *Does the New Testament Imitate Homer? Four Cases from the Acts of the Apostles* (New Haven, CT: Yale University Press, 2003).

[53]Ibid., 2-4.

[54]Ibid., 7.

[55]Ibid., 3.

[56]Ibid., 19-145. The Acts's episodes are the following: the Cornelius episode (Acts 10:1–11:18); Paul's farewell at Miletus (Acts 20:18-35); the selection of Matthias (Acts 1:15-26); Peter's prison escape (Acts 5; 12).

[57]Karl Olav Sandnes, "*Imitatio Homeri*? An Appraisal of Dennis R. MacDonald's 'Mimesis Criticism,'" *JBL* 112 (2005): 715-32.

he comes to an indication is the following: "In fact, the preface to the Gospel of Luke *seems* to imply that the author set out to compose a history *of sorts*."[58] It is not clear what generic classification MacDonald assigns to Acts by this phrase. From the context of his work (especially pp. 146-51), it appears that he considers it inferior history because the author invented material. This leads to a second observation. Concerning the historical reliability of Acts, MacDonald is not at all optimistic. He states concerning Luke: "He not only wrote up stories; he made up stories in the interest of advancing his understanding of the good news of Jesus Christ."[59] MacDonald disagrees with a number of scholars who view Luke's literary achievement as consisting primarily in arranging of material.[60] For him, Luke "created each of these stories as fictions to imitate or emulate famous stories in the *Iliad* and without the benefit of preexisting traditions."[61] The following logic seems to be at work here: *either* Luke is simply an assembler of traditions *or* he is an inventor of stories. In this way MacDonald does away with a significant bloc of Acts scholarship that argues for use of traditional material in a creative yet historically responsible manner (see below). Further, MacDonald's logic betrays a positivist understanding of historiography. For him it appears that originality necessarily entails invention. Yet, as we will show in chapter three, authorial originality (such as is seen in emplotment and point of view)[62] is not antithetical to faithful use of sources and reporting of the past.

Acts is not an ancient epic. While it is true that Acts shares some of the purposes of epic (such as the strengthening of a community's identity), this does not make it an epic any more than a dish with beef and tomato sauce is necessarily a lasagna. Not only is there a flawed understanding of genre in this view, but also the parallels adduced, when looked at in detail, fail to convince.

---

[58]MacDonald, *Does the New Testament Imitate Homer?*, 146; emphasis added.

[59]Ibid., 147.

[60]But is this a fair characterization of what scholars say about *Acts*? When it comes to the *Gospel*, many scholars do have a tendency to view Luke's work as cutting and pasting; but this is hardly the view in the case of Acts. MacDonald seems to be erecting a straw man that he can easily demolish.

[61]MacDonald, *Does the New Testament Imitate Homer?*, 146.

[62]By "emplotment" I refer to the historian's shaping of tradition into a narrative with a beginning and end.

Acts as an ancient novel. One genre of the Greco-Roman period that has generated discussion among classicists in the last forty years or so is the ancient novel. Whereas previously the ancient novel had been viewed with suspicion in the light of the great Greek and Roman classics, beginning in the early 1970s it began to be rescued from the fringes.[63] Two publications marked the ascendancy of the novel as a proper subject of study for the ancient world: the user-friendly English anthology of the novels edited by B. P. Reardon in 1989 and the excellent, large collection of studies edited by Schmeling and published by Brill in 1996.[64] Cross-fertilization between the different disciplines has been happening, with the result that the Society of Biblical Literature has a long-standing session named Ancient Fiction and Early Christian Narrative.

In biblical studies the author who has made formal and generic comparisons between Acts and the ancient novel with the most erudition and persuasion is Richard Pervo.[65] He has called attention to the motif of adventure, a constant in the ancient novel and the Acts of the Apostles. Examples of adventure shared by Acts and the novels include incarceration, persecution, intrigue, riots, trials, shipwreck and travel.[66] Pervo argues that while Acts certainly seeks to instruct through these adventures, it also attempts to entertain—and this is exactly what the ancient novels sought to do in their narration of adventures. In addition, Pervo argues that the literary style of Acts does not match that of the ancient historians, fitting much better with popular writings such as the novels.[67] In his early monograph Pervo argues without much equivocation that when these features are taken into consideration, Acts should be viewed not as ancient history but as an ancient novel that gave rise to the apocryphal Acts: "When the content of Acts, with its high proportion of exciting episodes, legendary presentations, and brief speeches, is taken into account, the scale tilts even more sharply toward the

---

[63]For the rise of the study of the ancient novel in classical scholarship, see Gareth Schmeling in *The Novel in the Ancient World*, ed. Gareth Schmeling (Leiden: Brill, 1996), 1-9.

[64]The former is B. P. Reardon, ed., *Collected Ancient Greek Novels* (Berkeley: University of California Press, 1989). For the latter, see footnote 63.

[65]See Richard Pervo, *Profit with Delight: The Literary Genre of the Acts of the Apostles* (Philadelphia: Fortress, 1987); idem, *Acts: A Commentary* (Minneapolis: Fortress, 2009).

[66]Pervo, *Profit with Delight*, 12-57.

[67]Pervo, *Acts*, 17.

historical novel."[68] By contrast, in his massive commentary published twelve years later, Pervo appears to have changed his mind. At one point he states: "Acts is a history."[69] When one reads Pervo's comments in the following paragraphs, however, it is clear that he has not actually changed his mind. First, immediately after his comment above, he continues: "The author has produced a coherent story in conformity with a plan, and his subject includes historical persons, places, and events."[70] But one can make this same comment of a Hemingway or Vargas Llosa novel. As we have seen, the issue of truth-claims toward the past is a necessary ingredient to differentiate between the historical novel and history. It thus appears that when Pervo says that Acts is "a history," he is using that phrase in a way similar to the French expression *une histoire* or the Spanish *una historia*, where the indefinite pronoun makes all the difference between understanding *histoire* or *historia* as history or as a story. I cannot see why Pervo would use this expression when what he wants to say, as we shall see presently, is that Acts is a type of ancient novel. This only brings confusion to the debate.

Second, his statement toward the end of his discussion on genre is telling: "Luke's achievement as a historian lies more in his success at creating history than in recording it."[71] The book of Acts, it appears Pervo is saying, because it speaks of historical characters and places, is a repository of knowledge of the early church that its author has creatively woven together in order to move his readers toward a new horizon. His concern was not to be faithful to the past but rather to *use* the past in order to create a future for his community. Acts is thus primarily parasitic of the past in the way that a contemporary historical novel may use the Elizabethan age to spin a tale in order to entertain readers. In this way, although Acts is not history, it *creates* history.

By way of assessment it must be said that Pervo is correct in calling attention to the similarities between Acts and ancient novels, especially one of the early ones, i.e., Chariton's *Callirhoe*. There are some striking similarities

---

[68] Pervo, *Profit with Delight*, 137.
[69] Pervo, *Acts*, 15.
[70] Ibid.
[71] Ibid., 18.

between Acts and this novel. For example, Chariton's syntax is very similar to that of Acts (especially the second half of Acts). We find in both the type of "intermediary" Hellenistic prose (as Lars Rydbeck puts it[72]) that is free of classicizing tendencies. It is neither the barbarous (from a Greek perspective) paratactic syntax of some parts of the Septuagint or the Atticizing Greek with remarkable freedom of word order that is found in some of the later novels.[73] Another example of strong similarity is the use of speeches in Acts and the novel: both prefer short, direct speeches rather than the long, elaborate pieces one often finds in historians, which are moreover often cast in indirect speech.[74] One last example to give is the similarity of scenes found in both Acts and the novels. Particularly impressive are the episodes in *Callirhoe* in the theater at Syracuse (1.1.11-13) and the trial of Mithridates (5.4.5-6), which are strikingly similar to the assembly at Ephesus in Acts 19:28-41 and the trial of Paul before Festus, Agrippa and Bernice in Acts 25:23–26:1, respectively.

Although I can appreciate some of the parallels drawn by Pervo, there are still significant differences between Acts and the novel. These variances make a classification of Acts as an ancient novel improbable. First, as far as *theme*, the indisputable theme of the novels is Eros, romance between lovers. The lovers are usually separated by cruel fate only to be eventually reunited after considerable danger and adventure. If this is one of the core features that marked out the novelistic genre, then the ancient reader could not have possibly considered Acts a novel. Second, we may speak of *tone*. There is an overall sobriety and economy of expression in Acts that makes it look like a docile pet in comparison to the verbose, glittery and dramatic aura of the novels. Third, there is the matter of *authorial voice*. The narrator of Acts, once the preface is finished, is less intrusive in breaking into the flow of the narrative to give his opinion on a matter.[75] By contrast, the authors

---

[72]Lars Rydbeck, "Bible," in *RPP*, 2:12-13. See also B. P. Reardon's comments in his introduction to the translation of *Callirhoe* in *Collected Ancient Greek Novels*, 17-21.
[73]Ewen Bowie, "The Ancient Readers of the Greek Novels," in *The Novel in the Ancient World*, 88, calls the novels by Achilles Tatius, Longus and Heliodoros "sophistic."
[74]On which, see Richard Pervo, "Direct Speech in Acts and the Question of Genre," *JSNT* 28 (2006): 285-307.
[75]See Alexander, *Acts in Its Ancient Literary Context*, 158-59. For some examples, see the section "Acts as a Historical Monograph" in this chapter.

of the novels constantly intrude. The narrator in Chariton, for example, repeatedly sticks his head into the narrative to give a "word of wisdom" about the machinations of Eros.

It is to the credit of Pervo that he has blown the whistle on the repeated assertion that an ancient reader would have immediately thought of Acts as an example of classical history. As we shall see below, Acts is not an example of one of the great histories of the Greco-Roman epoch. But Pervo's own solution is also incorrect. Despite some strong similarities, there is a cluster of internal and external differences that shows that Acts does not belong to the ancient novel genre.

Acts as history. The traditional view of Acts's generic affiliation is that it is an example of history. Even those authors, like F. C. Baur and E. Haenchen, who dismissed the historical reliability of Acts viewed the document as an example of history. To be sure, due to what they viewed as the incorrigible theological tendencies of the author, they considered Acts to be full of errors and fabrications: to them Acts was bad history, but history nonetheless. We can say that despite the recent proposals sketched above (i.e., epic and novel), the dominant view continues to be that Acts belongs to the genre of history.[76] However, what exactly is meant by *history* is now vigorously debated. The conclusion of Thomas Phillips seems to me to be on target: "Is Acts history or fiction? In the eyes of most scholars, it is history—but not the kind of history that precludes [*sic*] fiction."[77] History, however, is a very broad genre, and so there have been numerous suggestions as to what specific type of history Acts is. Since these proposals have been competently surveyed in other places, I will limit the discussion here to my own proposal for the genre of Acts and justifications for this proposal.[78] I will conclude by noting the interpretational gains of a reasonable grasp of this genre.

---

[76]See the bibliography in Craig Keener, *Acts: An Exegetical Commentary* (Grand Rapids: Baker, 2012), 1:51, 90-91.

[77]Thomas E. Phillips, "The Genre of Acts: Moving Toward a Consensus?," *CBR* 4 (2006): 365-96, quotation on 385.

[78]See Phillips, "Genre of Acts"; Darryl Palmer, "Acts and the Ancient Historical Monograph," in *The Book of Acts in Its Ancient Literary Setting*, ed. A. D. Clarke and Bruce Winter (Grand Rapids: Eerdmans, 1993), 1-30. Most recently see Keener, *Acts*, 1:51-115; and Sean A. Adams, "The Genre of Luke and Acts: The State of the Question," in *Issues in Luke-Acts: Selected Essays*, ed. Sean A. Adams and Michael Pahl (Piscataway, NJ: Gorgias, 2012), 97-120.

Acts as a historical monograph. It is my suggestion that Acts is *a Hellenistic historical monograph in the Jewish tradition.* The term *historical monograph* did not exist in antiquity and as such is a modern label. Nevertheless, it is clear from Greco-Roman literature that such a type of historical genre did in fact exist. Consider the following examples.

The Hellenistic historian Polybius makes a contrast between "universal histories" and histories that are κατὰ μέρος or ἐπὶ μέρους—that is, "particular histories" that *concentrate on a particular subject and a limited time period.*[79] Consider the following statements:

> A historian should likewise bring before his readers under one synoptical view the operations by which she [Fortune] has accomplished her general purpose. Indeed it was this chiefly that invited and encouraged me to undertake my task; and secondly the fact that none of my contemporaries have undertaken to write a general history.... As it is, I observe that while several modern writers deal with particular wars [κατὰ μέρος πολέμους] and certain matters connected with them, no one, as far as I am aware, has even attempted to inquire critically when and whence the general and comprehensive scheme of events originated and how it led up to the end. (Polybius 1.4. LCL)

He further adds:

> We can no more hope to perceive this [movements of Fortune] from histories dealing with particular events [τῶν κατὰ μέρος γραφόντων] than to get at once a notion of the form of the whole world, its disposition and order, by visiting, each in turn, the most famous cities, or indeed looking at separate pictures of each.... He indeed who believes that by studying isolated histories [διὰ τῆς κατὰ μέρος ἱστορίας] he can acquire a fairly just view of history as a whole, is ... much in the case of one, who, after having looked at the dissevered limbs of an animal once alive and beautiful, fancies he has been as good as an eyewitness of the creature itself in all its action and grace.... Special histories [τὴν κατὰ μέρος ἱστορίαν] therefore contribute very little to the knowledge of the whole and conviction of its truth. (Polybius 1.4. LCL)

---

[79]See the important essay, on which I here depend, by Darryl Palmer cited in footnote 78 above, esp. 5-8.

As ancient authors were inclined to do in their prefaces, so here Polybius seeks to enhance the value of his work by criticizing the works of contemporaries in the same field. Polybius indicates that writing comprehensive history—which is what he is doing—is the most useful. In the process he censures those historians who choose to write isolated histories dealing with discrete events over a relatively short period of time. His statements show that there existed a subset of historiography that fits the description of what we call a historical monograph.

We get a further sense of the existence and nature of the historical monograph from Cicero's correspondence with his close friend Atticus. Cicero tells Atticus: "I have sent you a copy of my account of my consulship in Greek" (*Letters to Atticus* 1.19). Writing a few months later he informs Atticus that he has received the latter's evidently revised form of Cicero's consulship account. Cicero tells Atticus that he is still not content with the memoir and has thus sent a copy to Posidonius for elaboration. He asks Atticus to disseminate the book in Athens and other Greek towns, "for I think it may add some luster to my achievements" (*Letters to Atticus* 2.1). Interestingly enough, he adds that he will send Atticus some speeches, presumably to be added to the work. Cicero goes on to mention a number of the speeches, including the one reported by Sallust in the Catiline debacle. Cicero thus envisions a historical work that treats a short period of time (his consulship) focusing on a particular figure (Cicero himself) with a number of speeches. Importantly, in another correspondence still dealing with Cicero's desire to have his deeds and words published (*Letters to Friends* 5.12), he brings up Greek models that are similar to what he envisions, thus showing that there existed a tradition for the historical monograph.[80]

Besides the indirect evidence mentioned above, we actually possess two historical monographs by the Roman historian Sallust: *War with Catiline* and *War with Jugurtha*. These monographs are limited in subject and the

---

[80]On this, see especially Eckhard Plümacher, "Die Apostelgeschicte als historische Monographie," in *Les Actes des Apôtres. Traditions, rédaction, théologie*, BETL 48 (Leuven: Leuven University Press, 1979), esp. 461-62, where he emphasizes that Cicero's description of the historical monograph is not original with the Roman politician but has a long tradition among the Greeks. I have been helped in much of the above discussion by Plümacher's essay as well as Palmer, "Historical Monograph," 11-13.

length of period they cover,[81] and, as historian Ronald Syme suggests, have a tendency to concentrate on one individual.[82] They also include a large amount of material cast in direct speech.

To sum up, both by what we read from ancient authors as well as extant examples, we find a species of historiography that is different from the universal histories of Herodotus or Polybius. This type of history, which modern scholars call a historical monograph, has a more concentrated focus in terms of time period, subject and characters. The historical monograph, as we can observe from Cicero and Sallust, includes narrative and speeches, being particularly rich in the latter. In addition, in terms of narrative management, the historical monograph appears to be episodic in nature. A number of scholars have come to the conclusion that Acts fits well with the ancient historical monograph.[83] They draw attention to the following important parallels: devotion to a relatively short period of time; limited focus on the subject (for Acts, the spread of the gospel from Jerusalem to Rome); episodic nature; concentration on one or two characters; and a rich amount of direct speech. This is the sort of *cluster* of external and internal features that allows us to align a work with a particular genre.

There is, however, a glaring difference between the historical monograph as explained above and Acts: the Greco-Roman historical monograph is decidedly focused on the affairs of the state such as war and politics. The role of the gods is sidelined—*precisely* because history as conceived by the Greeks had to exclude the work of the gods to be worthy of the name history.[84] It was to epic that description of the actions of the gods swooping in and out of Olympus to guide the fate of people belonged. The historian, to be sure, could report supernatural or religious events found in his sources or informants. However, he should bring in a measure of rationality by adding: "that is as they say." According to Loveday Alexander, this way of

---

[81]Although, to be fair, in the case of *Catiline* there is a digression on the ancient history of Rome (6-14), a sort of *Archaelogia* in imitation of Thucydides 1.2-19.

[82]Ronald Syme, *Sallust* (Berkeley: University of California Press, 1964), 68-69, although he is referring primarily to *Catiline*. I owe this reference to Palmer, "Historical Monograph," 5.

[83]See the survey in Keener, *Acts*, 1:90-115.

[84]On this, see John Marincola, *Authority and Tradition in Ancient Historiography* (Cambridge: Cambridge University Press, 1997), 117-27, with copious primary sources cited.

dealing with the supernatural was used to full advantage by Herodotus (the so-called father of history) and became the possession of future Greek and Roman historians.[85]

Acts, on the other hand, is unashamedly *theocentric*.[86] What is underlined is the unstoppable movement of the word (λόγος) from Jerusalem to Rome because God impels this movement. The narrative of Acts, in contrast to Greco-Roman history, is saturated with God's breaking in to historical affairs to move them in the direction he wishes. Does this fundamental difference disqualify Acts from being a historical monograph? I do not believe so. It is here that my previous remark on Acts as a historical monograph with a *Jewish* influence comes into place. What I am suggesting is that Luke took the well-known form and structure of the Greco-Roman monograph and appropriated it to communicate an essentially theological message of salvation through Jesus Christ. There are two questions that need to be addressed in order to substantiate this position. First, did Luke have Jewish models and precedents in using the historical monograph to highlight a movement of God? Second, is it in fact true that Acts portrays God as the mover of the Christian mission, or does Luke express the impartiality one encounters in Greco-Roman historians?

The first question can be answered in the affirmative. The main model Luke possessed for a theological history is the Old Testament, which is without question his main source of intertextuality. The historical books of the Old Testament concentrate on God's powerful judgment and salvation in a global theater on behalf of his people. These works demonstrate that God is God and worthy of glory. They also help define Israel as God's people.[87] Not that the Old Testament historical books were conceived as

---

[85]See Loveday Alexander's excellent essay, "Fact, Fiction and the Genre of Acts," in *Acts in Its Ancient Literary Context*, 133-63, esp. 136-47. See also Marincola, *Authority and Tradition*, 118, where he notes the three options the historian had when dealing with the supernatural: avoid it, "rationalize" it, or report it but leave the readers to decide on its truthfulness.

[86]One could argue trinitarian, since at different stages God, Christ and the Holy Spirit, respectively, lead the Christian mission. God guiding the mission: Acts 1:24-26; 2:47; 4:24-30; 10–11; Jesus: Acts 16:7; 18:9-10; 23:11; the Holy Spirit: Acts 13:2-4; 15:28; 16:6.

[87]On Old Testament historiography as Acts's genre, see Brian Rosner, "Acts and Biblical History," in *The Book of Acts in Its First Century Setting*, ed. Andrew D. Clarke and Bruce W. Winter (Grand Rapids: Eerdmans, 1993), 65-82. Jacob Jervell in his commentary on Acts has also highlighted Luke's dependence on the Old Testament, going as far as to state: "There is for Luke only one history of meaning, namely the

historical monographs; rather, in them Luke had an example of history written from a theological perspective. The question we must ask is whether there were other historians, contemporary with Luke, who found their understanding of history in the Old Testament and who at the same time deployed the Greco-Roman historical monograph, thus blazing a trail for others. Again the answer is yes. As Darryl Palmer has ably shown, 1–2 Maccabees and 1 Esdras take a Jewish conception of history and yet are solid examples of the Greco-Roman historical monograph.[88] The most impressive of these in terms of comparison with Acts is 2 Maccabees. Like Acts, the epitomator of 2 Maccabees is able to blend with impressive dexterity the Greek and Jewish elements of historiography. This is most concentrated in the preface (2 Macc 2:19-32), where the use of a preface in itself shows Greek affinities. In addition, there are numerous Greek historical cliché terms: τοῖς τῆς ἱστορίας διηγήμασι (24), ψυχαγωγία (25), ὠφέλεια (25), πραγματεία (31).

Last, one can compare Lucian, *How to Write History* 23 to 2 Maccabees 2:32, where both comment on the necessary balance between the preface and the body of the history itself. And yet, in the same preface, the epitomator does something that is most Jewish. He says that he will also write about "the heavenly apparitions which occurred" (τὰς ἐξ οὐρανοῦ γενομένας ἐπιφανείας) in 2 Maccabees 2:21 and of "the Lord who was gracious with all goodness to them [who fought for Judaism]" in 2 Maccabees 2:22. He thus combines the conception and structure of the Greco-Roman historical monograph with a Jewish theological view of events. Daniel Schwartz nicely summarizes the stance of the author:

> There is no need to choose between these two models [Greek and Jewish], just as there is no need to choose, with regard to specific topoi, between Jewish antecedents and Greek ones. True, our author was not a biblical

---

history of Israel. The history of the nations is of no interest and without meaning because only the history of the people of God is the history of God with the world. . . . Luke himself writes his history as a part of biblical history" ("Es gibt für Lukas nur eine Geschichte von Bedeutung, nämlich die Geschichte Israels. Die Geschichte des Völker ist uninteressant und ohne Bedeutung, weil allein die Geschichte des Gottesvolkes die Geschichte Gottes mit der Welt ist. . . . Lukas selbst schreibt seine Geschichte als einen Teil der biblischen Geschichte") (*Die Apostelgeschichte*, KEK 3 [Göttingen: Vandenhoeck & Ruprecht, 1998], 78).

[88]Palmer, "Historical Monograph," 18-21, 27-28. On 1–2 Maccabees and their similarities to Acts, see Padilla, *Speeches of Outsiders*, 64-74.

author. But he was a Jewish author. Moreover, he was one of those happy people who was able to express a synthesis between two identities in a way that approached an integrated whole. We term this synthesis "Jewish-Hellenistic," but for our author it was simply "Judaism," which was a legitimate and respected way to be Greek.[89]

If I had to choose the literary convention operative in the writing of Acts, I would say that it is most comparable to the one evinced in the work of 2 Maccabees.[90] I am not suggesting that Acts is *genetically* related to this or other Jewish-Hellenistic works.[91] What I am suggesting is that before Luke wrote there were already authors writing history from the Jewish perspective who used the historical monograph as a genre to help them communicate. Luke probably belongs to the same literary soil.[92]

The second question—does Acts present God as directly breaking into history to superintend the movement of the mission?—can also be answered affirmatively. There is an issue of method here, however: Do we depend solely on editorial comments to address the question, or are there other ways of assessing Luke's way of saying "This is the work of God"? I will argue in chapter five that the speeches of the apostles serve as authoritative commentaries that affirm an action as the work of God. For this chapter I will concentrate on editorial statements as well as direct interruptions into affairs by God or his messengers. Consider the following:

- Acts 1:9-11: "When he had said this, as they were watching, *he was lifted up*, and a cloud took him out of their sight. While he was going and they were gazing up toward heaven, suddenly *two men in white robes* stood by them. They said . . ."

- Acts 2:2-4: "And suddenly from heaven there came a sound like the rush

---

[89]Daniel R. Schwartz, *2 Maccabees* (Berlin: Walter de Gruyter, 2008), 66.

[90]For a similar conclusion, see Gregory Sterling, *Historiography and Self-Definition: Josephos, Luke-Acts and Apologetic Historiography*, NovTSup 64 (Leiden: Brill, 1992), 387. However, note that he does not classify Acts as a historical monograph but rather as "apologetic historiography."

[91]Although this must not be offhandedly discarded, as Josephus used 1 Maccabees as a source in *Jewish Antiquities* 12.241–13.214.

[92]Similarly, Sterling, *Historiography and Self-Definition*, 369, speaking of the similarities between the author of Acts and Josephus: "The author of Luke-Acts thus shared common historical and historiographical traditions with Josephos. This does not mean that Luke-Acts is dependent upon Josephos, but that they were cut out of the same bolt of cloth."

of a violent wind, and it filled the entire house where they were sitting. Divided tongues, as of fire, appeared among them, and a tongue rested on each of them. *All of them were filled with the Holy Spirit.*"

- Acts 2:47: " . . . praising God and having the goodwill of all the people. And day by *day the Lord added to their number those who were being saved.*"

- Acts 5:19: "But during the night *an angel of the Lord opened the prison doors, brought them out . . .*"

- Acts 8:39-40: "When they came out of the water, *the Spirit of the Lord snatched Philip away*; the eunuch saw him no more, and went on his way rejoicing. But Philip found himself [εὑρέθη] at Azotus."

- Acts 9:3-18: Description of the risen Lord appearing to Saul.

- Acts 10:3: "One afternoon at about three o'clock *he had a vision in which he clearly saw an angel of God coming in and saying to him, 'Cornelius.'*"

- Acts 10:9-16: Peter's vision of the opened heaven and unclean animals being lowered down.

- Acts 11:21: "*The hand of the Lord was with them*, and a great number became believers and turned to the Lord."

- Acts 12:6-11: Peter delivered from prison by an angel of the Lord.

- Acts 12:23: "And immediately, *because he [Herod] had not given the glory to God, an angel of the Lord struck him down*, and he was eaten by worms and died."

- Acts 13:2: "While they were worshiping the Lord and fasting, *the Holy Spirit said, 'Set apart for me Barnabas and Saul . . .'*"

- Acts 16:14: "A certain woman named Lydia, a worshiper of God, was listening to us; . . . *The Lord opened her heart* to listen eagerly to what was said by Paul."

- Acts 18:9-10: "One night *the Lord said to Paul in a vision*, 'Do not be afraid, but speak and do not be silent; for I am with you and no one will lay a hand on you to harm you, for there are many in this city who are my people.'"

- Acts 19:11-12: "*God did extraordinary miracles through Paul,* so that when the handkerchiefs and aprons that had touched his skin were brought to the sick, their diseases left them, and the evil spirits came out of them."

- Acts 23:11: "That night *the Lord stood near him and said,* 'Keep up your courage! For just as you have testified for me in Jerusalem, so you must bear witness also in Rome.'"

These examples *show* God (sometimes by means of messengers) intervening in history to guide the mission; by means of editorial comments they also *tell* of an action as directly being the work of God.[93] In contrast to Greco-Roman historians, Luke does not coolly distance himself from the affirmations of his narrative concerning God's involvement. He writes in the same manner as Old Testament historiography and Second Temple works such as 2 Maccabees.

Having established (1) the existence, features and use of the historical monograph in both the Greco-Roman and Jewish milieu, and (2) the similarities of Acts to the historical monograph, it is important to offer one more piece of evidence for support. Although this piece of evidence could have been offered under (1) or (2) above, I have decided to discuss it separately because of its importance and the amount of discussion it has generated. I am referring to the preface of the Gospel of Luke. As I will offer a close reading of the preface in the following chapter, I can now only provide a sketch of how it supports the view of Acts as a historical monograph. I will do this by making three observations, two negative and one positive.

First, it should be noted that even if we do not hold to Luke and Acts as belonging to the same genre, this does not preclude our use of the preface to *Luke* as a generic indicator for *Acts*. While the Gospel of Luke is more than likely an ancient biography, Acts, as we have been arguing, is better understood as a historical monograph. Thus we have two different genres.[94]

---

[93]For other examples, see Jean-Noël Aletti, *Quand Luc Raconte: Le Récit comme Théologie* (Paris: Les Éditions du Cerf, 1998), 22-24.

[94]But see David Aune, *The New Testament in Its Literary Environment*, LEC 8 (Philadelphia: Westminster, 1987), 77, who states: "Luke does not belong to a type of ancient biography for it belongs with Acts, and Acts cannot be forced into a biographical mold."

Nevertheless, given the clear connections that both prefaces establish with each other, it is clear that Luke intended his readers to read his second volume in light of the preface to his first volume.[95] As Richard Burridge suggests, the fact that the genre of biography and history overlapped in the Hellenistic period may have made it possible for Luke to use two separate genres in one essentially unified work.[96] As such, we may confidently state that the preface to the Gospel of Luke is the generic gateway to the Acts of the Apostles.

Second, it should be noted that while rhetorical prologues are not only the domain of history, nevertheless, given the other historiographic traits we have already noted about Acts, the prefaces *do* further strengthen the viability of Acts as a historical monograph. In other words, the argument is cumulative, and as such the prefaces play an important part in it.[97]

Third, we should not forget that the preface to Luke, in fact, teems with historiographic markers. The following terms in Luke 1:1-4 would have raised the historical expectations of the readers: διήγησις (BDAG, 245, citing Diodorus Siculus, *Library of History* 11.20.1; Lucian, *How to Write History* 55; and Polybius 3.36.1; see also 2 Macc 2:32); πρᾶγμα (Josephus, *Jewish War* 1.1, 2, 4 [twice], 5 [thrice]; *Jewish Antiquities* 1.3, 5, 8); αὐτόπτης (Cadbury, "Commentary," in *BegChr* 2:498-99); ἀκριβῶς (Cadbury, "Commentary," 504).

True, as Alexander points out, these terms also cluster in the prefaces of scientific treatises.[98] However, given that what follows in the Gospel and Acts is clearly a narrative and not a scientific treatise, the prefaces, especially the one to the Gospel, provide support for the view that Acts is a historical

---

[95]See the careful argument for this view in I. Howard Marshall, "Acts and the 'Former Treatise,'" in *The Book of Acts in Its Ancient Literary Setting*, 163-82, esp. 172-80.

[96]Burridge, *What Are the Gospels?*, 237-39.

[97]This must be said in light of Alexander's carefully argued hypothesis that the prefaces to Luke and Acts align most closely with the prologues of scientific treatises. See her groundbreaking work, *The Preface to Luke's Gospel: Literary Convention and Social Context in Luke 1.1-4 and Acts 1.1*, SNTSMS 78 (Cambridge: Cambridge University Press, 1993). Alexander has a tendency to minimize or downplay the alignment of the prefaces with historical works while overplaying their alignment with scientific works. She reaches, in my opinion, a more credible proposal in her subsequent work, "The Preface to Acts and the Historians," in *Acts in Its Ancient Literary Setting*, 21-42. Speaking of the preface of Acts, she states concerning its characteristics: "Where they occur in historiography, they cluster on the margins of the genre [history], where it is furthest from epic or rhetorical pretension and closest to the scholarly, scientific side of the Ionian *historia*-tradition" (41).

[98]Alexander, *Preface*, 102-46.

monograph.[99] One may retort by saying that since the preface is the entry point into the narrative it is especially powerful in guiding generic expectations. As such, as a matter of the preface *alone*, the readers may not have been sure that a work of history was to follow, given that many of the terms in the preface cluster in scientific writings. But is it not anachronistic to think that the original audience of Luke-Acts dove right into the books without any extratextual information about them? Since "publication" in the ancient world happened when a work was read to the public, it is likely that the reader/performer would have said a few words (perhaps many!) about the work that was about to be read. This was almost certainly the case in Pauline communities (e.g., Eph 6:21-22; Col 4:7-9, 16-17), and it probably obtained as well in other Christian circles. As such, there would have been "an entry before an entry," where the hearers of Acts, having been prepared aurally for the subject of the work that was about to be read, would not have been deterred from understanding Acts as a historical narrative despite the apparent scientific terms in the preface. This aural introduction would have cleared any gray areas concerning the generic affiliation of the work, encouraging the hearers to expect a work of history. And so we come back to the issue of cumulative evidence: when the form, subject, features and—yes— the preface are combined, it is most likely that the genre of Acts would have been understood as a historical monograph.

It is time to summarize. In the search for a proper literary genre for the Acts of the Apostles, I have discarded two proposals that have gained momentum in recent time: these are the ancient epic and the ancient novel. Along with the majority of scholars I have suggested that Acts is best viewed as belonging to the genre of history. But it is necessary to be more precise, since the ancient category of history is very broad. I proposed the historical monograph as a defensible candidate. We focused on the subject, size, features and relation to the past of the historical monograph, noticing impressive external and internal similarities to Acts. As far as the clear religious aspect of Acts, we noticed that already in Jewish soil we encounter use of the historical monograph suffused with divine intervention.

---

[99]Or a piece of history in general.

These types of works probably paved the way for Luke's use of the historical monograph.

We now bring this chapter to a close by sketching two ways in which the identification of Acts as a historical monograph can help us in interpretation.

CONCLUSION—ACTS AS HISTORICAL MONOGRAPH: HOW DOES IT HELP?

First, *it encourages the reader to view the events narrated as actually having occurred; however, it does not guarantee accuracy.* When, through the signals sent in the text, the reader and writer reach an agreement on the genre of the work, certain expectations follow. In the case of the historical genre, the expectation is that the historian will tell the truth—namely, that the events narrated in the text will correspond to how things happened in the world outside the text. It is imperative to grasp this, for if Acts is not an example of historiography but is rather a novel or epic, then we have no business expecting the author to tell us things as they happened; it would be a ridiculous expectation on our part. Should a person be upset at Cervantes if it turned out that Don Quixote did not really exist as he describes him in Spain of the seventeenth century? We would say that person is completely out of touch with the way literature works. Similarly, if Acts is a novel, the whole discussion of historical accuracy would be superfluous. On the other hand, if the genre *is* history, it is a legitimate and healthy aim to ask whether the things he narrates are true or not.

But we should not fall into another mistake: Acts is in the genre of history, therefore it logically follows that the contents will be accurate. This in fact does not follow, for the profession of historian is not coterminous with truth telling. In other words, historians often tell lies![100] Thus, although accepting the genre of Acts as history is an invitation for us to trust the accuracy of its contents, we still must check Luke's performance to determine the veracity of its account. We will argue in the next chapter that Luke is a most reliable historian, but this conclusion is not entirely based on the identification of Acts as a work of history.

---

[100]This was the case especially in the ancient world. See the helpful, if exaggerated, positions of C. Gill and T. P. Wiseman, eds., *Lies and Fiction in the Ancient World* (Exeter, UK: University of Exeter Press, 1993).

Second, accepting Acts as a historical monograph *invites us to expect the author to be an eyewitness and/or interviewer of those who participated in the events narrated.* In the most serious tradition of Greek historical writing, the qualification of the historian as a participant and interviewer of eyewitnesses is essential. Marincola indicates that these methods "serve as one of the most prominent means of claiming the authority to narrate contemporary and non-contemporary history."[101] The technical term for the first of these methods is *autopsy*.[102] We find this tradition in Herodotus with his extensive travels in order to see the evidence for himself and interview eyewitnesses. Thucydides is keen to highlight his role as an eyewitness in order to bolster the credibility of his account (e.g., 1.1, 22). Polybius continues this tradition in his criticisms of Timaeus (12.23-28), whom he accuses of being an "armchair" historian. This is contrasted with active participation in events or interrogation of participants. Lucian, *How to Write History* 29, parodies the armchair historian, who in order to hide his inadequacy begins his history by alluding to Heraclitus: "Ears are less reliable than eyes. I write then what I have seen, not what I have heard." Those historians, then, whom both ancients and moderns consider to be concerned with accuracy (especially Thucydides and Polybius) and who set the course for the method of history writing in antiquity, emphasize *autopsy* and enquiry.[103]

I would suggest that the acceptance of Acts as a historical monograph encourages us to view the author as participant and inquirer of participants. In fact, it is likely that the use of αὐτόπται in Luke 1:2, the first-person pronouns in the prologue ("of the events that have been fulfilled among *us*" [Lk 1:1], "just as they were handed down to *us*" [Lk 1:2], "it seemed to *me*" [Lk 1:3; my translation]) and the conspicuous "we" passages from Acts 16 forward are subtle nudges to the readers to view Luke as participating in

---

[101] Marincola, *Authority and Tradition*, 63.

[102] In addition to ibid., 63-86, see the helpful work of Samuel Byrskog, *Story as History—History as Story: The Gospel Tradition in the Context of Ancient Oral History*, WUNT 1.123 (Tübingen: Mohr Siebeck, 2000), 48-65. Some of the citations of ancient historians above come from Byrskog.

[103] Herodotus has more of a checkered record, especially with the ancients. See Plutarch, *On the Malice of Herodotus*. See also Arnaldo Momigliano's exquisite essay, "The Place of Herodotus in the History of Historiography," in *Studies in Historiography* (London: Weidenfeld and Nicolson, 1966), 127-42.

autopsia and enquiry.[104] He thus presents himself as a conscientious historian, a posture that, as we shall see in the following chapters, has significant repercussions for how we understand Luke's theology in the context of early Christianity.[105]

There are other ways in which the recognition of Acts as a historical monograph helps us in interpretation. Since these overlap with other matters referring to the nature of history and how Luke writes history, we defer them to the next chapter.

---

[104]See Aune, *New Testament*, 122-24, with the important quotation from Polybius 36.12; Claus-Jürgen Thornton, *Der Zeuge des Zeugen: Lukas als Historiker der Paulusreisen*, WUNT 1.56 (Tübingen: Mohr Siebeck, 1991).

[105]Again, it must be emphasized that Luke's *claim* to be a conscientious historian is not *proof* that he actually was. The determination of his credibility, to the extent that we can check it, rests on a number of factors, not just his self-presentation in the prologue.

three

How Luke Writes History

In the previous chapter we established that in composing Acts Luke wrote as a historian. We teased out how this affects our appreciation of his work. In this chapter we want to continue to work out those implications. In particular, we want to defend three broad assertions. First, we want to establish that Luke was a *theological* historian. That is, his purpose in writing Acts was not just to provide satisfaction to antiquarian curiosity to a second generation of Christians; neither was it an attempt to provide dry chronicling so that his readers could have a neat "chronology book" of the early church; still, his work was not just documentary history (*just the facts, please*).[1] Although not devoid of any of these interests, Luke writes as a theologian who wants to assure his readers that in the events of the early church he narrates, the mighty arm of God was working to save.

The second broad assertion we wish to defend is that Luke's theological history is couched in beautiful, indeed sometimes unforgettable, *narrative*. He is a raconteur whose theological message is seriously impoverished when we do not closely follow the shape of his narrative. In fact, there are occasions when the *way* he tells something is as theologically significant as *what* he tells.

Last, we want to defend the proposition that Luke's writing as a theologian in attractive narrative does not preclude the possibility that he

---

[1] For the different types of historiography and their application to Acts, see Daniel Marguerat, *The First Christian Historian: Writing the "Acts of the Apostles,"* trans. Ken McKinney, Gregory Laughery and Richard Bauckham, SNTSMS 121 (Cambridge: Cambridge University Press, 2002), 8-13, building on Ricoeur.

writes as a *responsible* historian. For some, the possibility that Luke could be a theologian *and* historian is not very plausible. To the extent that Luke's theological truth-claims are statements about transcendence and not purely immanent reflections, the Enlightenment has taught us to look at such attitudes with deep suspicion. But it should be noted that this is a distinctively modern attitude (and one, we may add, not always shared by those outside the Western European intellectual heritage). Luke, as we will argue, certainly believed that he could write as a theologian while being a sober historian; we must take him seriously if we are to do justice to his work.[2] For others, the positing of Luke as writing an artistically pleasing narrative that can concurrently be faithful to historical facts will appear as lacking in critical rigor on his part. This may be the result of a positivist approach to historiography. However, both ancient and now postmodern historiography demonstrate that narrative emplotment (to mention one aspect of narrative) and sober historical reporting are not mutually exclusive. We shall thus argue in this chapter that Luke is a theological historian who presents his account of early Christianity with narrative verve while wishing to be viewed as a serious historian.

LUKE THE THEOLOGICAL HISTORIAN

Luke-Acts is narrated in the third person almost entirely. As such, Luke generally (we saw important exceptions in the previous chapter) does not intrude into the narrative to give a judgment or explanation in the first person. This does not mean, of course, that he is without judgments; it means that the majority of the times these are not stated explicitly, thus requiring of readers to look at narrative clues to apprehend the judgments of the author. This is the way of narrative.[3] One of the most notable exceptions to third-person narration is the preface to Luke (Lk 1:1-4). Here the voice of the author is not filtered through the story but found in the first

---

[2]On New Testament theology and its tendency to devalue the worldview of the New Testament while overvaluing modern epistemological constructs, see R. W. Yarbrough, *The Salvation Historical Fallacy? Reassessing the History of New Testament Theology* (Leiden: Deo, 2004).

[3]For an excellent explanation of this in what has already become a classic in biblical narrative, see M. Sternberg, *The Poetics of Biblical Narrative: Ideological Literature and the Drama of Reading* (Bloomington: Indiana University Press, 1985).

person, and as such more directly. Scholars have thus sensibly suggested that the preface plays a very important role in helping us understand the type of writer Luke is and what he is trying to accomplish. Below we will concentrate on specific terms of the preface that I believe show us that Luke intended to write a theological-historical narrative. In fact, I will show that Luke deftly combines terms and concepts that point to a fusion of history and theology.

The terminology in the preface to Luke. Luke uses a number of terms that would have raised historiographic expectations for his readers. At the same time, a number of the terms are loaded theologically. As we argued in the previous chapter, the preface describes the contents of Luke's two volumes. Let us now look at some of the salient terms.

1. πρᾶγμα (Lk 1:1 "Since many have tried to compose a narrative of the *events* [πραγμάτων] that have been fulfilled among us . . ."; my translation). BDAG, 858-59, provides a wide range of meanings for this word, from "thing, event" to "dispute, lawsuit." Given the context of Luke 1:1-4, a meaning of "event," "deed" or "fact" is plausible. Loveday Alexander states that the term, although occurring in historical writing, "is not characteristically used of the stuff of history."[4] I wish to show below, among other things, that this conclusion is misleading.

One of the historians who is most profitable to use in comparison to Luke is Josephus. His corpus is entirely extant, he is a contemporary of Luke and both write in a broad Jewish context. The term πρᾶγμα, as entries in Rengstorf's concordance of Josephus show, was copiously used by the historian. In many places it has the sense of "event" or "fact."

- *Jewish War* 1.1: Josephus emphasizes the greatness (μέγιστον) of the Jewish war, for which he says there have not lacked historians.[5] He criticizes some of these historians because they have not—in contrast to Josephus himself—taken part in the actions or events of the war (οἱ μὲν οὐ παρατυχόντες τοῖς πράγμασιν). Rather, they have depended on "hearsay" (ἀκοῇ) to put their narratives together. As a result they have

---

[4]Loveday Alexander, *The Preface to Luke's Gospel: Literary Convention and Social Context in Luke 1.1-4 and Acts 1.1*, SNTSMS 78 (Cambridge: Cambridge University Press, 1993), 112.

[5]Saying that the war one is writing about is the greatest in history is a cliché of ancient historians.

ended up falsifying the facts of the history (καταψεύδονται τῶν πραγμάτων). We can see that in the same paragraph Josephus can use the term πρᾶγμα to refer to both the "events" of the war as well as to the truthfulness of the events in recorded fashion. Thus the translation "facts" seems appropriate in the second example. Notably, in 1.6 he employs πρᾶγμα with ἀλήθεια.

- *Jewish War* 1.14: As in 1.1, the term is used with the verb παρατυγχάνω. This time Josephus states that because many historians of the past have participated in the events they narrate (τὸ παρατυχεῖν τοῖς πράγμασιν), they are able to give their account clarity (ἐναργῆ), a desired trait in ancient historiography (e.g., Josephus, *Against Apion* 1.25; Dionysius of Halicarnassus, *Roman Antiquities* 2.17).

- *Jewish War* 1.16: In contrast to the practice of Greek historians, who, according to Josephus, can be careless with the truth, Josephus writes responsibly. This is so because he understands that history is concerned with the truth; and in order to obtain the truth, the historian must work very hard at collecting the "facts" of what happened (μετὰ πολλοῦ πόνου τὰ πράγματα συλλέγειν). Here the πράγματα refer to the distillation of the events that become the actual historical writing. These facts must be in accordance with the events (ἀλήθεια, cognates of which are used twice in 1.16).

- *Jewish Antiquities* 1.3: In the writing of history, Josephus explains, there are different motivating factors. He counts himself among those who want to write a truthful account in order that it might be of usefulness (ὠφέλειαν) for the future. These authors, including Josephus, are further constrained to write history by the fact that they participated in the events they recount (τῆς τῶν πραγμάτων ἀνάγκης οἷς πραττομένοις παρέτυχον). As in *Jewish War* 1.6, Josephus links πρᾶγμα with παράτυγχάνω, highlighting the importance of participation in the events narrated for the writing of a truthful account (cf. also *Jewish Antiquities* 1.8).

- *Against Apion* 1.47: Josephus, in contrast to those writers of the Jewish war who were not acquainted with Palestine firsthand, can write a true account (ἀληθῆ τὴν ἀναγραφήν) because he was present in all the events (τοῖς πράγμασιν αὐτὸς ἅπασι παρατυχών). Again, Josephus links πρᾶγμα with παρατυγχάνω to argue for the superiority of his accounts with respect to truthfulness (cf. also *Against Apion* 1.56).

By way of conclusion it can be said that in Josephus, a historian contemporary with Luke, the term πρᾶγμα can, among other things, refer to the "events" as well as to the distillation of those events that make up the historical narrative. Assuming (for the sake of argument) that there is a faithful correspondence between the events and their distillation, we can call these latter "facts." Josephus underlines several times that in order for history to be accurate, the writer must have himself been a participant in the events or painstakingly have collected information from eyewitnesses. The evidence is overwhelming that, when used with other terms such as παρατυγχάνω, Josephus uses πρᾶγμα in a context that triggers in the mind the venerable tradition of *autopsia*. As we saw in chapter two, this is a tradition found in Greek historiography from Herodotus forward. This tradition of *autopsia* is employed by historians to call attention to the importance of eyewitness account—either by the historian himself or by those whom the historian interviews. Josephus wishes to portray himself as operating within this tradition.[6]

Is it possible that Luke, by employing the term πρᾶγμα in Luke 1:1 along with "among us" and αὐτόπται in Luke 1:2, is also wishing to place himself in the historical tradition of *autopsia*? That is, he is claiming to be a participant/eyewitness in some of the events he recounts ("among us") and also to gather his information from those who were eyewitnesses (αὐτόπται). Interestingly, Luke does not link πρᾶγμα with παρατυγχάνω as we saw in Josephus, although he does use the latter term in another passage (Acts 17:17). Instead, he uses a term that is distinctively theological.[7] This is the next word we examine.

2. πληροφορέω ("Since many attempted to compose a narrative of the events *fulfilled* among us . . ."). This word, which here appears as a perfect passive participle, has been shown to be the equivalent of the simpler

---

[6]See the comments to this effect by J. M. G. Barclay in *Against Apion: Translation and Commentary*, in *Flavius Josephus: Translation and Commentary*, ed. S. Mason (Leiden: Brill, 2007), 34n193.

[7]Alexander, *Preface*, 113, calls it "the rather mysterious passive participle."

πληρόω.[8] Luke uses the longer version probably because in prefaces it was conventional to use long-sounding terms, thus giving the discourse a sense of solemnity. This observation must be kept in mind, for while the compound form appears only here in Luke-Acts, the simpler form occurs numerous times. We thus have plenty of material to observe how Luke uses the term and then bring that information to bear on the meaning of the word in Luke 1:1.

The verb can be used with a reference to "filling," whether it be a place (Acts 2:2; 5:28), or person (Acts 5:3); it can also refer to "reaching" an age (Acts 7:23), or to days coming to "completion" (Acts 9:23). The use of the verb that is probably of greatest significance for Luke 1:1 is its use for the fulfillment of prophecy. The following examples are worth looking at in more detail.

• Luke 1:20: The angel Gabriel appears to Zechariah to announce the birth of John the Baptist and the eschatological, prophetic ministry that he will have. But apparently Zechariah has his doubts about this prophecy, and so he is chastised with muteness until the day John is born. Concerning the words of the prophecy, Gabriel tells Zechariah that they "will be fulfilled [πληρωθήσονται] in their time." It is clear that, with the use of the passive, the sense is that the prophecy will be brought to fruition by God's power.

• Luke 4:21: This is the episode that takes place at the synagogue of Nazareth. After reading the Scripture (Is 61:1-2), Jesus rolls up the scroll and says: "Today this scripture has been fulfilled [πεπλήρωται] in your hearing." Jesus' proclamation here is that the prophecy of Isaiah—that is, the healing of the broken and destitute by the anointed Servant—has now reached its fulfillment in his ministry. Notice again the use of the passive, suggesting that this is God's hand at work in bringing the prophecy to completion.

• Luke 24:44: This is the account of Jesus' postresurrection appearance to his disciples. After they are enabled to recognize him, Jesus speaks:

---

[8]See ibid., 111-12.

"These are my words that I spoke to you while I was still with you—that everything written about me in the law of Moses, the prophets, and the psalms must be fulfilled [δεῖ πληρωθῆναι, again in the passive voice]." This summary statement is then developed in Luke 24:45-49. Jesus opens the disciples' minds (Lk 24:45) and gives a closer explanation of what it is about the Messiah that has been fulfilled; but he will include something else about the fulfillment of Scripture that is surprising: "Thus it is written, that the Messiah is to suffer and to rise from the dead on the third day, *and that repentance and forgiveness of sins is to be proclaimed in his name to all nations, beginning from Jerusalem. You are witnesses of these things*" (Lk 24:46-48). In the words of Bovon, here Luke "provokes a new surprise," *for he now includes the preaching of repentance to the nations as part of the scriptural prophecy that will be fulfilled.*[9] In addition, Jesus makes the statements that the preaching is to begin from Jerusalem and that the disciples are witnesses. We thus have a bridge to Acts 1:8, which indeed serves as the template for the entirety of that book. What is critical to observe here is that the preaching to the nations—that is, *the content of the book of Acts*—is also part of scriptural prophecy that is to be fulfilled (πληρόω);[10] and this brings us back to the preface of Luke.

What is Luke referring to in Luke 1:1 when he speaks of the events that "have been fulfilled among us"? Although here the participle can simply be taken to mean "the things that *happened* among us," the fact that a verb synonymous with πληρόω is used and that it is used in the passive (as in the passages explained above) suggests to the reader that it should be understood in the sense of fulfillment of prophecy.[11] And as we saw above in Luke 24:44-50, part of this prophetic fulfillment includes the preaching of the

---

[9] François Bovon, *L'Evangile selon Saint Luc (19,28-24,53)*, CNT (Genève: Labor et Fides, 2009), 469. It is possible that the prophetic fulfillment only refers to the death and resurrection of the Messiah. However, the fact that "to be preached" (κηρυχθῆναι) is in the infinitive suggests that it goes together with the other two infinitives "to suffer" (παθεῖν) and "to be raised" (ἀναστῆναι). Thus that which is written is explained with three infinitives. For corroboration see especially Wilfried Eckey, *Das Lukasevangelium Unter Berücksichtigung seiner Parallelen. Teilband II: 11,1—24,53* (Neukirchen-Vluyn: Neukirchener, 2004), 991; I. Howard Marshall, *The Gospel of Luke: A Commentary on the Greek Text* (Grand Rapids: Eerdmans, 1978), 905-6.

[10] As David Pao has argued persuasively in *Acts and the Isaianic New Exodus*, WUNT 2.130 (Tübingen: Mohr Siebeck, 2000), 84-91.

[11] If Luke wanted simply to say that many have written about "the things that have *happened* among us," he could have used the much less theologically pronounced τὰ γενόμενα (cf. Lk 2:15).

gospel to the nations—that is, what we find in the book of Acts. It is thus probable that when Luke uses this word he has in mind not only the events related to the ministry of Jesus but also the ministry of the church. In principle, therefore, there is no reason why Luke himself should be excluded from the "us" of Luke 1:1, especially in view of the "we" passage of Acts. In this way Luke would be subtly suggesting that he was a participant in the events he narrates, thus meeting an important qualification of *autopsia*. More than likely, then, Luke is thinking of two stages: the fulfillment of prophecy in the ministry of Jesus (of which he was not a witness), and the fulfillment of prophecy in the ministry of the church (of which he *was* a witness).

We should add by way of conclusion that the use of πληρόω in an apparent sober and detached historical preface would have seemed strange to a Greek audience: the fulfillment of prophecy is not normally a topic for historians.[12] However, for a writer like Luke, whose bearings on historical writing are Jewish, it would not at all have been out of place to speak of God bringing his promises to fulfillment in the historical plane. Thus, his combination of the rather "secular" πρᾶγμα with the more "theological" πληροφορέω/πληρόω would have made sense to insiders—a Christian audience.

3. αὐτόπτης ("just as they were handed on to us by those who from the beginning were *eyewitnesses*"). BDAG, 162, renders this term as "eyewitness" and provides some documentation. The following examples show that the term is important in the context of historical writing.

- Polybius: In 3.4, Polybius explains that one of his goals in writing his history is to inquire on the present position of those states that had been conquered by Rome. Why does he have this particular goal? He states (as most ancient historians) that it is due to the greatness of the subject. Yet, he adds another reason: he was not only an "eyewitness" (αὐτόπτης) but he was even a "helper" (συνεργός) and, furthermore, an "administrator" (χειρίστης) in the events. The idea is that although being an eyewitness should have been sufficient, he could even top that, because he was a helper and further still an administrator. Thus he could provide an accurate report of the contemporary status of the states conquered by the

---

[12]See, rightly, Alexander, *Preface*, 113-14. Of course, the case is different in Epic, like the *Aeneid*.

Romans. Another example of the use of αὐτόπτης is found in 10.11. Polybius is about to describe the siege of New Carthage. To help his readers follow his narrative, he first provides a description of the city. Concerning the circumference of the city, he states that at the time of the siege it was "not more than twenty stades." Although some say that it measured forty stades, Polybius says this is not true. His own measurement should be followed because he did not receive it from "hearsay" (ἐξ ἀκοῆς, cf. Josephus, *Jewish War* 1.1), but rather he was an eyewitness who investigated carefully (αὐτόπται γεγονότες μετ᾽ ἐπιστάσεως). Thus his description should be viewed as accurate because he was an eyewitness. In book 12, which is a castigation of the historical methods of the historian Timaeus, Polybius criticizes Timaeus because the latter is mostly an "armchair" historian; he does not do the field work necessary to be an accurate historian, which includes observation. Although the term αὐτόπτης itself is only used twice in the book (12.4 and 12.28), the *concept* of *autopsia* is undeniable.[13] Polybius presents himself as a responsible historian, deeply concerned with the truth. One of the ways that he tries to persuade his readership of this standard is his commitment to *autopsia*.

- Josephus: The Jewish historian uses αὐτόπτης in *Against Apion* 1.55. Josephus is responding to those who have challenged the truthfulness of his previous accounts (*Jewish War* and *Antiquities*). Concerning the history of the war, he attempts to strengthen his credibility by highlighting his personal involvement. Thus he provides essentially three reasons that qualify him to tell the truth as a historian: he was "personally involved" (αὐτουργος), he was an "eyewitness" (αὐτόπτης), and he was not ignorant of anything that was said or done.[14] It is clear that Josephus is appealing to the tradition of *autopsia*.

---

[13]Here the discussion of John Marincola on Polybius, *Authority and Tradition in Ancient Historiography* (Cambridge: Cambridge University Press, 1997), 71-75, is crucial. On 12.4, notice that Polybius is outraged at Timaeus because even on those occasions where the latter was an eyewitness (αὐτόπτης γέγονε) he still did not give trustworthy reports.

[14]I follow here Barclay's translation. Barclay rightly notes that these qualifications are laid out in the form of a tricolon. Perhaps this softens what initially appears to be a sharp contrast between αὐτουργός and αὐτόπτης, as the construction is presented in a μέν . . . δέ contrastive. On this see Alexander, *Preface*, 39n36, who moreover suggests that Josephus is dependent on Polybius here.

- Dionysius of Halicarnassus: In his comparison of different historians (Herodotus, Thucydides, Xenophon, etc.), Dionysius comments on the Hellenistic historian Theopompus, clearly his favorite historian (*Letter to Pompeius* 6.3). Among the many qualities of Theopompus, Dionysius points to the former's careful research. He states that Theopompus was an "eyewitness" (αὐτόπτης) of many of the events he reported and also "kept company" (ὁμιλίαν ἐλθών) with those who participated in wars such as eminent men and generals, thus implying that he had interviewed these men. By calling attention to these activities, Dionysius is clearly drawing on the convention of *autopsia* and claiming it for Theopompus.

Although we have been concentrating on the term αὐτόπτης (since it appears in the Lukan preface), it should be noted that the convention of *autopsia* is not solely dependent on that term. For example, it would appear that Thucydides, although not using the particular word, is calling attention to *autopsia* in his methodological passage in 1.22.2-3. Concerning the events of the Peloponnesian War (τὰ ἔργα, in contrast to the speeches), Thucydides states that he did not trust chance informants. Rather, he writes of those events where he himself was present (ἀλλ᾽ οἷς τε αὐτὸς παρῆν). Of those events in which he was not present, it seems clear that he inquired of those who were eyewitnesses (παρὰ τῶν ἄλλων ... οἱ παρόντες τοῖς ἔργοις ἑκάστοις). *Autopsia* is clearly present here, even without recourse to specific terms such as αὐτόπτης.[15]

By way of conclusion on our investigation of αὐτόπτης, it can be said that in a number of authors the term is used in a context that shows historians as composing their works on the basis of personal investigation by observation (sometimes participation) and the interviewing of those who participated in the events being reported. It is this act of *autopsia* that is presented as securing the accuracy of the accounts. It is quite fascinating that Luke would employ the term αὐτόπτης in his methodological introduction in Luke 1:2. Is he thereby invoking the admired (at least by mouth!)

---

[15]*Pace* Alexander, *Preface*, 121, who minimizes Thucydides's claim to *autopsia* because he lacks the term αὐτόπτης.

tradition of *autopsia*? The answer, in view of the term used here and our previous observations, is probably yes.

At this point in our discussion of eyewitnesses it is important to observe that in Luke 1:2 he categorizes this group as also "ministers [ὑπηρέται] of the word." We thus have the combination αὐτόπται καὶ ὑπηρέται. Intriguingly, we find an almost synonymous combination in Acts 26:16, which I translate as follows: "But rise and stand on your feet. Because for this reason I appeared to you, to appoint you *servant and witness* both of the things you saw and of the things in which I will appear to you." The words italicized translate ὑπηρέτεν καὶ μάρτυρα, strikingly similar to αὐτόπται καὶ ὑπηρέται of Luke 1:2. Three observations are in order here.

First, as A. A. Trites has shown, the term μάρτυς can also be used of the witnessing of historical events, and as such is not very different from αὐτόπτης, although the former has a more juridical flavor.[16] Second, one may ask why Luke did not use μάρτυς in Luke 1:2, since this is a term that he was obviously fond of.[17] The answer may again be that in the preface Luke wants, at least partly, to present himself as a sober historian in the tradition of *autopsia*. Hence he used the more scientific term αὐτόπτης. Although Alexander may go too far, her statement is incisive: "But, as we saw in verse 1, Luke goes out of his way to avoid explicitly Christian language in the preface."[18] Third, it is of no little significance that in Acts 26:16 it is of *Paul* that it is said that he will be a servant and witness.

To sum up this section on αὐτόπτης, I would suggest that thus far in his brief behind-the-scenes description of what went into the composition of Luke-Acts, Luke is making two affirmations. First, he makes it clear that he has "received the traditions"[19] of the events of the ministry of Jesus and of the early church from those who "from the beginning" were eyewitnesses

---

[16]Allison Trites, *The New Testament Concept of Witness*, SNTSMS 31 (Cambridge: Cambridge University Press, 1977), 14-15, 55-56, 139.

[17]Ibid., 128, indicates that the word and its derivatives appear *thirty-nine times* in Acts.

[18]Alexander, *Preface*, 124.

[19]Παραδίδωμι. The term is used in the New Testament of the handing down of apostolic teaching. Note, however, that in other literature the verb is also used in the context of passing down historical information or opinion. See, e.g., Hecataeus of Abdera, *FGH* 3 F25, who speaks of the handing down of "a deed worthy of historical recording" (πρᾶξις ἱστορίας ἀξία); Diodorus Siculus, *Library of History* 37.1.1; and Dionysius of Halicarnassus, *Roman Antiquities* 4.64.3. Thus the verb is not restricted to religious or scientific language.

and servants of the word. He has thus satisfied one aspect of *autopsia*. Second, keeping in mind that Paul is also designated in Acts 26:16 as a "witness," and that Luke links himself to Paul through the "we" passages, it is probable that Luke is projecting himself as fulfilling another criterion of *autopsia*—namely, being present in some of the events he later recorded.

4. παρακολουθέω ("it seemed to me also, *having followed* everything from the beginning and carefully"; my translation). The participle translated "having followed" should be understood as causal. That is, *because* Luke has followed everything with such care he is able to write a truthful and orderly account to Theophilus. But what exactly does Luke imply when he says he has "followed everything"?[20] The verb παρακολουθέω can refer to (1) following someone physically;[21] (2) intellectual following so as to understand something;[22] (3) the following of sources;[23] (4) following events by personal participation/eyewitnessing or interviewing eyewitnesses.[24] More than likely Luke's sense in Luke 1:3 is a combination of options (2) and (4) above, although the weight falls on the gathering of information from eyewitnesses, not participation/eyewitnessing. The reason for this is that Luke states that his "following" was "from the beginning," and yet we know that he was not a first-generation Christian. Therefore he is not—in this particular verse—claiming direct participation *in the life of Jesus*. What he *is* doing is claiming to have been in touch with those who were able to provide a firsthand account of the Jesus event. It is this qualification along with the hints at personal participation (in Paul's ministry) in Luke 1:1-2 that allow Luke to write a narrative to Theophilus that will strengthen the latter's belief in the things he has been taught (Lk 1:4).

---

[20]I take the πᾶσιν to be neuter.

[21]E.g., Xenophon, *Hellenica* 4.5; Dionysius of Halicarnassus, *Roman Antiquities* 7.69, 72 ("accompany"); 11.40; Philo, *Embassy to Gaius* 359.1; Josephus, *Jewish War* 6.252 ("pursuing" in battle); Strabo, *Geography* 7.2.

[22]On this see especially Josephus, *Against Apion* 1.218, where the sense is an inability to follow the meaning of writings or records (γράμμασι). See also Epictetus 1.9, 17; 2.14; and Josephus, *Jewish Antiquities* 12.259 ("adherence").

[23]Alexander, *Preface*, 129-30.

[24]Josephus, *Life* 357; Josephus, *Against Apion* 1.53. For a similar but not identical conclusion on this with respect to Josephus, see D. P. Moessner, "'Eyewitnesses,' 'Informed Contemporaries,' and 'Unknowing Inquirers': Josephus' Criteria for Authentic Historiography and the Meaning of ΠΑΡΑΚΟΛΟΥΘΕΩ," *NovT* 37 (1996): 105-22.

Conclusion. We have given a good amount of space to exploring the preface of Luke due to the fact that this is the only place (apart from some brief words in Acts 1:1-4) where the author pulls back the curtain to allow his readers to see how he operates. Some encompassing statements are now in order.

First, Luke is linking, at least in part, the narrative composition of the πολλοί in Luke 1:1 with the tradition handed down by the eyewitnesses and ministers of the word. More than likely, then, he is not being critical of the πολλοί. Rather, as often happens in ancient prefaces, the author highlights the importance of his own work by means of comparison. What would have been striking to ancient readers familiar with this rhetorical move is how Luke refuses to engage in bitter polemics that were de rigueur in ancient prefaces. On the contrary, he leads one to believe that at least some of the πολλοί received their tradition from authoritative tradents (i.e., those who carried the tradition forward). But then why not simply substitute πολλοί with "brothers" or "servants" or other "Christian" vocabulary? Why πολλοί? The answer is that Luke—in his preface at least—is determined to follow ancient convention, where the insertion of πολλοί was elementary. More than likely Luke wants to show in his preface that he was no ignoramus; he knew how to write in a literary manner. This would add credibility to his account.

Second, I believe it is clear that Luke is appealing to the ancient conception of *autopsia* to bolster the credibility of his account. On the one hand, he has reached out to participants of the events by direct interviewing.[25] On the other hand, with his use of ἡμῖν in Luke 1:1 along with the other clues that we have seen above, he is claiming to have been an eyewitness/participant of at least some of the events that are described in his second volume. Luke thus presents himself, even if he does this modestly, as meeting the double criteria of *autopsia*; and this means that he wants his readers to view him as a serious, sober historian.[26]

---

[25]"*The tradition available to the author was, according to the Lukan perspective, rooted in its entirety in the oral history of persons present at the events themselves*" (Samuel Byrskog, *Story as History—History as Story: The Gospel Tradition in the Context of Ancient Oral Historiography*, WUNT 1.123 [Tübingen: Mohr Siebeck, 2000], 232; emphasis original).

[26]These claims do not *prove* that Luke was such a historian. Josephus, for example, is keen on his meeting of

But, third, as we saw, Luke uses a theologically loaded term in πληρόω; and he also uses "insider" Christian language such as ὑπηρέτης. Luke wants to make clear that he is not operating strictly within the guidelines of Greek historians by assuming a detached and skeptical attitude toward the divine in human affairs. That is, Luke happily affirms the breaking in of transcendence into history.[27] In his case this means that the God of Israel is bringing salvation and judgment by the risen Christ through the Holy Spirit. God is at work in the Christian movement, the Way. This attitude might have disbarred him from the ancient (and modern) historical profession. But to people who had gained their worldview from the Old Testament, saying that God was at work in a tangible way in our world would not have been problematic. Luke is a historian-theologian.

LUKE THE STORYTELLER

Luke, we have argued, provides us with a direct statement of how he went about composing both of his volumes on Jesus and the early church. But what does this look like in practice, for our purposes in the book of Acts? How does he take the *bruta facta* of his research, emplot it and eventually provide us with a beautiful narrative through which he constructs his theology? In what follows we call attention to three procedures he employs.

Luke compresses information for theological effect. It is probably the case that Luke had a significant amount of traditional material when he set about to compose the Acts of the Apostles. Yet, as every historian knows, it is impossible—and unhelpful to the reader—to pass down into the final historical piece all the traditional material accumulated during research. The historian must thus choose to exclude and include, and this with a purpose in mind. The result of this aspect of historical writing—or better, the *planning* of historical writing—is that often historians only present a summary, a distillation of the material assembled. Luke falls into this category.

---

the qualifications of *autopsia*, often trumpeting this; but we know that in many places he greatly exaggerates—not to say distorts—his accounts. The question of Luke's reliability cannot be settled by the preface.

[27]I wonder whether Luke would have expressed himself as I have in this sentence: it strikes me how much of the Enlightenment heritage my words presuppose!

He summarizes long periods of time; he telescopes events; he gives only the gist of a speech. In this section I want to concentrate on his compressing or telescoping of events, which he does with a theological aim in mind. But before examining some of the cases in the book of Acts, it will be helpful to look at one of the most stunning cases of telescoping in his first volume. The example comes from the resurrection account found in Luke 24:1-53. To put the matter bluntly at the outset: Luke presents all the events recorded in Luke 24 as if they happened in one day. Yet, from Matthew, John and Acts itself, it emerges that these events did *not* happen in one day. Let us have a closer look.

There are four scenes in this chapter: (1) the angelic announcement at the tomb to the women and Peter's investigation of the tomb (Lk 24:1-12); (2) the meeting of Jesus with the disciples on the road to Emmaus and his breaking bread with them (Lk 24:13-35); (3) Jesus' appearance to his disciples in Jerusalem (Lk 24:36-49); and (4) the ascension (Lk 24:50-53). There are three "chronological" markers in this chapter, excluding Luke 24:1. After Peter investigated the empty tomb and marveled, a new scene opens. Luke states that "in the same day" (ἐν αὐτῇ τῇ ἡμέρᾳ) two disciples were heading toward the area of Emmaus when Jesus meets them. The narrative thus leads us to understand that the empty-tomb experience of the women and Peter "on the first day of the week" and the meeting on the way to Emmaus happened on the same day.

After Emmaus, Jesus appears to the Twelve (there were probably others as well). But all we are told as far as chronology in Luke 24:36 is that, "as they were speaking," Jesus himself appeared to them. The impression is given that this is all still happening on the same day. Last, we come to the ascension in Luke 24:50. But again Luke's chronological marker is very vague. He connects the previous narrative with the ascension by means of a simple "and" (δέ). Then Jesus is taken to heaven; what a long and eventful day this has been! But did Luke really believe that after his resurrection Jesus spent only one day with his disciples? The answer is no; and the proof of this is found in Acts.

In the preface to Acts, Luke recapitulates the events of his previous volume, "until the day when he was taken up to heaven after giving instructions

through the Holy Spirit to the apostles whom he had chosen" (Acts 1:2).
This verse clearly harks back to the final section of the Gospel of Luke,
specifically Luke 24:13-50, all of which apparently happened in one day. But
the next verse is crucial: "After his suffering he presented himself alive to
them by many convincing proofs, *appearing to them during forty days and
speaking about the kingdom of God*" (Acts 1:3). Luke, then, clearly understood that the risen Jesus had been with the apostles for longer than just
one day: in fact, he had spent forty days with them! So why is the presentation in Luke 24 made in such a way that the reader comes away thinking
that the resurrected Jesus had only been with his apostles for *one* day? It is
difficult to know. Perhaps one reason why Luke has condensed the appearance of Jesus and his teaching is that he wants to move his readers as
quickly as possible to the ministry of the apostles. Perhaps the point is that
it is now *the apostles* who will carry the teaching of the risen one to the
nations.[28] Whether our interpretation is accurate or not, the point must
not be missed that we have here clear proof that Luke compresses his material for (probably) theological reasons. The comparison of Luke 24 with
Acts 1 assures us that we are heading in the right direction when we speak
of Luke compressing material for theological effect.

Luke compresses by being selective. Is the Acts of the Apostles meant to
be a comprehensive history of the early church? Evidently not. Luke mentions the name of each of the Twelve apostles (Acts 1:12-26), and this, along
with the title in our Bibles of the "Acts of the *Apostles*" in plural, may initially suggest that the author will tell us about the mission of each one. But
we soon have to revise our expectation, for Luke concentrates his efforts
on two apostles. To be sure, we hear of others who were part of the Twelve
(e.g., James the brother of the Lord, John) as well as other prominent
leaders of the primitive church (e.g., Stephen, Barnabas, Philip). But these
fly across the screen with little development of their character or mission.
Naturally, we would like to know more: How did the gospel reach Egypt?
Did John have a mission outside Judea? Who initially brought the gospel

---

[28]See similarly O. Mainville, "De Jésus à l'Eglise. Etude rédactionnelle de Saint Luc 24," *NTS* 51 (2005):
192-211. I owe this reference to Bovon, *L'Évangile selon Saint Luc, IIId*, 411.

to Italy and Rome?[29] None of these questions is answered. Instead we are
led to focus on the actions and words of Peter and especially Paul. And
even with these two the presentation is selective.[30] Why has Luke left out
so much?

While there may be many reasons for this (lack of sources? lack of eyewitnesses? travel barriers?[31]), we can be certain that one of them was *selectivity*. This was a common practice of ancient historians, and thus we
should not be surprised to find Luke operating in a similar manner.[32] For
Luke, selectivity is driven by theological reasons. A good example of this
is found in his selective presentation of key characters, a selection that is
determined by one of his main theological themes—namely, the status of
Gentiles as full members of the people of God. Consider the following.

While it is true that *Peter* dominates the opening chapters of Acts as he
preaches to the Jews, it is of note that his lengthiest, consecutive appearance occurs in Acts 10–11. These chapters report the initial reception
of the gospel and the Holy Spirit by Gentiles. The amount of detail, especially in Acts 10, on the character of Peter and his mission is staggering in
view of Luke's usual economy. There is prolepsis, interpolation, paradox
and redundancy, to name some of his literary techniques.[33] It is clear that
in this selection of an event in the life of Peter the author is guiding us into
one of his essential theological points.[34]

James, the brother of the Lord, is not given much space in the narrative of
Acts, despite being the leader of the Jerusalem church. When there *is* some
character development, it also is done in the context of Gentile inclusion.
Thus we encounter him also in Acts 15. There he defends the inclusion

---

[29]It was not Paul (see Acts 18:1-3; 28:11-15), as strange as that may sound given the "necessity" of Paul's
preaching in Rome spoken of in the last chapters of Acts.

[30]For example, Paul mentions in 2 Cor 11:25 that he was shipwrecked "*three* times." But we only hear of one
in Acts.

[31]See the helpful comments of H. J. Cadbury, *The Making of Luke-Acts*, 2nd ed. (London: SPCK, 1968),
13-14.

[32]Ibid., 15-16. See also Byrskog, *Story as History*, 256-58.

[33]On this see Daniel Marguerat, *Les Actes des Apôtres 1-12* (Genève: Labor et Fides, 2007), 363-72.

[34]Note also that Peter's final appearance (Acts 15:7-11), his final testament as it were, concentrates on the
inclusion of the Gentiles: "And God, who knows the human heart, testified to them by giving them the
Holy Spirit, just as he did to us; and in cleansing their hearts by faith he has made no distinction between
them and us."

of Gentiles; but whereas Paul and Peter used mainly *testimony* to support their view, James uses *biblical exegesis* from Amos to bolster the argument (Acts 15:14-18). And in this way he brings to conclusion the Jerusalem Council: yes, the Gentiles *can* be full members of the people of God without circumcision.

What about *Paul*? He certainly dominates the second half of the book. Yet, Acts should not be viewed as a biography of Paul. In fact, the reader may be surprised to know that Luke's presentation of Paul is quite selective. A number of foundational texts speak to this. Consider Acts 9:15: "But the Lord said to him, 'Go, for he [Paul] is an instrument whom I have chosen to bring my name before *Gentiles* and kings and before the people of Israel.'" Speaking to Jews at Pisidia after they have rejected the gospel, Paul and Barnabas state: "It was necessary that the word of God should be spoken first to you. Since you reject it and judge yourselves to be unworthy of eternal life, we are now turning to the *Gentiles*" (Acts 13:46). Paul quotes the words of Jesus to him in Acts 22:21: "Go, for I will send you far away to the *Gentiles*." Again recounting his commission, Paul repeats for his audience the words of Jesus: "I will rescue you from your people and from the Gentiles—to whom I am sending you to open their eyes so that they may turn from darkness to light and from the power of Satan to God, so that they may receive forgiveness of sins and a place among those who are sanctified by faith in me" (Acts 26:17-18). The closing scene in Acts has Paul, after his message was rejected by the Jewish leaders of Rome, stating: "Let it be known to you then that this salvation of God has been sent to the *Gentiles*; they will listen" (Acts 28:28). Luke, therefore, operates with selectivity with the purpose of etching in his readers' minds a theology of Gentile inclusion into the people of God through the ministry of Paul.

Luke compresses by epitomizing. A second manner in which Luke condenses his account is the technique of epitomizing.[35] Technically speaking, this refers to the abridgment of longer works.[36] As such, Luke does not epitomize in the way that, say, the author of 2 Maccabees does. However,

---

[35]For a helpful discussion, see Clare K. Rothschild, *Luke-Acts and the Rhetoric of History*, WUNT 2.175 (Tübingen: Mohr Siebeck, 2004), 213-87.
[36]Ibid., 217.

we may speak of Luke epitomizing in the sense of condensing his sources.[37] Clare Rothschild suggests that Luke employs "epitomizing language" for the purposes of persuasion.[38] We focus on two areas of epitomizing: hyperbole and summaries, which often occur together.

One way that Luke uses hyperbole is by his penchant for inclusive (and therefore often hyperbolic) language. At the day of Pentecost, we are told that there were in Jerusalem "devout Jews from *every nation* under heaven" (ἀπὸ παντὸς ἔθνους τῶν ὑπὸ τὸν οὐρανόν, Acts 2:5). But this is hyperbole, since the catalog of nations that follows (Acts 2:9-12) does not in fact record all nations. Luke wants to point out proleptically the universality of the people of God in the new era of the Spirit, and hence *every* is used. In Acts 2:42-47 we find one of the well-known Lukan summaries, where Luke gives a beautiful description of the early community. He uses hyperbole at least three times: "Awe came upon *everyone* [πάσῃ ψυχῇ, lit. "every soul" or "person"], because many wonders and signs were being done by the apostles. *All* [πάντες] who believed were together and had *all things* [ἅπαντα] in common" (Acts 2:43-44). Luke thus epitomizes by means of the summary and hyperbole. That the summary includes hyperbole can be seen from the fact that in Acts 5:1-11, the story of Ananias and Sapphira, we find two members who in fact did *not* live up to the qualities of the community stated in Acts 2:42-47. By epitomizing, Luke wants to highlight the golden age of the community in order to provoke imitation from the contemporary community.

Another example of epitomizing is found in the summary of Acts 4:32-37. Here Luke is again providing a summary of the golden age of the community: "Now the whole group of those who believed were of *one* heart and soul [καρδία καὶ ψυχὴ μία], and no one claimed private ownership of any possessions, but *everything* they owned was held in common [ἅπαντα κοινά]." Again, this statement is relativized by the following story of Ananias and Sapphira. We must thus understand the summary as an example of epitomizing by using hyperbole. The point being made is didactic for the contemporary community: adopt the unity, honesty and generosity

---

[37]Ibid., 218.
[38]Ibid.

of the early church as exemplified by Barnabas (Acts 4:36-37), *not* the dishonesty and duplicity of Ananias and Sapphira.

Three more examples of epitomizing by using hyperbole can be found, this time in the ministry of Paul. One of the emphases of Luke is that in the city of Ephesus the ministry of Paul met with an unusual degree of success (Acts 19:1-41). One of the ways that he demonstrates this is by his editorial comment in Acts 19:17-20. The statement is a commentary on Paul's extraordinary miracles and the failed exorcism of the sons of Sceva. After the evil spirit acknowledged Jesus and Paul, it overpowered and trashed the would-be exorcists. Luke then comments: "When this became known to *all* [πᾶσιν] residents of Ephesus, both Jews and Greeks, *everyone* [πάντας] was awestruck; and the name of the Lord Jesus was praised" (Acts 19:17). It is doubtful that *every single* dweller of Ephesus learned of this. Rather, Luke is epitomizing in order to underline the tremendous success of the word of the Lord in Ephesus.

The two other examples are found in the description of Paul's encounter with the crowd in Jerusalem (Acts 21:27-36). In Acts 21:27 we are told that the Jews from Asia "stirred up the *whole* crowed" (πάντα τὸν ὄχλον) near the temple area. And then in Acts 21:30 Luke tells us that "*all* the city was aroused" (ἐκινήθη τε ἡ πόλις ὅλη). It is questionable whether *every person* in the temple complex or in the city of Jerusalem was agitated and rushed to seize Paul.[39] This is best viewed as another example of epitomizing by hyperbole. In fact, the phrase used in Acts 21:30 (ἡ πόλις ὅλη) is found quite often in classical and Hellenistic literature to describe uncontrolled mob behavior in a city.[40] Luke uses this well-known hyperbole to underline the strong rejection of the gospel by the Jews in Jerusalem.

One controversial example in the book of Acts on which light could be shed by paying attention to epitomizing is the Jerusalem Council, found in

---

[39]Ernst Haenchen, *The Acts of the Apostles: A Commentary*, trans. R. M. Wilson (Philadelphia: Westminster, 1971), 616, "That immediately the entire city was thrown into uproar is impossible."

[40]Very close examples include Dionysius of Halicarnassus, *Roman Antiquities* 9.48.4; Josephus, *Jewish War* 1.253.2; and Dio Chrysostom, *Orations* 51.62. From the classical period see Demosthenes, *Against Midias* 80.2; *Against Aristocrates* 81.3; *Against Timocrates* 7.1. For a helpful article on mob violence similar to what we have in Acts 21–22, see M. Hubbard, "Urban Uprisings in the Roman World: The Social Setting of the Mobbing of Sosthenes," *NTS* 51 (2005): 416-28.

Acts 15:1-29. In fact, Rothschild views this passage as an important example of epitomizing.[41] The text presents problems on two main fronts. (1) Concentrating on Acts itself, the unity of theology and language between Paul and Barnabas on the one hand and Peter on the other sounds too good to be true. Peter sounds too much like Paul![42] Furthermore, we know that Peter and Paul did not always see eye to eye (e.g., Gal 2:11-14). And yet, they appear in great harmony in Acts 15. In short, the Lukan account appears intolerably tendentious and cannot, according to many, be true. (2) What is the relationship of Acts 15 to Galatians 2:1-10? On the one hand, there are some striking similarities.[43] On the other hand, there appear to be such discrepancies that either the accounts refer to separate events, or, if they refer to the same event, one of the authors is being dishonest. Luke usually emerges as the guilty party.[44] Although it is possible that the respective texts may be referring to different meetings on separate occasions in Jerusalem, the amount of overlap between the two texts is such that we opt to view the texts as referring to the same event. But how do we resolve the discrepancies, if they can at all be resolved? The amount of literature in itself shows that there is no simple solution. But perhaps scholars have not called sufficient attention to epitomizing? I suggest this as a way forward.

Epitomizing can be seen in a number of places in Acts 15, to which Rothschild has already pointed. I want to focus on the amount of epitomizing in the sphere of *chronology* that is noteworthy in this text. Specifically, it should be noted that after the Antiochean party has reached Jerusalem—that is, once the council proper begins—chronological markers for the duration of the meeting are vague: τε (Acts 15:4), δέ (Acts 15:5), τε (Acts 15:6), δέ (Acts 15:7), τότε (Acts 15:22). Consider Acts 15:4-6. In Acts 15:4 we are told that when the Antiochean party reached Jerusalem, "they were welcomed by the church and the apostles and the elders, and they reported all that God had done with them." In Acts 15:5 the party is contradicted by

---

[41]Rothschild, *Luke-Acts and the Rhetoric of History*, 281-83.
[42]Haenchen, *Acts of the Apostles*, 459: "This clearly does not represent the historical Peter's way of thinking."
[43]See the impressive list compiled by Craig Keener, *Acts: An Exegetical Commentary* (Grand Rapids: Baker, 2012), 1:244.
[44]For F. F. Bruce's comments on this tendency, see *The Book of the Acts*, rev. ed., NICNT (Grand Rapids: Eerdmans, 1988), 282-85.

some of the Pharisees, who said, "It is necessary for them to be circumcised and ordered to keep the law of Moses." And yet, in the next verse we are told, "The apostles and the elders met together [Συνήχθησάν τε οἱ ἀπόστολοι καὶ οἱ πρεσβύτεροι] to consider this matter."

This sounds out of place. Did not Acts 15:4 just say that the Antiochean party had been welcomed by the apostles and elders? Why does Luke repeat what he said in Acts 15:4?[45] Or is it possible that the council took a number of days, and that Luke is attempting to epitomize and compress the entire council into one day (which is exactly what he did with the resurrection account on Luke 24, as we saw above), and hence we have a somewhat clumsy repetition in Acts 15:6? I would suggest that in fact Luke is epitomizing in Acts 15: he is completely focused on communicating to the audience the acceptance of the Gentiles without circumcision by the mother church and chief apostles. More than likely, then, the Jerusalem council took more than one day. Would this example of epitomizing help solve some of the discrepancies between Acts 15 and Galatians 2? It may be that some of the things that Paul reports as having occurred in the meeting but that are omitted by Luke could be explained by noting that the council took a number of days, thus allowing for many meetings where different business was discussed.

Let me conclude this section on epitomizing by speaking somewhat personally, lest we think that this matter is "all academic." In fact, failing to grasp this literary technique of Luke can cause serious damage by creating the equivocated expectation that miracles happened every day in Acts! As a Hispanic, I have at times inhabited an ecclesial world that has been profoundly impacted by Pentecostalism and charismatism. In this context, as is well known, miracles play a prominent role in evangelism and worship. Often I have found this emphasis helpful; I have been challenged to be more open to God's miraculous intervention. At other times, however, I have found that the expectation of a miracle *every week* has been destructive for many churchgoers. They are encouraged to expect "mountaintop" experiences of the presence of God *regularly*. The justification? The book of

---

[45]If one retorts that the party from Antioch was absent in the deliberation of Acts 15:6, to this it can be answered that this is not the case, as the context clearly shows.

Acts. We are told that in the early church God was potently present all the time. There we see powerful healings, speaking in tongues, angelic experiences and so on. Since Jesus Christ is the same yesterday, today and forever, we should expect the same today.

This is not in itself the problem; rather, it is the expectation that this should happen *every day*. The book of Acts, with a miracle on almost every page, is said to sanction this attitude. But then these churchgoers do not experience the miraculous each week. They cope with this in different ways: maybe there is something wrong with *me*; maybe I just don't have enough faith. Others proceed to *manufacture* an experience weekly, not reflecting on the possible psychological and physiological damage this "auto-frenzing" can cause. Others simply reject Scripture because it does not match with their experience, and walk out of the church.

This constant expectation for the miraculous should not be based on the book of Acts. I am convinced that it is a misreading of Acts, a failure to grapple hermeneutically with Luke's compressing and selectivity. Luke is highlighting the *high points* of the early church where miracles must thus be stressed for the purpose of persuasion. But this is simply the way history is written. To confuse the highlights with the mundane can create false expectations.

Luke presents a cohesive narrative for theological purposes. The cohesiveness of the narrative is to be apprehended in its teleological dimensions. That is to say, Luke presents early Christianity as inexorably moving forward in its mission of the proclamation of the gospel. This unstoppable surge can only occur because *God* is the ultimate source of the church. But God uses servants. The first one in the link is of course Jesus of Nazareth (Acts 4:27): he is the Lord and Christ (Acts 2:36) and also the "pioneer" (ἀρχηγός) (Acts 5:31). The Twelve, along with other apostles and servants (e.g., Stephen, Barnabas), link back to Jesus and then forward to Paul. These servants are thus used by God, through the Holy Spirit, to move the word forward to the "end of the earth" (Acts 1:8). To the extent that they are dependent on Jesus, who grants them the Holy Spirit (Acts 2:32-34), they labor under God's power. We can thus speak of apostolic cohesiveness (with Jesus as the "pioneer") that is used by God for the purposes of witnessing.

This does not mean that the movement is free of tensions (see Acts 5:1-11; 15:1-29, 36-41) or persecution (see Acts 4:1-22; 5:17-41; 7:54-8:3; 9:1-2, etc.). Yet, God uses even these obstacles to forward the mission. In short, there is a solidity in the church that stems from God and as such accomplishes his will. Luke's message in this is the confirmation that the Christians, both Jews and Gentiles, are the people of God. Put differently, the point is that Christianity is a movement of God.

But how does Luke accomplish communicating this statement by means of narrative? Daniel Marguerat has proposed three "unifying procedures" that help readers apprehend narrative unity and thereby "unity of . . . salvation history."[46] I follow two of Marguerat's procedures but sometimes use different examples to illustrate them; I add a third.

Prolepsis. This procedure refers to "a projection toward the future of the story."[47] Like the morsel that gives us a taste of the main dish coming, so prolepsis gives us an indication of something that will become significant later in the narrative. There are two powerful examples of prolepsis related to the theme of the salvation of the Gentiles. The first is in Acts 1:8: "But you will receive power when the Holy Spirit has come upon you; and you will be my witnesses in Jerusalem, in all Judea and Samaria, and to the ends of the earth." This passage has been taken as something of an *exact* template for Acts. While there is some validity to this view, it becomes problematic when we wish to use it as a neat descriptor of consecutive stops for the gospel.[48] For example, while it is true that Jerusalem is the first place where the apostles testify to Jesus, the province of Judea is already included in the initial proclamation.[49] Thus Acts 2:9, in cataloging the representatives of the nations on the day of Pentecost, states: "Parthians, Medes, Elamites, and residents of Mesopotamia, *Judea* and Cappadocia, Pontus and Asia." Consequently, the view that Acts 1:8 presents a sharp, sequential (*first* Jerusalem, *then* Judea) geographic template is mistaken. In fact, already in Acts 2:11 we hear of "visitors from Rome" present at Pentecost,

---

[46]Marguerat, *First Christian Historian*, 49-59.

[47]Ibid., 49.

[48]Thus rightly, Pao, *Acts and the Isaianic New Exodus*, 93, 95n141.

[49]This is hinted at in the construction of Acts 1:8: ἔν τε Ἰερουσαλὴμ καὶ πάσῃ Ἰουδαίᾳ. This is best translated as "both in Jerusalem and also in all Judea."

thus somewhat spoiling the suspense of the last chapters of Acts, where reaching Rome with the gospel seems to be an important goal that is in jeopardy. Rather, from the point of view of geography, we would find better justification in saying that Acts 1:8 shows us that Luke is working with a *Jewish* mental map, in which Jerusalem is understood to be the center of the world.[50]

From the perspective of the theological goal of Acts, while not completely denying the traditional understanding of Acts 1:8, I suggest that we also understand it as proleptic of the mission to the Gentiles. In this respect, the phrase "the ends of the earth" is fascinating. What is Luke referring to here? There is considerable debate on the matter. Possibilities include Ethiopia, India, Spain and Rome.[51] The exact phrase, ἐσχάτου τῆς γῆς, however, is not foreign to the Old Testament. In Deuteronomy 28:49 it is used to refer to a faraway Gentile nation that will take Israel captive. In Jeremiah 16:19 this is in some ways reversed: it is now the nations that will realize their idolatrous folly and will come to Yahweh ἀπ' ἐσχάτου τῆς γῆς. The context is clearly eschatological. This eschatological framework is most visible in the use of the phrase in Isaiah. In Isaiah 45:22 the nations (οἱ ἀπ' ἐσχάτου τῆς γῆς) are commanded to repent and be saved. In Isaiah 49:6 Yahweh has raised his servant Jacob, who will be restored in order that God's salvation might reach ἕως ἐσχάτου τῆς γῆς, the exact phrase of Acts 1:8.[52] Luke himself, in the speech of Paul and Barnabas in Acts 13:47, quotes Isaiah 49:6 to provide scriptural justification for taking the gospel to the Gentiles. It is clear, therefore, that we should understand the phrase in Acts 1:8 to refer to the Gentiles.[53] As such, all Gentiles in the book of Acts who receive the gospel—from the Ethiopian in Acts 8 to the Ephesians in Acts 19—can represent the ends of the earth. The phrase is thus an expansion of Luke 24:47 and becomes proleptic for the rest of Acts.

---

[50]See Loveday Alexander, *Acts in Its Ancient Literary Context: A Classicist Looks at the Acts of the Apostles*, LNTS 298 (London: T&T Clark, 2005), 72-75. Pao, *Acts and the Isaianic New Exodus*, 86n95, links the geographic phrase "beginning from Jerusalem" to Is 2:3; 51:4.

[51]*Ethiopia*: Herodotus 3.25; Strabo, *Geography* 1.1.6. *India*: Demosthenes, *Epistulae* 4.7.6; Strabo, *Geography* 1.1.8. *Spain*: Strabo, *Geography* 1.1.8 (the west end of the earth); *Rome*: *Psalms of Solomon* 8.15. See further Earle Ellis, "'The End of the Earth' (Acts 1:8)," *BBR* 1 (1991): 123-32, who prefers Spain; and now Keener, *Acts*, 1:697-711.

[52]Interestingly, Tobit 13:13 echoes Is 49:6.

[53]Thus also Pao, *Acts and the Isaianic New Exodus*, 93-95, but further grounding his interpretation on Is 49:6.

A second example of prolepsis is found in Acts 2 with the miraculous speaking in tongues (Acts 2:1-13).[54] The description of the coming of the Spirit in Acts 2:2-3 is done in such a way so as to evoke an epiphany: "suddenly," "a roar from heaven," "violent wind" and "fire." The terminology immediately brings to mind the descent of God on Mount Sinai described in Exodus 19:16-25. What is interesting is that in the Exodus passage it is God who descends; in Acts it is the Holy Spirit.[55] Once *all* (notice the extensive use of πάντες in these verses) the disciples have been filled with the Holy Spirit and speak inspired speech (ἀποφθέγγομαι, Acts 2:4), Luke provides the catalogue of nations and the sneering of some as they hear the disciples speaking in tongues (Acts 2:13). This is followed by Peter's sermon (Acts 2:14-40). We will devote significant space to this sermon in chapter five; thus only the following main comment is necessary for this specific section.

Peter grounds his explanation of the tongues event in Scripture— namely, Joel 2:28-32 (LXX 3:1-5). Adding the words "in the last days" (Acts 2:17) to make sure that the audience understands the eschatological context of Joel,[56] Peter explains the event as the fulfillment of the pouring out of the Spirit on *everyone* in God's household. This event is accompanied by apocalyptic signs (Acts 2:19-20) and a promise that "everyone" who calls on the name of the Lord will be saved (Acts 2:21). Thus what the crowds in Jerusalem have witnessed is not drunkenness on the part of Jesus' disciples, but rather the fulfillment of the eschatological promise of the Holy Spirit. This means that the time for universal (catalogue of nations, Acts 2:5-11) salvation through Jesus Christ has dawned.

The pouring out of the Spirit along with the speech of Peter sets the course for the remainder of Acts. As such, this event (outpouring and speech) provides a prolepsis for the rest of Acts. But are Gentiles in mind here, or just the Jewish diaspora? It is clear from the rest of the narrative that many of the disciples (Peter certainly) understood the Old Testament promises as referring to naturally born Jews or proselytes, not uncircumcised Gentiles. But God will make it clear (Acts 10–11; esp. Acts 11:19-21)

---

[54] On this see also chapter five.

[55] This is one of many trinitarian "nudges" in Luke-Acts.

[56] This is implicit in the context of Joel.

that the Spirit will be poured out on *all* who believe—Jews (including proselytes) and non-Jews. In fact, as the narrative progresses outside Judea we see multiple conversions of Gentiles. The prolepsis of Acts 2 is thus concretized in the remainder of the book.[57]

Syncrisis. Marguerat defines syncrisis in the following way: "It consists in modeling the presentation of a character on another in order to compare them, or at least to establish a correlation between the two."[58] Syncrisis is found in Luke-Acts in the form of parallelisms. The observation of these parallelisms has, as Susan Praeder noted, been part of modern Lukan scholarship since the nineteenth century.[59] It is agreed that at a broad level the following parallels are present: Jesus—Peter; Jesus—Paul; Jesus—Stephen; Peter—Paul. With respect to the chain of Jesus → Peter → Paul, there are parallelisms in the areas of miracles, trials and (excepting Peter) journeys.[60] Luke clearly wants to show that there is a strong connection between these three characters. But what does he want do with this syncrisis? I suggest, among a number of possibilities, the following two.

First, syncrisis is used in Acts for the purpose of legitimation. Concentrating on Paul, we know that the apostle was a controversial figure in early Christianity. Perhaps the most troublesome issue (apart from that of the place of Torah) was related to his call: Was he a legitimate apostle of Jesus Christ? Thus the question in Corinth was: Do not his many sufferings and lack of rhetorical power show that he is not an apostle? And in Galatia: Did he not actually receive his gospel from the Jerusalem authorities? Let us imagine how this may have affected those Christians who had converted directly under Paul or under one of his disciples. They may well have been wondering whether the gospel that they had received was genuine. The rehabilitation of Paul may thus have been one of the goals in the composition of Acts. By means of syncrisis Luke links Paul to both Jesus and Peter.

---

[57] See also James M. Scott, "Acts 2:9-11 as an Anticipation of the Mission to the Nations," in *The Mission of the Early Church to Jews and Gentiles*, ed. Jostein Ådna and Hans Kvalbein, WUNT 1.127 (Tübingen: Mohr Siebeck, 2000), 87-123.

[58] Marguerat, *First Christian Historian*, 56.

[59] See Susan M. Praeder, "Jesus-Paul, Peter-Paul, and Jesus-Peter Parallelisms in Luke-Acts: A History of Reader Response," in *SBL 1984 Seminar Papers*, ed. Kent Harold Richards (Chico, CA: Scholars Press, 1984), 23-39.

[60] For the biblical texts, see ibid., 34-37.

Paul heals like Jesus and Peter; Paul suffers persecution like Peter and especially like Jesus. In fact, Paul's journey to Jerusalem is patterned after Jesus' own journey of prospective suffering to that city. Last, Paul preaches like Jesus and Peter, but especially like the former. In this respect, the curious ending of Acts is intriguing. Twice in Acts 28:23-31 Paul's preaching is summarized as having as its content the kingdom of God. This was also the theme of Jesus' preaching (Lk 4:43; 8:1, 9; Acts 1:3). And so Paul heals like the Master, suffers like the Master and preaches like the Master. The point is clear: Paul is a legitimate apostle of Jesus Christ.

Second, syncrisis is used to prod the readers to *imitatio* of Jesus and his apostles. In proclamation, witnessing and suffering, the chain that began with Jesus and was continued with the apostles is at present to continue with the readers of Acts.

Dramatic irony. This is the last example of how Luke unifies his narrative theologically. By dramatic irony we are referring to the irony of the theater. Dramatic irony exploits the gap that exists between the characters in the story (the dramatis personae) and the audience outside the story. Usually a statement is made by one of the characters that contains a surplus of meaning for the audience, thereby showing that the speaker has said more than he or she realizes. Dramatic irony is often found in the Bible in order to show the limitations of human knowledge and cleverness; positively, it is employed to highlight God's sovereignty.[61]

Luke uses dramatic irony throughout both his volumes in a very rich way. To provide just one example before moving to the uses in Acts, one may recall the scene on the way to Emmaus (Lk 24:13-29). Jesus, who is not recognized by the disciples, plays the ignorant when, after the disciples speak of the events that have just happened in Jerusalem, he asks: "What are you discussing with each other while you walk along?" Cleopas is apparently irritated at the stranger's ignorance and responds: "Are you the only stranger in Jerusalem who does not know the things that have taken place there in these days?" (Lk 24:17-18). But Jesus is *precisely* the one who knows best what has just happened in Jerusalem!

---

[61]See further Osvaldo Padilla, *The Speeches of Outsiders in Acts: Poetics, Theology and Historiography*, SNTSMS 144 (Cambridge: Cambridge University Press, 2008), 13-14, 128-30, 159-61.

The disciples are ignorant of this, but the readers know better. By this irony Luke shows that the disciples are "foolish" and "slow of heart to believe" (Lk 24:25).[62]

In the book of Acts I suggest that there is a controlling dramatic irony. This use of irony provides us with a hermeneutic to grasp the dynamics of the narrative. This irony is found on the lips of Gamaliel in Acts 5:35-39. Gamaliel intervenes in the deliberation of the Sanhedrin. The council is at a loss on what to do with the disciples of Jesus. It has already done much in an attempt to silence them: warnings, arrest and a beating. But the disciples have not stopped; if anything, they have grown even bolder. Apparently there is only one last recourse: execution. At this juncture Gamaliel intervenes. The council should be careful on how it acts, the wise Pharisee warns. It should let time pass. These sorts of messianic movements, he says, are not new: we have the examples of Theudas and Judas, who, after drawing people to themselves, were extinguished and their movements came to nothing. Perhaps, Gamaliel suggests, this is what will happen with these disciples of Jesus. But it may be that this movement has divine backing, and so the council must be patient. Gamaliel concludes: "If this plan or this undertaking is of human origin, it will fail; but if it is of God, you will not be able to overthrow them—in that case you may even be found fighting against God!" A key term is the one translated by the phrase "fighting against God," just one word in Greek: θεομάχοι.

The θεομάχος, or "god-fighter," is a well-known figure in Greek literature.[63] He appears mostly in Greek drama as one who resists the cult of the god Dionysius and pays the price with his own destruction. Perhaps the best-known god-fighter in this context is the Theban king Pentheus as presented in Euripides's tragedy *Bacchae*. The concept of the god-fighter made its way into Jewish literature—and thus we have a closer background to Acts. In 2 Maccabees 7:19 King Antiochus Epiphanes is called a God-fighter by one of the seven brothers who is martyred. The king opposes the

---

[62]On Luke's use of dramatic irony for profoundly christological use, see C. Kavin Rowe, *Early Narrative Christology: The Lord in the Gospel of Luke*, BZNW 139 (Berlin: Walter de Gruyter, 2006), esp. 208-16.

[63]To be noted is that, in contrast to Luke, classical and Hellenistic literature prefers the verbal form. See, e.g., Euripides, *Bacchae* 45, 325, 1255; *Iphigenia in Aulis* 1408; Xenophon, *Economics* 16.3; Diodorus Siculus, *Library* 14.69; Epictetus, *Discourses* 4.1. But see the term used in the vocative in Lucian, *Zeus Rants* 45.

true worship of Yahweh and as such engages in a war against him. He is warned of future destruction.

The term θεομάχος is also found twice in Josephus, when the historian quotes Manetho.[64] As J. Weaver points out, although the term is not used in *Jewish Antiquities* 14.310, nevertheless the concept is clearly present. In this last example, classic hubristic characters of the Old Testament such as Pharaoh and Sennacherib are used.[65] Those who engage in god-fighting put themselves against the deity and thus can only expect future retribution. Weavers sums up well the dynamics of the god-fighter: "To be called a θεομάχος was, in other words, to be put on notice that one's future is in serious jeopardy."[66] The flip side of this is the implicit legitimation of those who follow the deity that the θεομάχος opposes. That is, when there are god-fighters present in a narrative, the readers are conditioned to expect persecution against the followers of the deity; but they are also conditioned to expect the victory of the persecuted because they stand on the side of the deity. And this brings us back to the speech of Gamaliel.

When Gamaliel warns the council that if the Jesus movement endures, it would mean that it is from God, Luke is employing dramatic irony. For some of the characters in the story (i.e., the Sanhedrin), the possibility that the movement will endure is presented as unlikely: notice that the examples that Gamaliel uses to compare to the Jesus movement have all failed! But for the readers, who have the rest of the narrative as well as the historical advantage of seeing Christianity grow, Gamaliel has just stated far more than he realizes. By means of dramatic irony Luke takes what is a possibility for the characters in the story and turns it into an affirmation for the readers outside the story: the Jesus movement will move forward even in the face of persecution.[67] By extension, in using the term θεομάχοι, Luke invites the readers to be on the alert for those who will unsuccessfully

---

[64]Josephus, *Against Apion* 1.246, 263.

[65]J. B. Weaver, *Plots of Epiphany: Prison-Escape in the Acts of the Apostles*, BZNW 131 (Berlin: Walter de Gruyter, 2004), 135.

[66]Ibid., 134.

[67]I have developed this further in Padilla, *Speeches of Outsiders*, 106-34. For a similar conclusion, see J. A. Darr, "Irenic or Ironic? Another Look at Gamaliel," in *Literary Studies in Luke-Acts: Essays in Honor of Joseph B. Tyson*, ed. R. P. Thompson and T. E. Philips (Macon, GA: Mercer University Press, 1998), 121-40.

attempt to halt the movement—in fact, those who will end up unwittingly moving it forward. The dynamics for the remainder of the narrative are now set by means of dramatic irony. Marguerat reaches the same conclusion: "The irony of God consists in integrating even the actions of his enemies in order to make them contribute to the advancement of the Word 'to the ends of the earth' (1:8)."[68] But who are the θεομάχοι? Below I sketch the two principal ones.

Perhaps surprisingly, the first God-fighter is none other than Paul in his pre-Christian identity as Saul. Luke clearly presents Paul as a God-fighter, primarily through his composing of Paul's conversion/call (Acts 9:1-29; 22:3-21; 26:9-20). Consider the following three observations.

First, the description of Paul's attitude in Acts 9:1 resembles the attitude of a god-fighter. We are told that Paul was "breathing threats and murder" (ἐμπνέων ἀπειλῆς καὶ φόνου). Although the form ἐμπνέω is not very common before the New Testament, the synonymous πνέω is. It primarily occurs in its metaphoric use in poetic literature.[69] Intriguingly, in Euripides's *Bacchae* (a work that we previously saw as highlighting the motif of the god-fighter) it is used of that archetypal god-fighter, Pentheus. The king, in his fight against Dionysius, is described as θυμὸν ἐκπνέων (620; see also 640)—that is, "breathing fury."

Second, note that in Paul's recounting of his conversion before Agrippa, he reports the Lord as saying to him, "'Saul, Saul, why are you persecuting me? *It hurts you to kick against the goads*'" (Acts 26:14). This last expression is also found in Euripides's *Bacchae* 794, and is part of a dialogue between King Pentheus and the god Dionysius where the god warns the king that to fight against him is useless and painful. It is like kicking against the goads.[70]

---

[68]Marguerat, *First Christian Historian*, 108.

[69]See, e.g., Homer, *Iliad* 2.508, 536, where it refers to breathing "fury" (μένος); Sophocles, *Electra* 610; Euripides, *Iphigenia in Taurus* 288, πῦρ πνέουσα καὶ φόνον ("breathing fire and murder"); *Phoenician Women* 454, δεινὸν ὄμμα καὶ θυμοῦ πνόας (cf. also 876). For the metaphoric use in prose literature, see Xenophon, *Hellenica* 7.4.32; Dionysius of Halicarnassus, *Roman Antiquities* 7.35.3; and Wisdom of Solomon 15:11. Particularly instructive is Philo, *Moses* 2.240, where those who "breathe great things" (οἱ μέγα πνέοντες) are also called "boasters" (οἱ ἀλαζόνες). Some of these references I owe to the treasure of a work on the term by P. W. van der Horst, "Drohung und Mord schnaubend (Acta IX 1)," *NovT* 12 (1970): 256-69.

[70]We are not suggesting that Luke's use of Euripides proves direct dependence on the latter. The proverb

Last, the couching of Paul's conversion as occurring in the context of an epiphany leads us to view him as a God-fighter. That the encounter with the risen Jesus is portrayed as an epiphany is certain. There is light ("brighter than the sun," Acts 26:13), suddenness (Acts 9:3; 22:6), prostration (Acts 9:4; 22:7; 26:14), double-calling of Saul's name (Acts 9:4; 22:7; 26:14) and overpowering of the enemy. The epiphany recalls the encounter with Moses (Ex 3:4-6); but it is even closer to epiphanies of Second Temple literature, especially those involving Heliodorus (2 Macc 3:1-39) and Philopator (3 Macc). Paul is thus presented as a God-fighter who attempts to stop the Jesus movement. Yet, he is overpowered by the risen Christ and ironically serves as the greatest propagator of the Christian message.

The second God-fighter is an entity—namely, those Jews who oppose the gospel. The Jerusalem authorities and the Jews from Asia Minor are singled out by Luke as foes of the gospel. They arrest the apostles and believers (Acts 4:3), threaten them (Acts 4:21), flog them (Acts 5:40), order them to stop speaking in the name of Jesus (Acts 5:40) and persecute them (Acts 8:1). Unwittingly, they aid in the expansion of the gospel to Samaria (Acts 8:4) and Antioch (Acts 11:20). The Jews from Asia Minor are virulent in their persecution of the believers, particularly Paul. They stone Paul (Acts 14:19-20), accuse him and his companions of treason (Acts 17:5-7), charge him before the proconsul Gallio (Acts 18:12-13), incite a mob lynching while he is in the temple (Acts 21:27-36), plot an ambush to kill him (Acts 23:12-15) and bring charges against him for causing sedition (Acts 24:2-8). They unwittingly aid in the movement of Paul to Rome, where he is destined to preach the gospel (Acts 23:11). They are clearly presented as God-fighters. In fact, there is an intriguing textual variant in Acts 23:9 that harks back to Gamaliel's warning against God-fighting. Here Paul is taken to the Sanhedrin (Acts 23:1) when he notices that there are both Sadducees and Pharisees present. He exploits the situation by exclaiming that he is on trial for his belief in the resurrection (Acts 23:6). This triggers a vigorous argument, where some of the scribes of the Pharisees

---

was well known in antiquity (e.g., Pindar and Aeschylus). Rather, it is likely that the sentiment of the futility of fighting against the god had spread through the Mediterranean. On this see Weaver, *Plots of Epiphany*, 133-36.

state: "We find nothing wrong with this man. What if a spirit or angel has spoken to him?" (Acts 23:9). Immediately after these words, some manuscripts of the Majority text and Byzantine family (L, 323) add: μὴ θεομαχῶμεν—"Let us not be God-fighters." Although the reading is not original, it nevertheless shows how in antiquity these actions of the Jews could be depicted as God-fighting.

Conclusion. In this section we have concentrated on Luke the storyteller. We have seen that although in his preface Luke wished to present himself as a historian, he nevertheless wanted to be viewed as a *theological* historian. We have argued that in order to advance his main theological emphases, he wrote his history like an artist. He availed himself of numerous narrative procedures: telescoping, epitomizing, selectivity, prolepsis, syncrisis and dramatic irony.[71] By using these, he produced a cohesive effect that in turn provokes in the reader a sense of the theological unity of his work. This unity can be called *missional unity*: the word of the Lord goes forth victoriously from Jerusalem to the ends of the earth, reaching both Jews and Gentiles. Under this canopy (or, from a different perspective, *supporting* the canopy) fit the motifs highlighted above. Those who take the gospel to the ends of the earth imitate Jesus in word and deed (syncrisis). These servants encounter resistance from θεομάχοι, God-fighters, who unwittingly aid in the progress of the gospel (dramatic irony). All this progress is presaged by the command of the risen Jesus in Acts 1:8 and the speaking in tongues of Acts 2 (prolepsis). In short, Luke has taken the different characters and events of early Christianity and emplotted them to produce a satisfying and persuasive account.

LUKE THE HISTORIAN

We began this chapter by looking at some of the key terms of Luke's preface. We suggested that Luke clearly wanted his readers to understand his double work as a form of theological history. Having seen in the previous section how Luke constructed and communicated his theology through narrative, we conclude this chapter by returning to the matter of history.

---

[71]Others could have been included, such as repetition and humor.

For certain readers, my forthcoming attempt to persuade that Acts is in some sense history may seem to have been undermined at my own hands by the previous section on narrative: Did we not speak of eminently *literary* procedures such as telescoping, syncrisis, prolepsis and so on (not to mention the involvement of the supernatural)? Are these not features primarily found in novelistic or epic literature—that is, fictive literature? In fact, it was the literary procedure of syncrisis (among other things) that led the father of modern criticism of Acts, F. C. Baur, to question its historical caliber. For syncrisis is nothing if not the inclusion and exclusion (and shaping) of data to show links between characters. And this was unacceptable to Baur:

> It is certainly apparent that a decided apologetic feeling lies at the root of his [Luke's] statement, and therefore it must be doubtful whether we can have a purely historical relation from him: and it can scarcely be denied that possibly, if not probably, he has in many cases ignored the true history, not only negatively, by ignoring actions and circumstances which bear essentially on his subject matter, but also positively.[72]

As we can see from Baur—and he has been followed in this by many—it is the combination of narrative management with an apologetic end that renders the historical reliability of Acts suspect.[73] Persuasion—which to a large extent necessitates the use of *rhetoric*—and history seemingly cannot go together.

But according to whom? To ask this question is to embark on some of the essential elements of the nature of history. Both the lack of specialization of this author as well as the limitations of space preclude a sustained discussion. Nevertheless, a sketch is possible that does not require these but that can be informative for our understanding of Acts as history. The plan is to provide an overview of the study of historiography with the emphasis falling on two developments: the professionalization of history in the nineteenth century and the revival of history as narrative in the postmodern

---

[72]F. C. Baur, *Paul the Apostle of Jesus Christ: His Life and Works, His Epistles and His Teachings*, trans. A. Menzies (Peabody, MA: Hendrickson, 2003), 11.

[73]A point made time after time by Haenchen in his massively influential Acts commentary for the Meyer series. See esp. 98-110; 112-16.

period. These will then be brought to bear on the historical nature of Acts.

The professionalization of history. When historians speak of the professionalization of history, the name of Leopold von Ranke is usually invoked as its founder. As Georg Iggers has indicated, this is true in a number of ways. Under educational reforms brought about by Wilhelm von Humboldt, the German university was to become a place of research, producing results that would make citizens recipients of *Bildung*—that is, intellectual and aesthetic education. For this to be accomplished, the different branches would need experts, professionals who would do the work in a manner consistent with *Wissenschaft*. It was in this context that Ranke was called to the University of Berlin in 1825.[74] Ranke devised a method that called for historians to base their work on primary sources.[75] They would do this by going to the state archives and sifting through the relevant documents in as objective a manner as possible. A strong philological base was necessary to do this competently, and so the students received training in this area. Ranke inculcated this method on numerous future historians through the famous seminar.[76]

Ranke's historiographic method can thus be summarized as comprising the following: search of primary sources primarily through archives and seeing the past in its own terms. It is in this last area that Ranke has been misunderstood, with the result that he has been wrongly viewed as espousing a positivistic view of history. There was, in fact, something of a tension in Ranke's understanding of history. For while he wanted to present the past "as it actually happened," he did not consider the final goal of history as merely the chronicling of facts.[77] For Ranke, once the historian had toiled in reconstructing the past accurately, it was then time to go beyond the "mere events" to an intuition of the spiritual realities behind them. Iggers and others have argued that Ranke should be viewed as a panentheist, and that this was fundamental for how he understood history:

---

[74]Georg Iggers, *Historiography in the Twentieth Century: From Scientific Objectivity to the Postmodern Challenge* (Middletown, CT: Wesleyan University Press, 1997), 23-24.

[75]Perhaps "consolidated" would be more accurate than "devised," since in some of these he was not original.

[76]Iggers, *Historiography in the Twentieth Century*, 25-26.

[77]Perhaps Ranke's most famous phrase. For debate on the meaning of this phrase, see *The Theory and Practice of History*, ed. and with introduction by Georg Iggers (London: Routledge, 2011), xiv.

"His religious belief has been repeatedly described as panentheism which, in contrast to pantheism, recognized the separateness of all human existence from God, yet sees the reflection of God in all existence. The historian's task resembled that of a priest; he was to decipher the 'holy hieroglyph' contained in history."[78] Consider the following statements, one of them coming from Ranke's letter to his closest brother, Heinrich.

> In all of history God dwells, lives, can be recognized. Every deed gives testimony to Him, every moment preaches His name, but most of all, it seems to me, does so the connectedness of History (*Zusammenhang der großen Geschichte*).[79]
>
> History is distinguished from all other sciences in that it is also an art. . . . History is a science in collecting, finding, penetrating; it is an art because it recreates and portrays that which it has found and recognized. Other sciences are satisfied simply with recording what has been found; history requires the ability to recreate.[80]
>
> It is not necessary for us to prove at length that the eternal dwells in the individual. This is the religious foundation on which our efforts rest. We believe that there is nothing without God, and nothing lives except through God.[81]

In Ranke's conception of historiography, the historian was to research documents without any residue of bias; but this should lead to a grasping of the concrete movement of God in the affairs of humans, especially the state, *L'État*. Ranke was no positivist.[82] Thus when we include Ranke in the professionalization of history, this must be viewed from the perspective of his insistence on objective archival research and his passing of this ideal to a future generation of university professors. But as often happens, the disciples take the master's views and push them in different horizons. In particular,

---

[78]Ibid., xvi.

[79]Ibid., 4.

[80]Ibid., 8.

[81]Ibid., xxviii.

[82]This must be said in light of the fact that Ranke has become the whipping boy of much scholarship. He is often blamed as the destructor of the literary qualities of history. See recently Claire Clivaz, *L'Ange et la Sueur de Sang (Lc 22, 43-44). Ou Comment on Pourrait Bien Encore Écrire L'Histoire* (Leuven: Peeters, 2010), 19-20, 154, 175, who latches on to Ranke's statement that history must be "farblos und unschön" to castigate him as the one who has sawn asunder history and narrative. Overlooked in this is the fact that Ranke himself wrote history in a very elegant narrative form.

with the emphasis on archival research and philological exactitude in the interpretation of the documents, there was a tendency with professional historians, particularly at the beginning of the twentieth century, to pay less attention to the rhetorical features of history. Georg Iggers notes: "The literary qualities which had constituted an integral part of the persuasive power of the great historians of the nineteenth century . . . receded in significance as a new generation of historians trained in the techniques of archival research tended to minimize the rhetorical qualities of historical writing."[83] This tendency to minimize the literary quality of historical writing on the part of many professional historians—indeed this tendency to *undervalue* it—would be repeated in France and the United States.

As in Germany, the professionalization of history in France emerged in the context of educational reforms. The indefatigable minister of public education, Victor Duruy, installed as such in 1863, lamented over the ruinous state of French education, particularly in history.[84] Comparison with the German university system served as both the cause for his shame over the French system as well as an example to emulate.[85] Prior to his appointment, Duruy had encouraged the brightest of those who had passed the *agrégation* examination to travel to Germany in order to learn the science of history from its university professors. These men proved to be the core of professional historians of the newly formed École Pratique des Hautes Études of 1868. William Keylor states: "In the same year a select group of young historians who were steeped in German methods of historical scholarship received appointments as *répétiteurs* at the new school. On a very modest scale, these young érudits began to introduce the modern conception of historical study into French higher education."[86]

How did this essentially German method impact French historiography? It is useful to ponder the comments of perhaps the most influential

---

[83]Georg Iggers, *New Directions in European Historiography*, rev. ed. (Middletown, CT: Wesleyan University Press, 1984), 26. On the minimization of rhetoric in history, due in part to the influence of Ernst Bernheim's *Lehrbuch der Historischen Methode*, see further Byrskog, *Story as History*, 21-22.

[84]William R. Keylor, *Academy and Community: The Foundation of the French Historical Profession* (Cambridge, MA: Harvard University Press, 1975), 20-22.

[85]Ibid., 22-25.

[86]Ibid., 27.

French historical theorist of the late nineteenth and early twentieth century, Charles Seignobos. Although not without his own misunderstandings of the German perspective, his comments allow us to see the French historiographic situation as it was being influenced in the early twentieth century.[87] Seignobos, on the one hand, criticized those in the French historical profession who, inspired by their particular understanding (or misunderstanding) of the German model, were espousing a form of positivism. In the words of Keylor: "He expressed grave reservations about the fashionable belief that the historian is obligated to suppress his own personality and let the facts speak for themselves."[88] Seignobos did not believe that history was a science in the way of the natural sciences, *les sciences naturelles*. There was a subjective aspect of reconstruction and generalization that made history different from the natural sciences.[89]

On the other hand, Seignobos welcomed the German insistence on investigation of original documents and the excoriation of the rhetorical. He hoped this would cure what he felt was an excessive focus on the form or literary aspect of history as practiced in France. He believed that this amateurish way of writing history would be remedied by the departments of history of the Sorbonne.[90] With the development of the *Annales* school a greater emphasis was laid on the place of statistics in professional history.[91] The place of narrative and rhetoric in history was thus diminished, although it would be revived toward the middle of the twentieth century.

---

[87]On Seignobos, see ibid., 75-82, who speaks of the historian's occasional misconception of the Germanic method. Further on Seignobos, see Pim den Boer, *History as a Profession: The Study of History in France, 1818—1914*, trans. Arnold J. Pomerans (Princeton, NJ: Princeton University Press, 1998), 295-300. To be recalled is that, along with Charles Langlois, Seignobos wrote what was probably the most influential textbook on historical method in French for the period: *Introduction aux études historiques* (Paris: Hachette, 1898), English translation, *Introduction to the Study of History*, trans. G. G. Berry (New York: Henry Holt and Company, 1926).

[88]Keylor, *Academy and Community*, 78.

[89]"History, which began by being a form of literature, has remained the least methodical of the sciences" (Seignobos, *Introduction to the Study of History*, 214). "'Historical analysis' is no more real than is the vision of historical facts; it is an abstract process, a purely intellectual operation. The analysis of a document consists in a *mental* search for the items of information it contains" (ibid., 216).

[90]See Keylor, *Academy and Community*, 79-80.

[91]See Elizabeth Clark, *History, Theory, Text: Historians and the Linguistic Turn* (Cambridge, MA: Harvard University Press, 2004), 66-71.

The professionalization of history in the United States was linked with the ideal of complete objectivity with greater zeal than had been the case in Germany and France. This story has been well told by Peter Novick, so there is no need to rehearse it here.[92] There is one area, however, that I think is worth looking at in some detail as it has immediate repercussions for our study. This has to do with the American understanding of the German term *Wissenschaft*. As is well known, many of those who would become the pioneers of the historical profession in American universities studied in Germany during the nineteenth century.[93] According to Novick, while there, these future historians became obsessed with the German concept of *Wissenschaft*—as *they* understood it.[94] They were to some extent correct in giving the term the definition of "science." However, they allowed the English linkage of "science" with the *natural* sciences to distort their understanding of *Wissenschaft*. As Fritz Ringer has clarified, this is a mistake. His comments are worth quoting at some length:

> In German usage, any organized body of information is referred to as *eine Wissenschaft*, with the indefinite article. At the same time, all formal knowledge, and the collective activity of scholars in obtaining, interpreting, and ordering it, may be rendered *Wissenschaft*, or, more commonly, *die Wissenschaft*, with the definite article. Thus, *die Wissenschaft* must be translated as "scholarship" or "learning," rarely as "science," and *eine Wissenschaft* simply means a "discipline."[95]

Thus when Ranke and other German historians spoke of history as *Wissenschaft*, they were not attempting to bring it into conformity with the natural sciences, and thereby obtain for history the objectivity that was supposed to be the indispensable mark of the natural sciences. Again, Ringer is helpful: "The German historian was not only certain that his field of work was a discipline; he also knew that it was a *Geisteswissenschaft*, a humanistic discipline by definition. This gave him a starting advantage in

---

[92]Peter Novick, *That Noble Dream: The "Objectivity Question" and the American Historical Profession* (Cambridge: Cambridge University Press, 1988).

[93]Ibid., 21-24.

[94]Ibid., 24-31.

[95]Fritz Ringer, *The Decline of the German Mandarins: The German Academic Community, 1890–1933* (Cambridge, MA: Harvard University Press, 1969), 102-3.

any argument against an advocate of 'scientific' methods in history."[96] Novick suggests that a failure to grasp this nuance of the term led the early American historians to enshrine history as another example of the empirical sciences.[97] Frederick Jackson Turner credited Ranke with this advance: "That inductive study of phenomena which has worked a revolution in our knowledge of the external world was applied to history."[98]

The emphasis on scientific objectivity led to an obsession with "the facts only" that began a shift in the method of presentation. Novick notes the fascinating effect of this on journalism toward the end of the nineteenth century. He quotes Lincoln Steffens: "Reporters were to report the news as it happened, like machines, without prejudice, color, and without style; all alike. Humor or any sign of personality in our reports was caught, rebuked, and, in time, suppressed."[99] This "scientific" manner of reporting was to be the hallmark of professional historians. As opposed to "amateurs" like George Bancroft, William Lothrop Motley and others, who presented history in narrative manner, professional historians were to be austere and dry in their manner of presentation.[100] The "purification" of history by cleansing it from the literary was, on the whole, a significant ethos in the professionalization of history in the young nation.[101]

Let us sum up on the professionalization of history as it bears on Acts: If the only history that can be considered genuine is that which most closely approximates the (idealized) model of the natural sciences with its connotations of objectivity, austerity and neutrality, what can be said about a work like the book of Acts, which evidently does not reflect such ideals? For many biblical scholars the dicta that emerged from the professionalization of history have been adopted in the assessment of Acts's claim to be taken as serious history. Although the guidelines for analysis

---

[96]Ibid., 103.

[97]One should add that a failure to understand *Wissenschaft* as well as *the epistemological ethos opened by an understanding of the term* is what led to the American distortion. Sometimes Novick seems to hang all of the misconception on a single word; this does not seem realistic.

[98]As quoted in Novick, *That Noble Dream*, 28-29.

[99]Ibid., 43.

[100]Ibid., 44-46.

[101]We have not mentioned British historiography because, although certainly adopting some of the German ideas, it nevertheless was less keen than France and the United States.

are often not stated explicitly, one can see the overall effect in the criteria that are used to determine the possibility of truthfulness of different portions of Acts. The following quotations are representative:

- H. J. Cadbury: "In the fiction of the speeches, in indifference to dates and to other minor data, in objectivity and in many other traits ... Luke belongs to the ancient rather than to the modern standards."[102] And because Luke does not attain to modern standards, Cadbury is as a whole skeptical of the historical truthfulness of Acts.[103]

- Ernst Haenchen, on the historical plausibility of the speech of Peter in Acts 15: "The whole theory with which Luke reconciles the legitimacy of the Gentile mission without the law . . . with Antioch's struggle for the recognition of its mission to the Gentiles is an imaginary construction answering to no historical reality."[104] For Haenchen believes that this example of *syncrisis* between Peter and Paul is far too tendentious. History worthy of respect must not be so rhetorically invested.

- Alan Segal: "The description in the Acts of the Apostles of Paul's sudden conversion on the road to Damascus is primarily the creation of Luke, Paul's biographer, for Paul never describes his conversion directly." And later: "Luke's description of Paul is not impartial biography either, for it was intended to dramatize the early church's journey from Judea into the gentile world."[105]

These statements are most revealing. The first is really a non sequitur: the fact (if it is a fact) that Paul never gives a detailed account of his conversion in his writings does not mean that Luke had to invent it. Paul could have passed it down orally either to Luke himself or to others, thus leading to the emergence of a tradition on which Luke could have drawn. The only way in which Segal's statement is not logically flawed is if he assumes that

---

[102]Cadbury, *Making of Luke-Acts,* 320.

[103]To be fair to Cadbury, he does mention (ibid., 368) that the modern standards of historiography are themselves also deficient in some areas. Yet, both in the work cited as well as in some of his essays in the *Beginnings of Christianity* series, one detects a skeptical strain.

[104]Haenchen, *Acts of the Apostles,* 463.

[105]Alan Segal, *Paul the Convert: The Apostolate and Apostasy of Saul the Pharisee* (New Haven, CT: Yale University Press, 1990), 3, 4.

Luke wrote his second volume with only *written* material as his source. *But this is itself an assumption based on the modern, professional way of writing history, which often eschewed oral sources.* Segal's second statement also assumes the professionalization of history: it appeals to a lack of partiality and literary creativity as necessary for a faithful historical account.

Other examples could be cited.[106] The point is that with the professionalization of history a number of criteria have been put in place that can certainly lead to skepticism of a work like Acts. Biblical scholars have drawn on these, the result often being a marginalization of Acts as a dependable historical source.[107]

Postmodern historiography and the revival of history as narrative. The conception of historiography that began in the nineteenth century and that we called the professionalization of history has been slowly in decline. This has been significantly influenced by the rise of postmodern currents in the humanities. Peter Burke has provided a set of contrasts that helpfully show the tendencies of postmodern historiography.[108] First, whereas traditionally history was focused on politics, postmodern history is concerned with all the human activities. Second, there is a concern in postmodern historiography with structures instead of purely concentrating on narrative of events. Third, postmodern history is preoccupied not just with the deeds of "great men," but also with the lives of "ordinary people." The phrase "history from below" tries to capture this. Fourth, whereas modern history is based almost exclusively on documents, postmodern history is more open to other sources of evidence such as the visual, oral and statistical. Fifth, postmodern historians widen the array of questions to be asked of the causes of historical events, whereas traditional historians appeared to be too narrow in their examination of causes (i.e., *one* cause for *x* to do this). Last, the traditional paradigm as a whole viewed history as objective.

---

[106]G. Lüdemann, *Early Christianity According to the Traditions in Acts: A Commentary,* trans. John Bowden (Minneapolis: Fortress, 1989), 1-18.

[107]One can also mention *theology* as a catalyst for the minimization of the historical worth of Acts. This has been well examined by Scott Shauf, *Theology as History, History as Theology: Paul in Ephesus in Acts 19,* BZNW 133 (Berlin: Walter de Gruyter, 2005), noting the influence of Hans Conzelmann.

[108]Peter Burke, "Overture: The New History, Its Past and Its Future," in *New Perspectives on Historical Writing,* ed. Peter Burke (University Park: Pennsylvania State University Press, 1992), 2-6. Burke uses the phrase "the New History."

Postmodern historiography, Burke explains, sees this differently:

> However hard we struggle to avoid the prejudices associated with colour,
> creed, class, or gender, we cannot avoid looking at the past from a particular
> point of view. . . . Our minds do not reflect reality directly. We perceive the
> world only through a network of conventions, schemata and stereotypes, a
> network which varies from one culture to another.[109]

In another chapter in the work cited above, Burke adds what is essentially a seventh feature—namely, the return of narrative: "For some years
now there have been signs that historical narrative in a fairly strict sense is
making another comeback."[110]

I could further distill Burke's contrasts into three broad trends that are
seen in postmodern historiography. There is a sense in which all three
could be understood under the heading of "subjectivity" or "situatedness."[111]
First, postmodern historiography calls attention to the frameworks *through
which* we apprehend the past (and the present). These frameworks could
be religion (or lack thereof), customs, ethnicity, gender, language and so
on. When looking at the past, these structures function as spectacles that
inevitably affect what we see. This means, among other things, that there
is no such thing as a value-free history.

Second, postmodern historiography stresses the "pastness of the past."
The past, being what it is, can never be accessed directly. The present in-
stantaneously vanishes into the past, never to be grasped in immediacy.
This means that our interaction with the past is always indirect, even when
dealing with texts or monuments.[112] The gap that opens between the
present of the historian and the past events she is recounting can never be
bridged entirely; a leap needs to be made, which is nothing less than the
imagination (hopefully kept from going off the rails by documents, testimony, etc.). This renders the task of the historians as less than an objective operation.

---

[109]Ibid., 6.

[110]Burke, "History of Events and the Revival of Narrative," in *New Perspectives on Historical Writing,* 234.

[111]For what follows, see also Clark, *History, Theory, Text,* 17-28.

[112]For some helpful and stimulating thoughts in this area, see David Lowenthal, *The Past Is a Foreign Country* (Cambridge: Cambridge University Press, 1985), esp. 185-259.

Third, postmodern historians have pointed out that the events that make up the *bruta facta* of the past do not contain in themselves the type of narrative order and explanations of causality that is essential in a work of history. That is, historical events do not come with tags explaining how they relate to other historical events. No, it is the task of the historian to string these together, thereby creating a plot (this action is called *emplotment*); and this plot is, as it were, in the historian's head, not in the facts themselves. This is, therefore, the "fictive" substructure that is part of any historical work.

Few, if any, professional historians today reject these insights, even if they add nuances in various places. There are, however, some postmodern philosophers and historians who have taken them to an extreme. In the matter of the very helpful category of emplotment, for example, the conclusions of Hayden White are notable. He is convinced that history borrows its plots from essentially fictive literature such as tragedy, comedy and so on. Thus in order to interpret the historical material, historians must impose on it fictive frameworks; and these frameworks determine what and how the historians see. This results in a blurring (if not a complete effacement) of the lines between history and fiction.[113]

A more defensible understanding of the joining of the fictional (plot) and the historical is put forward by Paul Ricoeur. While appreciative of White's insights on emplotment,[114] Ricoeur is concerned that White "runs the risk of wiping out the boundary between fiction and history."[115] The reason is that White overemphasizes the rhetorical framework to such an extent that the trace of the past that acts as a force on the historian is left behind. Things like documents, which allow us to arbitrate on the truthfulness of the historical interpretation put forth by the historian, cannot be easily put aside in a genre that obliges us to look at the past.[116] Ricoeur's

---

[113]See Hayden White, *Metahistory: The Historical Imagination in Nineteenth Century Europe* (Baltimore: Johns Hopkins University Press, 1973); ibid., *The Content of the Form: Narrative Discourse and Historical Representation* (Baltimore: Johns Hopkins University Press, 1987).

[114]See Paul Ricoeur, *Time and Narrative*, trans. Kathleen Blamey and David Pellauer (Chicago: University of Chicago Press, 1988), 3:152-54.

[115]Ibid., 154.

[116]Ibid: "In other words, a sort of tropological arbitrariness must not make us forget the kind of constraint that the past event exercises on historical discourse by way of known documents, by requiring of this discourse an endless rectification."

notion of emplotment preserves the complexity of the relation between history and fiction; it fights, on the one hand, against the naivete of (call it) tranparentism and, on the other, against a thoroughgoing fictiveness of imaginative literature: "These two prejudices both have to be fought against."[117] For Ricoeur, therefore, there is a fictive element to history in the operation of emplotment, whereby the historian takes the disparate events of the past and organizes them into a plot with a view to telling a story that has an ultimate aim. But the use of emplotment need not lead to erasing the frontiers between history and imaginative works such as the novel.[118]

What is the significance of this understanding of history—that is, a history that can (and must) integrate the literary and rhetorical into its fabric while not being denied its place as a genre that is directed to the past in a way that is different from the imaginative genres? Among other things, understanding history in this way creates a space for a book like Acts— which, like other ancient historical works, is suffused with the literary—in the generic category of history. What the professionalization of history took away, with its (as a whole) rejection of the literary and rhetorical, postmodern historiography has given back with its acceptance of the literary as a legitimate part of the historical. Or, perhaps more accurately, some of the insights of postmodern historiography (in its nonextremist articulations) have reminded us that history is not less history if it admits to being a closer relative to literature than has previously been accepted. In fact, some historians today are writing history in unencumbered, attention-grabbing style, not dissimilar in presentation to ancient history. For example, Carlo Ginzburg (who is no postmodern relativist!) has written a history of sixteenth-century Italy that, it seems to me, is very similar to ancient history. To be sure, he has done meticulous research of the inquisitorial papers in the *Archivio della Curia Arcivescovile*, yet he presents

---

[117]Ibid., 155.

[118]Indeed, as Kevin Vanhoozer explains, for Ricoeur the past would be unintelligible if historical works did not find recourse in the region of narrative (i.e., emplotment), for narrative helps makes sense of our "temporal chaos" by creating order: "Narrative is a poetic strategy for transforming natural time (*chronos*) into meaningful or human time" (*Biblical Narrative and the Philosophy of Paul Ricoeur: A Study in Hermeneutics and Theology* [Cambridge: Cambridge University Press, 1990], 91).

his research in a rich literary manner, including dialogues and speeches.[119] Narrative history *is* making a comeback.

To conclude this section it may be helpful to note the work of Francis Watson with respect to biblical history (in his case the Gospels) and the dividends that may be gained when using the literary category of emplotment. Watson follows Ricoeur in his understanding of emplotment: "The synthesis of heterogeneous particulars that creates the plot is an act of the imagination, determined in historiography not only by surviving traces of the past but also by the historian's point of view and delimitation of his or her subject-matter."[120] Watson notes that the Gospels are richly emplotted works, with a beginning, middle and end leading to a firm telos. This has led some to relocate the Gospels to the region of fiction.[121] But this is unnecessary if one understands that history itself is not without need of emplotment: "Yet, if historiographical as well as fictional narrative is emplotted, then the characteristically 'literary' focus on the emplotment of the gospels need not proceed by assimilating these texts to fictional texts."[122] Watson thus suggests that we understand the Gospels as "narrated history."[123] In this way Watson is able (to my mind satisfactorily) to go beyond the traps of "modernist" historiography's positivism and postmodernity's fictionalizing of history. I suggest that his conclusions can easily work beyond the Gospels to Acts.

CONCLUSION

In this chapter we have attempted to put forth and sustain the thesis that the Acts of the Apostles is intended to be read as *theological history*. We paid particular attention to the preface of Luke, the reader's entry point into the narrative, which as such conditions the expectations of the reader on what is to come. On the one hand, doubtless Luke's terminology is

---

[119]Carlo Ginzburg, *The Cheese and the Worms: The Cosmos of a Sixteenth-Century Miller,* trans. John and Anne Tedeschi (Baltimore: Johns Hopkins University Press, 1980).

[120]Francis Watson, *Text and Truth: Redefining Biblical Theology* (Grand Rapids: Eerdmans, 1997), 56.

[121]Or to the patronizing *Kleinliteratur* (e.g., Bultmann, Dibelius), because they did not match the standard of so-called professional history of the period.

[122]Watson, *Text and Truth,* 56.

[123]A phrase that, in view of what Watson has just said, would be tautological; but he is working in the context of history understood as purely scientific.

pointing the reader to the historical convention of *autopsia*, even if this is expressed in understated fashion.[124] On the other hand, a number of terms in the preface did not fit easily within the received templates of Greco-Roman history. They were theological: "fulfilled," "ministers of the word." The narratives that followed in both volumes showed God's intervention in the world through his servant Jesus Christ and his apostles. This is theological history.

In the second place we showed that in order to communicate this theological history Luke availed himself of several literary practices: in addition to the basic operation of emplotment that is part of every history, he used telescoping, epitomizing, syncrisis and so on. These are rhetorical procedures that are used to persuade the reader. But this raised a question: Should not Acts, by being so literary in its constitution, be doubted as a serious piece of history? This led to the final section.

The professionalization of history that arose in the nineteenth century was, as a whole, suspicious of the literary and rhetorical in works of history. These "subjective" aspects did not fit well with the conception of history as a science. Postmodern historiography, however, has recovered the narrative and thus literary substructure of history. Historians today, therefore, are more willing to accept "narrated history" as legitimate. This has helped, in some ways, to "rehabilitate" the book of Acts as a rightful example of history.

This chapter has been something of an attempt to clear the ground for the following. To be sure, I believe that I have proffered strong arguments to confirm that Acts should be viewed as a legitimate piece of historical work. What we have not yet done is provide specific examples to suggest that Acts is a *responsible and truthful* historical account. One of the reasons

---

[124]But it may be this understated style, which stands in stark contrast to some of the flourishes of other historians (e.g., Josephus), that gives credibility to his statement. Byrskog's suggestion hits home: "If they [early Christian writers] solely were to defend the veracity of their records with rhetorical and narrative means, without at the same time attempting to be true to their actual proceedings, *a much more forceful and direct way* of anchoring the writings in the oral history of the eyewitnesses would indeed have been in line with contemporary practice" (*Story as History,* 249; emphasis added). To put it bluntly, had Luke shouted loudly the way other historians did in the matter of *autopsia*, we may have more reasons to suspect his testimony.

for this gap is that others have already done excellent work in this area.[125] Nevertheless, I think that a contribution could be made here, and that on the subject of the speeches in Acts. Thus the following chapter, although not exclusively dealing with the matter of the truthfulness of the speeches, nevertheless will be concerned with this important aspect.

[125]For example, Colin Hemer, *The Book of Acts in the Setting of Hellenistic History*, WUNT 1.49 (Tübingen: Mohr Siebeck, 1989), a meticulous piece of work that unfortunately is overlooked (by some) in discussions of Acts's accuracy. See also now Keener, *Acts*.

four

THE SPEECHES IN ACTS (PART ONE)

The Speeches in Their Ancient Context

THE PREVIOUS CHAPTER WAS concerned with Luke as a theological historian who cast his work in narrative form. We suggested that both the manner of writing history in the ancient world and the insights from postmodern historiography help us view Acts as a historical work. The canons of modernist historiography, which for some students of Acts caused embarrassment before the historical tribunal of the university, have been eclipsed. Investigating Acts from the perspective of ancient historiography (a perspective whose validity has been strengthened by postmodern historiography) has encouraged us in proceeding with integrity as we examine Acts as history.

But saying that Acts can be legitimately viewed as belonging to the genre of history is not the same thing as saying that it actually *is* historical: the firm decision by an author to write in a particular genre does not guarantee success. And so we must examine the author's *performance*, as far as that can be checked. Some authors have done good work in this area, primarily by means of comparison with literary and epigraphic sources outside Acts.[1] What I intend to do in this chapter is to explore the performance of Luke as historian by concentrating on the speeches. This

---

[1] The best examples are Colin Hemer, *The Book of Acts in the Setting of Hellenistic History*, WUNT 1.49 (Tübingen: Mohr Siebeck, 1989), and Craig Keener, *Acts: An Exegetical Commentary* (Grand Rapids: Baker, 2012–2014), 1:90–220.

differs slightly from the authors pointed out above in two ways. First, the comparison will not be global but rather specific to Luke's performance as a speech reporter. Second, the approach can be seen as an exercise in moderate reader-response criticism. That is, I want to ask the question: How would more or less acculturated people of the first century have viewed the speeches in Acts? Would they have been inclined to accept them as faithful reports or otherwise?

It is difficult to obtain sure answers to these questions for obvious reasons: we do not live in the first century; and who exactly are these "more or less acculturated people"? How can we know how these people thought, given that the majority of the literature was written by the elite? Yet, I think some progress can be made because we do possess a lot of material on speeches to compare, both actual written speeches and precepts by rhetoricians on the composition of speeches. Thus the approach overlaps with those who compare Acts to outside sources, but it differs in that the comparison is not to the *realia* of the ancient world. The comparison has more to do with the literary texture and style of the speeches of Acts vis-à-vis those of Greco-Roman historians.

The chapter that follows this one will attempt to answer the question: What is Luke doing with the speeches? More specifically, What theological themes is he advancing through the speeches? To that end we will look at the main speeches of Acts in order to sketch theological themes that emerge from them. In this respect it will be important to link the speeches examined to their respective narrative contexts. There is a hermeneutical back-and-forth here: the narratives help us make sense of what Luke is doing with a particular speech; but the speech throws light on what Luke is doing with narratives, which in turn helps us make sense of the speeches, and so on.

THE REPORTING OF SPEECHES IN ANCIENT HISTORY

It would be a hermeneutical mistake of the gravest type to force Luke's manner of speech reporting into our contemporary mold. It would be similar to judging, for example, the aesthetics of biblical Hebrew poetry as deficient because it had different standards from modern English poetry. In both cases the mistake is in thinking that *our* standards should be timeless and universal: as if God, in inspiring the Bible, was leapfrogging the original audience because the only audience that matters is the contemporary one, you and I! This is not the way the Bible is written. God addresses the original audience in its language, worldview and so on. It is our duty as biblical interpreters to understand the ancient context in order to actualize the meaning of the Bible for the present responsibly.[2] If what emerges is uncomfortable for us, so be it. The desire to force God to inspire the Bible in a way that our assumptions about the world are confirmed can be idolatrous.

Thus when asking about Luke's habits of presenting speeches we must ask what ancient historians, Greco-Romans in particular, thought of this.[3] There is good and bad news here. The good is that we have a number of ancient authors who have left us descriptions and prescriptions on the topic of speech reporting. The bad is that the statements of these historians have proved particularly difficult to interpret. Let us then look at these statements and attempt to understand what might have been both Luke's standards and the expectations of his audience.

Thucydides (fifth century BCE). The first statement of method on speech reporting that we possess from a Greek historian is that of the great Athenian Thucydides, renowned for his *Peloponnesian War*. Prior to the narration proper of the initial causes of the war (1.24), Thucydides provides us with a programmatic declaration of how he went about composing his history. The statement on the composition of speeches is so important in itself and for the posterity of Greco-Roman history that it needs to be quoted in full:

> As to the speeches that were made by different men, either when they were about to begin the war or when they were already engaged therein, it has been difficult to recall with strict accuracy the words actually spoken, both for me as regards that which I myself heard, and for those who from various other sources have brought me reports. Therefore, the speeches are given

---

[2]This is basic hermeneutical stuff. For further development see Grant Osborne, *The Hermeneutical Spiral: A Comprehensive Introduction to Biblical Interpretation* (Downers Grove, IL: InterVarsity Press, 1993).

[3]This does not exclude the practice of Hellenistic-Jewish historians. As I indicated in chapter two, Jewish historians writing in the historical-monograph genre (e.g., 2 Macc) already had incorporated some of the canons of Greek historiography into their work.

in the language in which, as it seemed to me, the several speakers would express, on the subjects under consideration, the sentiments most befitting the occasion, though at the same time I have adhered as closely as possible to the general sense of what was actually said.[4]

The complexity of this statement, both in syntax and concept, has generated more literature than we can discuss here. Roughly speaking, two interpretations have been offered.

On the one hand, there are those who think that Thucydides has gone beyond conceptual tension and actually contradicted himself. According to this view, it is impossible to reconcile the concepts of "the sentiments most befitting the occasion" and "I have adhered . . . to the general sense of what was actually said." The historian cannot have it both ways. The usual conclusion is that Thucydides was not very concerned with reproducing actual speeches; he was instead keen on using the speeches for dramatic purposes, primarily to advance his own opinions.[5]

On the other hand, there are those scholars who perceive in the statement a true tension. It is argued that Thucydides is being more or less transparent with his readers about the problems he faced in composing the history of the war. He is committed to historical accuracy in a way that others before him were not (1.21; 1.22.3-4). Can that accuracy even extend to the different speeches given during the war (1.22)? Thucydides puts the difficulties of accomplishing this before his readers' eyes. Yes, he admits, it *has* been difficult to remember with accuracy those speeches that he himself heard or that informants brought to him. In fact, it is quite impossible to provide a verbatim account of what was said. So what to do, given his commitment to accuracy rather than "a prize-essay [ἀγώνισμα] to be heard for the moment" (1.22.4)?

A number of scholars at this point suggest that we have to grant Thucydides a certain amount of subjectivity in his procedure of reporting

---

[4]Thucydides 1.22.1. The translation is that of C. F. Smith in the LCL.

[5]See especially Simon Hornblower, *A Commentary on Thucydides* (Oxford: Clarendon Press, 1991), 1:59. There has been a tendency in German-speaking work on Thucydides to view the historian as not concerned with accuracy (e.g., E. Meyer, A. Grosskinsky). I owe this observation to A. W. Gomme, *A Historical Commentary on Thucydides* (Oxford: Clarendon Press, 1959), 1:143-47. Could this be one of the reasons why Acts scholarship in Germany (e.g., Dibelius, Conzelmann, Wilckens), to the extent that it views Luke as operating within the realm of Greek historiography, has been skeptical of the historical accuracy of the speeches?

speeches—*but that this subjectivity does not render his reports false.* Thus as far as the *content* of the speeches is concerned, he does his best to provide a summary (probably integrating some *ipsissima verba* here and there whenever possible) of what was said; as to the *form* of the speeches, Thucydides allows his historical knowledge and imagination to help. Thomas F. Garrity paraphrases the end of the Thucydidean passage in this way: "And as for the form . . . of the speeches, in whatever way I thought the individuals would have said what was required, more or less, on a given occasion, that is the form (or 'manner') in which the speeches have been presented (by me)."[6] Thus Thucydides is committed to provide a faithful gist of what the speakers said, even if he adorns this in form by allowing the speakers to sound as they should, given their background and situation. And *yet*, lest anyone thinks that this last element would give the historian excessive freedom, he ends with a rejoinder: "Though at the same time I have adhered as closely as possible to the general sense of what was actually said."[7]

In my opinion, this second view does better justice to the statement of Thucydides. Whether one believes that the historian actually behaved this way or not is something else. He may have been attempting to deceive his audience precisely by acting as if he were really concerned to present the truth of the speeches in order to gain their confidence. Although possible, this seems perverse; and in fact most scholars of Thucydides believe him to have been, on the whole, a conscientious historian.

Thucydides became a massively popular historian in the centuries to come. Even in the second century CE there were those who attempted to imitate him. The view about the composition of speeches that we find in his programmatic statement influenced future historians—whether or not these historians actually lived up to his relative high standards.

Polybius of Megalopolis (second century BCE). Polybius is one of the few surviving historians who is keen to express his philosophy of history

---

[6]Thomas F. Garrity, "Thucydides 1.22.1: Content and Form in the Speeches," *AJP* 119 (1998): 361-84, at 373.

[7]Those who provide good arguments for the position presented above include Garrity, "Thucydides 1.22.1"; Gomme, *A Historical Commentary on Thucydides*, 142-48; D. Kagan, "The Speeches in Thucydides and the Mytilene Debate," *Yale Classical Studies* 24 (1975): 71-94. See also the important study of Stanley Porter, "Thucydides 1.22.1 and Speeches in Acts: Is There a Thucydidean View?" *NovT* 32 (1990): 121-42.

throughout his work. As Brian McGing has argued, Polybius knew and even imitated two of the classics of Greek historiography—namely, Herodotus and Thucydides.[8] He mentions the former historian (8.11.3); there are sections of Polybius where it is highly probable that the historian is following Thucydides.[9] One important example of this is found in Polybius 3.31.12-13, where he states that a history with only narrative and no analysis leaves you "with a prize essay [ἀγώνισμα], but not a lesson, and while pleasing for the moment, [it is] of no possible benefit for the future." The similarities to Thucydides 1.22.4 are striking, including the use of the term ἀγώνισμα, which we saw above was used by the historian in his famous passage. It would appear from this that Polybius is portraying himself as writing history in the tradition of Thucydides. Whether he is imitating Thucydides directly or simply following a tradition with a current flowing from Thucydides is immaterial.

If Polybius is then in some sense writing in the "tradition" of Thucydides, it is not surprising that he shows a conscientious approach to the reporting of speeches. His statements on the reporting of speeches are concentrated in the fragmentary book 12, and are stated in the form of polemics against another historian, Timaeus. In a word, Polybius accuses Timaeus of fabricating speeches. In the process of his accusations, we learn of Polybius's views of speech reporting. Consider the following:

> But to convince those also who are disposed to champion him [Timaeus] I must speak of his principle, above all in composing public speeches, harangues to soldiers, the discourses of ambassadors, and, in a word, all utterances of the kind, which, as it were, sum up events and hold the whole history together. Can anyone who reads these help noticing that Timaeus has untruthfully reported them in his work, and has done so for set purpose? *For he has not set down the words spoken nor the sense of what was really said*, but having made up his mind as to what ought to have been said, he recounts all these speeches and all else that follows upon events like a man in a school of rhetoric attempting to speak on a given

---

[8]Brian McGing, *Polybius' Histories* (Oxford: Oxford University Press, 2010), 52-61.
[9]On this see ibid., 58-61. Emilio Gabba, *Dionysius and The History of Archaic Rome* (Berkeley: University of California Press, 1991), 61, is more certain: "Thucydides and his imitator Polybius. . . ."

subject, and shows off his oratorical power, but gives no report of what was actually spoken.[10]

The peculiar function of history is to discover, in the first place, the words actually spoken, whatever they were, and next to ascertain the reason why what was done or spoken led to failure or success. (12.25b1)

But a writer who passes over in silence the speeches made … and in their place introduces false rhetorical exercises and discursive speeches, destroys the peculiar virtue of history. (12.25b.4)

According to Polybius, the duty of the historian—and something that Timaeus does *not* do—is to preserve either a transcript of a speech or a summary.[11] This is crucial, for in the opinion of Polybius the main goal of history is usefulness (ὠφέλια); and this usefulness is dependent on the truthfulness of the accounts—particularly speeches—which the historian provides.[12] Thus a historian should stay away from using speeches to show rhetorical prowess; and certainly a speech that never occurred should not be fabricated.

In assessing Polybius's standard for speech reporting, we must keep the following in mind. First, we should remember that his statements are made in the context of polemics. Polybius is quite vicious in his criticism of Timaeus. It may thus be that he is exaggerating the faults of Timaeus and thereby claiming for himself standards that no historian could or did meet. In this way he could crush the competition.[13] Second, and emerging from the first point, is the question of whether Polybius meets his own standards. McGing concludes by suggesting that at least prebattle speeches, not only in Polybius but in most ancient historians, are "close to a complete fiction."[14] Aside from these very dramatic types of situations, McGing has a more positive conclusion: "There seems to be a reasonably good chance that Polybius did, on the whole, abide by his own standards."[15]

---

[10]Polybius 12.25a3-5, LCL translation.

[11]F. W. Walbank, *A Historical Commentary on Polybius*, vol. 2, *Commentary on Books VII-XVIII* (Oxford: Oxford University Press, 1967), 386, helpfully paraphrases that Timaeus produces "neither a transcript nor an accurate résumé of the actual speech."

[12]See F. W. Walbank, *Polybius, Rome and the Hellenistic World: Essays and Reflections* (Cambridge: Cambridge University Press, 2002), 10-11, 231-41.

[13]See McGing, *Polybius' Histories*, 88-90.

[14]Ibid., 88.

[15]Ibid., 90.

Dionysius of Halicarnassus (first century BCE). Writing from Rome
at the turn of the century, Dionysius is essential to grasping how at least
one cultivated man of the period understood the methods of historiography. We can see his own method in practice in his multivolume *Roman
Antiquities*; but for our purposes his critical essays are of more value. One
of the most famous of his essays is *Thucydides*.[16] Here he dedicates chapters
34-49 to an examination of the speeches of Thucydides. His comments can
serve as something of a "reception history," thereby shedding some light
on how a certain strand of historiography viewed matters with respect to
speeches.[17]

The operative term in Dionysius with respect to speeches in a historical work is *fit*. He uses various words to refer to this concept: πρέπω,
ἐπιτήδιος and especially προσήκω. As he examines the speeches of
Thucydides, he asks: Are they a good fit? Consider the following
statement to help in clarification:

> Those who have admired Thucydides immoderately, crediting him with
> nothing less than divine inspiration, seem to have been affected in this way
> by the sheer multitude of his ideas. If you take a speech and relate it to the
> particular circumstances in which it was made, and point out that one ar-
> gument was inappropriate for use *by these persons on this occasion*, and an-
> other was unsuited for use in *those circumstances and at such a length*, his
> admirers take offence. (*Thucydides* 34)

Dionysius, to be sure, does esteem the ideas and arguments in Thucydides's
speeches; but he also finds a disconnect between the speeches and the
circumstance, length and person making the speech. Yet, this is not always
the case, Dionysius adds. In the attack on Plataea in book two of Thucydides,
we find the following good qualities: "Thucydides assigns to both sides
[Lacedaemonian king and Plataean envoys] speeches such as each might

---

[16]I use the LCL version translated by Stephen Usher.

[17]Important in this respect is Gabba, *Dionysius*, 60-92. He argues that there were at least two strands of
historiography that had reached to the Roman period—namely, the Herodotean and the Thucydidean.
The former was broader in focus (memorable events, geography, ethnography), while the latter was decidedly political in focus, Polybius being the best example during the time of the Republic. According to
Gabba, whatever strand Dionysius belonged to, he certainly was not of the Thucydidean-Polybian one
(65). This accounts for some of the criticism leveled at Thucydides on the part of Dionysius.

naturally have made. *They are suited to the characters of the speakers and relevant to the situation*, and neither inadequate nor overdone" (*Thucydides* 36). Again, the main question asked is that of appropriateness or fit: Does the speech reported fit with what we know of the person and the circumstances in which it was (purportedly) given? In fact, chapters 34–40 of *Thucydides* (a long section!) are all concerned with this question of fit. It thus appears that for Dionysius, unlike Polybius, whether the speech reported in the work actually was spoken or not is of no consequence.

But then in chapter 41 Dionysius appears to address the question of factuality. With respect to the dialogue between the Athenians and Melians in book five of Thucydides, he states the following: "From what the historian writes about himself in the previous book, it is easy to deduce that he neither was present at this meeting nor took part personally in the discussion, nor received a report of it from any of the Athenian or Melian spokesmen" (*Thucydides* 41). Clearly, Dionysius is referring to Thucydides 1.22 where, as we have seen, the historian speaks of the difficulty of remembering the speeches in which he was either present or of which he received a report from those who were present. Dionysius is suggesting that Thucydides did not fulfill either of these requirements in the Melian dialogue, but still went ahead and composed a speech—that is, *invented* a speech. But then Dionysius seems to backtrack a bit, for he asks: "It now remains to consider whether he has composed the dialogue in such a way that it is consistent with the facts [εἰ τοῖς . . . πράγμασι προσήκοντα . . . διάλογον] and fits the character of the delegates to the meeting." He then quotes the second part of Thucydides's methodological statement of 1.22— that is, "adhering as closely as possible to the general sense of what was actually said." The reader now expects that Dionysius will provide his final verdict: yes, the speech is true; or no, it has no basis on the facts.

But the reader (at least this one!) is disappointed. For Dionysius immediately falls back on the issue of "fit." The category of true versus false is suspended, and Dionysius simply states that the Melian dialogue is "inferior by comparison with the earlier one"; or one may also translate: "I do not praise this dialogue" (οὐκ ἐπαινῶ τὸν διάλογον τοῦτον). He then works through a number of speeches in Thucydides and submits them not to the criterion of truth, but to that of fit. It is as if the preoccupation with the veracity of a speech is of little or no importance to Dionysius. He simply has moved on from Thucydides's standards. Another possibility is that Dionysius has interpreted the Thucydidean methodological statement *solely* through the category of fit. In the words of Earle Hilgert: "It appears that for Dionysius, Thucydides' principle of 'adhering as closely as possible to what was actually said' means, first and foremost, that the speech be 'appropriate to the circumstances and befitting the persons' involved."[18] If that is the case, then Dionysius (in his opinion) is not at all going against the grain of the passage from Thucydides. This raises the question: Was this the way that Thucydides was being understood around this period (i.e., *fit*, not "true versus false")? Hilgert, following Plümacher, believes so.[19] Let us now look at one more author.

Lucian of Samosota (second century CE). He was an essayist and satirist of great erudition. As far as we know he never himself composed a history. Nevertheless, he wrote a fascinating essay, *How to Write History*, which in its prescriptions and proscriptions allows us to form some ideas about how both the educated and uneducated were writing history around this period.[20]

Lucian feels obligated to write an essay on the subject because at the moment "every single person is writing history" (*History* 2).[21] In fact, there is an attempt at imitating the classics: "Nay more, they are all Thucydideses, Herodotuses and Xenophons" (ibid.). The majority of Lucian's precepts have to do with the narrative sections of histories—that is, the description of actions. Here Lucian complains that a commitment to reporting what actually happened (τοῦ ἱστορεῖν τὰ γεγενημένα) is missing (7). This is unacceptable, since, unlike poetry, history *cannot* allow "embellishments" (κομμώματα) like myths, eulogies and exaggerations (8). Since

---

[18]Earle Hilgert, "Speeches in Acts and Hellenistic Canons of Historiography and Rhetoric," in *Good News in History: Essays in Honor of Bo Reicke*, ed. L. Miller (Atlanta: Scholars Press, 1993), 83-109, at 85.

[19]Ibid., 87-88.

[20]I follow André Hurst, *Lucien de Samosate: Comment Écrire l'Histoire. Introduction, traduction et notes* (Paris: Belles Lettres, 2010), xv, in accepting 166 CE as a more or less terminus post quem for the redaction of this work.

[21]The moment was the Parthian War of 162–165 CE. Edition used is the LCL translated by Kilburn.

the goal of history is "usefulness" (τὸ χρήσιμον), and usefulness can only come from the truth (9, cf. Polybius), the historian must aim at truth above all else: only to Truth must the historian sacrifice (40). In fact, history cannot admit even a small lie (7). It must be repeated that all these comments are made in the context of description of *actions* in history. The standards are very high.

What about the speeches? Lucian makes the following short comment: "If a person has to be introduced to make a speech, above all let his language suit his person and his subject [ἐοικότα τῷ προσώπῳ καὶ τῷ πράγματι οἰκεῖα λεγέσθω], and next let these also be as clear as possible. It is then, however, that you can play the orator and show your eloquence" (58). The concepts as well as the terminology used by Lucian will remind the reader of Dionysius's comments.[22] The main concern of the historian in reporting a speech is once again "fit." The speech must fit the character of the person delivering it as well as the circumstances in which it was given. This is the requirement, the essential criterion. Once the historian has taken care of this, then he can "play the orator" and "show your eloquence." The phrase "play the orator" translates the infinitive ῥητορεῦσαι. The term is used several times in the Lucianic corpus.[23] The verb can be used with either a negative or positive connotation, depending on who is the orator. When someone like Odysseus (famed for his eloquence and persuasiveness) is giving a speech to Achilles asking him to rejoin the forces of the Achaeans, the connotation is positive. But when someone is trying to be an orator who does not have the qualifications, then the use of the term can be sarcastic or pejorative. Given the context of section 58, the term should not be viewed as ironic or negative. Rather, Lucian is saying that once the historian has fulfilled the "fit" requirement, he should adorn the speech with all the qualities of oratory.

The second phrase, "show your eloquence," translates ἐπιδεῖξαι τὴν τῶν λόγων δεινότητα. A *TLG* search of the phrase (minus τῶν λόγων) for the period around Lucian shows that the phrase was used beyond the realm of oratory or history. Thus it could be used of the demonstration of military

---

[22]Thus also Gert Avenarius, *Lukians Schrift zur Geschichtsschreibung* (Meisenheim/Glan: Hain, 1956), 150-51.
[23]See, e.g., *How to Write History* 26; *Zeus Rants* 14, 29, 32; *The Dead Come to Life* 29; *A Slip of the Tongue* 2.

ability, or artistic skill.[24] Two examples in the realm of rhetoric come very close to Lucian. In Plutarch's *Pompey* (77.4.2), he speaks of Theodotus, who was able to persuade others because of "a display of his powerful speech and rhetorical art" (Θεόδοτος δὲ δεινότητα λόγου καὶ ῥητορείαν ἐπιδεικνύμενος). The phrase is strikingly similar to Lucian, suggesting that perhaps it was a stock phrase for the demonstration of ability in a person's area of professional expertise.

Even closer to Lucian is Josephus in *Jewish Antiquities* 1.2. In the proem, as was often the case in introductions to historical works, the author is seeking to establish his own authority vis-à-vis other writers. Josephus thus seizes on the matter of motivation, claiming that he is constrained to write the *Antiquities* in order to provide for the readers the truth of the events. He contrasts himself with those who write history because they are "eager to display their literary skill and to win the fame therefrom expected."[25] The phrase "eager to display their literary skill" translates ἐπιδεικνύμενοι λόγων δεινότητα. The similarity to Lucian, down to the sandwiching of λόγων, is remarkable. This supports the idea that it was a stock phrase.

Josephus, then, uses the phrase in a negative fashion—but that would be too simple. It would be better to say that Josephus has a problem, not with displaying one's skill in itself, but with those who write history *primarily* to show their rhetorical skill and not for the sake of truth. In other words, one should not write history *with the primary goal* of exhibiting "cleverness in discourse."[26] Although both narrative and speeches are in view here, the emphasis, with the use of λόγων, falls on speeches. Josephus certainly appears to take full advantage of those occasions in the *Antiquities* where he can show his "cleverness in discourse." In any case, Josephus is criticizing those who write history for the primary purpose of introducing

---

[24]On the former, e.g., Plutarch, *Pyrrhus* 8.2.6; *Timoleon* 21.5.2; *Lucullus* 36.7.2; on the latter, e.g., Dio Chrysostom, *Orations* 12.45.5.

[25]Translation is that of Thackeray in the LCL.

[26]This is how Louis H. Feldman, *Judean Antiquities 1-4*, in *Flavius Josephus: Translation and Commentary*, ed. S. Mason (Leiden: Brill, 2000), 3:3, translates the phrase. And I think it is an improvement on Thackeray (which is hard to achieve!) because with the term *discourse* we can see the overlap between history and rhetoric that was prevalent during the time of Josephus. On this important matter, specifically with respect to Josephus, see the careful work of Pere Villalba, *The Historical Method of Flavius Josephus*, ALGHJ 19 (Leiden: Brill, 1986).

speeches where they can show off their rhetorical skill. Lucian would probably agree with Josephus. However, the former is more open in encouraging historians—once the criteria of personality and circumstance have been met—to use speeches in order to please and persuade the readers. Perhaps the French translation of Lucian by Hurst catches the spirit of the statement the best: "However, this is a time in which we will tolerate a demonstration of eloquence and you will then have the opportunity to show your competence in the area of speeches."[27]

Conclusions. By the time that Luke wrote the Acts of the Apostles, it appears that criteria for speech reporting in history had undergone a shift from Thucydides. If our interpretation of the Athenian historian is correct, it was his method to provide speeches that fit the occasion while at the same time staying as close as possible to what the speakers actually said. Thucydides did not intend to provide a transcript, and we must remember that quotation marks did not exist in the ancient world. He would thus summarize the speeches, undoubtedly using historical imagination. However, he saw it as his duty to remain faithful to the speech event—not deviating from the sentiments of what was actually said.

Polybius had (or at least professed to have had) standards like those of Thucydides. For him it was unthinkable to invent a speech. To be sure, he had to summarize speeches in his own language.[28] Nevertheless, he felt obligated to report truthfully on what was said. According to Polybius, this was not the case with Timaeus, who actually fabricated speeches. Even if Polybius is exaggerating in his polemics against Timaeus, we can perceive from the former that for other historians there seemed to be little obligation in providing faithful summaries of what was spoken.

When we reach the first century CE we find in Dionysius of Halicarnassus more relaxed criteria on speech reporting in histories: the criterion of truth is secondary (if it has any place at all) to that of fit. The criteria for judging a speech were those of fit with the personality of the speaker and the circumstance of the speech. Maybe the criteria were relaxed even from

---

[27]"Toutefois, c'est un moment dans lequel on tolérera une démonstration d'éloquence et tu pourras alors exhiber tes compétences en matière de discours" (Hurst, *Lucien de Samosate*, 39).
[28]For which he apologized in 29.12.

the time of Thucydides; or perhaps they were relaxed as time went on;[29] or perhaps the concept of "relaxing criteria" is the wrong one, because it implies that future historians understood Thucydides in the stricter sense of reporting (in summary) what the speakers said. It could be that from the beginning Thucydides was understood as referring primarily to "fit." Another option, which does not necessarily exclude the view of "decline after Thucydides," is that which takes into account the influence of rhetoric in the writing of history. With rhetoric being the centerpiece of the tertiary level of Hellenistic education, it is probable that for many historians the most important thing became rhetorical display rather than adherence to the truth of a speech.

Lucian, in his treatise *How to Write History*, appears to have separate criteria for the historical narrative on the one hand and the speeches in the historical narrative on the other. While the truth of what happened was a sine qua non in the former, in the latter what mattered was once again fit—with the personality of the orator and the circumstance. Faithfulness to what was said is not mentioned; what is emphasized is appropriateness.[30] Once this criterion was met, the historian was encouraged to show his ability and competence in the speeches.

We seem to have before us a spectrum by the period when Luke wrote. On one end there are those historians who simply did not care whether the speech they introduced into their works was actually spoken or not. Introducing speeches was a rhetorical exercise meant to show how clever they were in oratory. The statements of Polybius and Diodorus Siculus show this.[31] On the other end of the spectrum, there are authors like Polybius and, on the Roman side, Tacitus, who not only were concerned with fit but also with

---

[29]Important in this respect is Charles Fornara, *The Nature of History in Ancient Greece and Rome* (Berkeley: University of California Press, 1983), 145-46, who argues that beginning with Callisthenes (fourth century BCE) the emphasis was laid on "fit," not reporting the summary of what was actually said. Cf. also Helen Homeyer, *Lukian, Wie man Geschichte schreiben soll. Herausgegeben, übersetzt und erläutert* (München: W. Fink, 1965), 276.

[30]Thus Avenarius, *Lukians Schrift*, 150, can say that the speeches "have little or nothing at all to do with the speeches actually given" ("Mit den wirklich gehaltenen Reden hatten sie [recorded speeches] wenig oder gar nichts zu tun"). The historian's duty was to make sure that the personality and circumstances were a fit with the speaker, something that was learned and practiced in the rhetorical school, as can be seen from Theon and Quintilian (ibid.).

[31]Diodorus Siculus, *Library of History* 20.1-2.2. He lived in the first century BCE.

giving a fair representation of what was actually said. Tacitus we can check by comparing the speech of Claudius as reported by him and the actual words of the speech preserved in the Lyons Tablet. Although Tacitus recasts Claudius's words into his own language, he most certainly provides a faithful summary of what the emperor actually said.[32] It is probably the case that authors like Polybius and Tacitus were in the minority. In the middle of the spectrum are those historians (as represented by Dionysius and Lucian) for whom the presentation of a speech was an opportunity to delight and persuade the audience. It was an opportunity to dramatize and thus bring emotion into the history, and so on. The most important criterion was fit, appropriateness. *However, all this presupposed that a speech had actually been given by person* x *in circumstance* y. You could (and should) adorn the speech; you could use it to forward your argument. *But you could not fabricate a speech event.* The following example could help in clarifying this position.

Suppose you were writing a history of the American Civil War and you wanted to include Abraham Lincoln's Gettysburg Address. Suppose that although you know that there certainly was such a speech, nevertheless you have no written sources for the speech; and certainly there are no eyewitnesses still living! But from other historical studies, you know quite a bit about Abraham Lincoln (his political thought, religious ideas, personality, etc.) and the circumstance of the Gettysburg Address. According to the stream represented by Dionysius and Lucian—the middle in my spectrum, and probably the majority of ancient historians—you were at liberty to put a speech on the lips of Abraham Lincoln. If your constructed speech fit well with Abraham Lincoln and the occasion of the speech, then as a historian you wrote "truthfully."

Biblical scholars have often misrepresented the data of ancient historians on the matter of speech reporting. Many have been too quick to say that for ancient historians, including the author of the Acts of the Apostles, speeches were *never* meant to preserve what the speakers actually said.[33]

---

[32]Tacitus, *Annales* 15.63 is also illuminating. Debating whether to introduce a speech of Seneca in his history, he opts for omission: "Since it has been given to the public in his own words I decline to recast it here." I owe both of these citations to Fornara, *Nature of History*, 153.

[33]E.g., Haenchen, Wilckens and Penner. Dibelius is more nuanced.

In my opinion this is not a scholarly conclusion. Others equally flatten the data by saying that the Thucydidean view (if there ever was such a view!) or the Polybian view was dominant in the first century.[34] This is also misleading. The situation, as is always the case in life, was more complex— probably even more complex than the spectrum I have suggested above. It is even possible, if not probable, that the methods of a historian in speech reporting varied within the same work. Thus if the historian is giving a speech of a character from the far past, it may be that all he could do was attempt a fit between speech and the character of the speaker and situation. But if the historian was including the speech of a contemporary character, he may well have been an eyewitness himself, known other eyewitnesses or have a record of the speech. In this case, the historian (unless he was a charlatan) would probably provide a summary of what the speaker actually said. The advantage of contemporaneity for accurate recording is in part what led Thucydides to write on the Peloponnesian War, as opposed to the ancient past (like Herodotus), where checking for accuracy was far more challenging.

With these complexities in mind, it is now time to attempt some testing of Luke's practice of speech reporting. Where may he fit in the spectrum presented above?

LUKE AS A CONSERVATIVE REPORTER OF SPEECHES

I want to argue in this section that in the Acts of the Apostles Luke should be viewed as a responsible reporter of speeches. To be sure, the speeches are given in his own words; he may add to clarify them; he is responsible for where they are placed in the narrative, and so on. He certainly does not provide a transcript.[35] Yet, I will argue that he is faithful in providing his audience a summary of what was actually said. In terms of the spectrum suggested above, I do not believe that Luke fabricated speeches in order to show his rhetorical ability. As I will demonstrate below, there are a number of reasons why this does not appear to be the case. Could he be representative

---

[34]See, e.g., Gasque, Polhill.

[35]Hemer, *Book of Acts*, 418: "The crucial question of historicity here concerns only the essential content of the speeches. We need not be concerned with any supposition that they are verbatim reports."

of the "middle" of the spectrum, certainly not fabricating a speech but primarily concerned with fit in the manner of Dionysius and Lucian? This is possible.[36] But if Luke is writing of contemporary events of which he was an eyewitness and for which there were other witnesses whom he could interview,[37] there is no reason why he would limit himself only to the criterion of fit. This is crucial, for one of the reasons why the criterion of fit was necessary was the lack of sources (oral and written) of the far past or of a far land.

Other authors have done competent work in showing the reliability of Luke as a reporter of speeches. Using the criterion of fit, Conrad Gempf has (convincingly to my mind) shown how there is a very good fit between the missionary speeches of Paul on the one hand, and his person and circumstances on the other.[38] Using the more rigorous criterion of "what was actually said," Steve Walton, in meticulously researched work, has shown that the speech of Paul at Miletus (Acts 20:18-35) is remarkably similar (even to the point of vocabulary) in the topic of leadership to 1 Thessalonians.[39] Others have noted that where Luke's practice of speech reporting can be checked—namely, in his treatment of Mark in his Gospel—Luke emerges as a conservative redactor of speeches. While he may improve Mark's syntax, for example, he nevertheless provides a truthful summary of the speech.[40]

My contribution in this area will be rather in a *via negativa*. That is, I want to show how Luke is *different* from what historians were taught to do—and actually did—in their presentation of speeches. I want to focus on two areas: brevity and pairing of speeches. The two overlap somewhat, but it is better to view them individually.

---

[36]See, for example, the careful work of Conrad Gempf, who argues that our main concern as interpreters of Acts should be with fit: "Public Speaking and Published Accounts," in *The Book of Acts in Its Ancient Literary Setting*, ed. Bruce Winter and Andrew Clarke (Grand Rapids: Eerdmans, 1993), 259-303; idem, "Historical and Literary Appropriateness in the Mission Speeches of Paul in Acts" (PhD diss., University of Aberdeen, 1988).

[37]See chapters two and three.

[38]Gempf, "Historical and Literary Appropriateness."

[39]Steve Walton, *Leadership and Lifestyle: The Portrait of Paul in the Miletus Speech and 1 Thessalonians*, SNTSMS 108 (Cambridge: Cambridge University Press, 2000).

[40]See F. F. Bruce, *The Speeches in Acts* (London: Tyndale, 1943), 8.

The length of the speeches in Acts. Writing in the first century BCE, the historian from Sicily Diodorus complained that historians were including in their works speeches that were too long. The following quotation helps us understand the situation on the ground:

> One might justly censure those who in their histories insert over-long orations or employ frequent speeches; for not only do they rend asunder the continuity of the narrative by the ill-timed insertion of speeches, but also they interrupt the interest of those who are eagerly pressing on toward a full knowledge of the events. . . . But as it is, some writers by excessive use of rhetorical passages have made the whole art of history into an appendage of oratory. Not only does that which is poorly composed give offence, but also that which seems to have hit the mark in other respects yet has gone far astray from the themes and occasions that belong to its peculiar type. Therefore, even of those who read such works, some skip over the orations although they appear to be entirely successful, and others, wearied in spirit by the historian's wordiness and lack of taste, abandon the reading entirely.[41]

Diodorus's vexation with long speeches is shared by modern readers of many Greco-Roman historians. Whether one is reading the first two books of Thucydides, or Hellenistic historians like Polybius or Dionysius, or Roman historians like Sallust, one is struck by the length of the speeches.[42] In comparison to, say, the Old Testament, the speeches in Greco-Roman history can be tediously long. As Diodorus indicates above, the purpose of these long orations was often to show off rhetorical ability. Below I provide two examples from Josephus. Note that these are actually *short* speeches in comparison to what Diodorus is complaining about! Yet, since we know the sources whence Josephus is drawing (i.e., the Old Testament), these examples can help the reader understand the issue at hand.

When Abraham had prepared the altar on which to sacrifice Isaac, Josephus reports the following speech from the patriarch:

> But when the altar had been prepared and he laid the chopped wood upon it and things were ready, he said to his son, "My child, having asked with

---

[41]Diodorus Siculus, *Library of History* 20.1.1-4, LCL translation.
[42]There are exceptions, e.g., Xenophon.

myriad prayers from God that you be born to me, when you came into life, there is nothing that I did not take trouble with regard to your upbringing, nor was there anything that I thought would bring me greater happiness than if I should see you grown to manhood and when I died, I should have you as the successor of my realm. But since it was by God's wish that I became your father and again since, as it seems best to Him, I give you up, bear this consecration nobly, for I concede you to God, who requires now to obtain this honor from us, in return for the fact that He has been a benevolent helper and ally to me. Since you were born (out of the course of nature), depart now from life not in a common fashion but sent forth by your own father to God, the father of all, by the rite of sacrifice. I think that He has judged that you are deserving to be removed from life neither by disease nor by war nor by some other of the afflictions that are conditioned by nature to befall humanity, but that He would receive your soul with prayers and sacrificial rites and would keep it near Himself. And you will be a guardian for me and supporter in my old age, wherefore also I especially reared you, by offering me God in place of yourself."[43]

One is struck at how Josephus takes the few words of Abraham from the Genesis text, "God himself will provide the lamb for a burnt offering, my son" (Gen 22:8), and launches into a long, beautiful and complex speech.[44] What only took a few seconds to read in the biblical text, now takes much longer in the rewritten version. I could take numerous examples from Josephus where we can compare his brief source to his drawn-out speech. Outside Josephus, this sort of protracted speech was common. It was done by the historian for several reasons, including the demonstration of rhetoric, which was believed to be appropriate—within limits—to the genre of history.

When one puts down a Greco-Roman history and picks up the Acts of the Apostles, the contrast in the length of speeches is striking. Some of the longer speeches in Acts, such as Peter's at Pentecost or Paul's at Antioch

---

[43]Josephus, *Jewish Antiquities* 1.228-231. Translation is that of Feldman.

[44]Feldman, *Judean Antiquities*, 90n706, actually views this speech as an example of the rhetorical exercise of *ethopoeia* (speech in character). Compare the much more conservative rewriting of the speech by Pseudo-Philo, *Biblical Antiquities* 32.2: "Behold now, my son, I am offering you as a burnt-offering and am delivering you into the hands of the one who gave you to me."

Pisidia, are short when read in comparison to the set pieces of Greco-Roman historians. The longest speech in Acts—that of Stephen—takes roughly six minutes to read. It is the most similar to the orations of characters in Greco-Roman historians; and yet, it is still shorter than most. We must also remember that Stephen's speech is really the exception in terms of length in Acts.

These comparative data can be interpreted in a number of directions. One option is to say that Luke lacked the type of rhetorical education needed to be competent in embellishing speeches. While I actually believe that Luke did not reach the highest level of rhetorical education and that this might have affected the length of his speeches, nevertheless it should be noted that one need not have reached the tertiary level in order to be able to embellish.[45] One may have needed to reach the tertiary level to embellish *with taste*, but embellishment could be done in bad taste, as both Diodorus and Lucian indicate. Thus a lack of education may be, but is not necessarily, linked to shorter, simpler speeches.

Another option is to say that the speeches in Acts are shorter than the Greco-Roman norm because Luke simply lacked material. Thus, for example, the speech of Peter in Acts 3:11-26 is relatively short because Luke only had limited sources for this early period of the church. Yet, this would only reinforce the portrait of Luke as a responsible reporter of speeches. For instead of embellishing short dialogues into long, elegant orations, he has gone against the current of Greco-Roman practice by refusing to put words into the speaker that were never said. This option also overlooks the probability that Luke was an eyewitness of many of the events in Acts involving Paul. In this scenario Luke—whether by memory or written notes or both—would have had plenty of material on which to draw to compose a speech. Thus he could have written very long speeches, keeping in mind that Paul appears to have been rather long-winded (spoke until midnight! Acts 20:7-12). Therefore even though it appears that Luke had plenty of material, he nevertheless presents speeches that are relatively short. I am suggesting that this means that Luke was not inclined to embellish speeches,

---

[45]See Osvaldo Padilla, "Hellenistic παιδεία and Luke's Education: A Critique of Recent Approaches," *NTS* 55 (2009): 416-37.

probably signifying that his intention was to provide simply a gist of what
the speakers said.

Pairing of speeches. One of the most conspicuous aspects of Greco-Roman
history is the pairing of speeches. When history is concerned with a war (most
often the case), the authors would include the generals' harangues to the respective armies. At other times the historians may include opposing speeches
on a specific topic.[46] Oftentimes we find pairing of opposing speeches at am-
bassadorial meetings.[47] Pairing of deliberative speeches, where there is argument on what direction to proceed, is common in assembly meetings
among the Greeks,[48] but not exclusive to them.[49] The pairing of speeches was
one way in which the agonistic character of Greek civilization was manifested,
as fierce competition permeated all aspects of Greek life (e.g., drama, athletics,
politics). In fact, the highest level of rhetorical education consisted in training
in declamation, where the exercises of *controversiae* and *suasoriae* prepared the
student to compose a speech-in-character arguing for one or another side of
a judicial case or deliberative occasion.[50]

Again, an example from Josephus is useful, since we possess the main
source from which he constructs the following pair of speeches. Notice
what Josephus does with the dialogue between Laban and Jacob found in
Genesis 31:25-32. Although long, this pairing of speeches is worth quoting
in full to give the reader a concrete example of the rhetorical practice:

> "Indeed, I gave you my daughters in marriage, reckoning that I would
> thereby increase your goodwill toward us. But you, having no regard either
> [οὔτε] for your own mother and the kinship which you have with me or
> [οὔτε] the wives whom you married or having a thought for the children of
> whom I am the grandfather, have used the way of war with me, carrying off
> my possessions, and inducing my daughters to run away from the one who

---

[46]One thinks of Herodotus 3.80-82 with the rival speeches on the three types of government.

[47]There are numerous of these. For a good example, see Thucydides 1.32-43 between the Corcyreans and
the Corinthians.

[48]Again see Thucydides 1.80-86 for a very good example among the Lacedaemonians—namely, Archidamus
versus Sthenelaidas. Note that while in 1.139 Thucydides clearly states that the Athenians held an assembly
and many gave their opinions, he only includes the speech of Pericles (1.140-144).

[49]See, e.g., the beautiful, deliberative speeches between Caesar and Cato in the Catiline debate (Sallust, *The
War with Catiline* 51-52).

[50]On the *controversiae*, see further Padilla, "Hellenistic παιδεία," 420-21.

fathered them; and you have gone, carrying off and removing the ancestral sacred objects that were honored by my forefathers and were deemed worthy of the same worship by me as by them. And these things, which not even those who have gone to war have done to the enemy, you, a kinsman and the son of my sister, the husband of my daughters, you, who have been a visitor and guest of my house, have done." When Labanos said this, Iakobos said in defense that God had implanted love of fatherland not in him alone but also in all, and that after so long a time it was proper for him to return to it. "And with regard to the plunder with which you charge me," he said, "you yourself would be found doing injustice before another judge; for in view of the gratitude that you ought to feel toward us and in view of what was guarded by us and increased in amount, how have you not missed the mark of justice in this case, being angry with me if we have taken a small portion of it? However, regarding your daughters, know that it is not through my wickedness that they follow me in departing, but through the just affection that it happens married women have toward their husbands. Therefore, they follow not so much me as their children."[51]

Josephus has significantly enriched the speeches in order to introduce the agonistic foundation of Greco-Roman historiography: notice how he pushes the analogy of war through the lips of Laban. In addition he has added pathos and solemnity to the speeches with the continued use of οὔτε. Last, the sense of rebuttal so dear in the rhetorical tradition is introduced by saying that Jacob ἀπελογεῖτο ("said in defense") to Laban. A historian of the Greco-Roman tradition should capitalize on any opportunity to bring out the polemical culture of rhetoric, and putting opposing speeches side by side was a preferred method.

One is therefore struck at the dearth of pairing of speeches in the Acts of the Apostles—even though there were ample opportunities for Luke to exploit. Consider the following examples.

At Philippi, Paul and Silas receive a serious accusation: "These men are disturbing our city; they are Jews and are advocating customs that are not lawful for us as Romans to adopt or observe" (Acts 16:20-21). The accusation is probably that of causing civic insurrection, a very serious charge

---

[51]Josephus, *Jewish Antiquities* 1.314-318. Translation from Feldman.

in the Roman world. This would have been an excellent opportunity for Luke to put in the mouth of Paul a counterspeech rejecting such a charge. No such speech comes. Paul's protest in Acts 16:37 is not a carefully worked rebuttal of the charges; it is simply an affirmation that Silas and he were uncondemned and have been wronged despite being Roman citizens.

At Thessalonica, an even more serious accusation is lodged: "These people who have been turning the world upside down have come here also, and Jason has entertained them as guests. They are all acting contrary to the decrees of the emperor, saying that there is another king named Jesus" (Acts 17:6-7). More than likely the charge is that of *maiestas*, treason. In light of the practice of Greco-Roman history, I find it remarkable that there is not an opposing speech of defense on the lips of Paul. Luke simply narrates that Paul and Silas are sent away covertly (by night!) to Berea. For a reader who is not sympathetic to the Christian movement, such action only seems to reinforce the charge of treason!

At Corinth, we once again find an accusation against Paul before the tribunal of Gallio. The accusation is similar to the one at Philippi in that there is a hint that Paul is causing civic disturbance by "persuading people to worship God in ways that are contrary to the law" (Acts 18:13). Again, this represents an appropriate opportunity for Luke to include a speech of Paul rebutting the charge. No such speech is presented. Instead, a third party comes to Paul's rescue, as it were: Gallio himself declares that the matter is simply a case of inter-Jewish issues (Acts 18:14-15).

Why does Luke not introduce rebuttal speeches—as is the norm in Greco-Roman history—in these scenarios that were so apposite for them? One possibility is that Luke has delayed the rebuttals only to present them before the readers toward the end of Acts—namely, in Acts 24 and 26: the speeches before Felix and Agrippa. The former, in fact, is the only example of pairing of opposing speeches in Acts. Perhaps this is the way Luke operated. But, as Loveday Alexander has noted, there is a danger in this strategy:

> Paul, certainly, is presented as innocent of the particular charge on which he was tried in Caesarea. . . . But he and his associates have incurred a number of other charges along the way which have never in so many words—that is, in the explicit terms we would expect of apologetic speech—

been refuted. Mud has a disturbing tendency to stick, and it is a dangerous strategy for an apologetic writer to bring accusations to the reader's attention without taking the trouble to refute them.[52]

I suggest that a reason for Luke's not pairing speeches despite excellent opportunities has to do with his habits as a historian. That is, he was simply unwilling to grant a speech to one of his characters where there had been none. It is possible that Luke did not pair speeches because he did not possess the type of rhetorical education where this would have been learned. In fact, as I said above, I do not believe that Luke had reached the highest level of rhetorical education. But one need not have reached this level to be aware of this rhetorical strategy. One could have executed it even if not taught formally how to do it. The result might have seemed amateurish to professional historians, to be sure, but the *attempt* to do it did not require the highest education. The fact that pairing of speeches is only found once in Acts suggests that we have a historian who is sufficiently conservative not to invent speeches.

CONCLUSION: BELIEVING THE SPEECHES

In this section I have been attempting to look at the speeches in Acts through the lens of a first-century reader. I have suggested that there would have been at least two areas that would have surprised this reader (or better, *hearer*)—namely, the unusual short length of the speeches and the lack of pairing of opposing speeches. The reader might have drawn a number of conclusions from this: perhaps the author lacked a rhetorical education; perhaps he was an amateur historian; perhaps he lacked sufficient sources. I am suggesting that a reasonable conclusion—without necessarily excluding any of the previous ones—was that the author operated in a very conservative and sober manner. Here was a historian who, although having ample opportunities to "play the orator and show his skill," instead reported speeches in a moderate manner. This in turn might have suggested that the historian was very concerned for accuracy and truth. Not that

---

[52]Loveday Alexander, *Acts in Its Ancient Literary Context: A Classicist Looks at the Acts of the Apostles*, LNTS 289 (London: T&T Clark, 2005), 198.

Luke was *un*rhetorical: he has a number of features in his work that show rhetorical care. In any case, it probably would have been an impossibility to compose a history in the first century that was untouched by the rhetorical strategies of the period. We are therefore not suggesting that Luke operated in a manner similar to the modern, (supposedly) detached journalist who reports speeches verbatim. The speeches are given in Luke's own language, and they are molded to address the situation at hand. Nevertheless, their brevity and lack of agonistic character suggest that they are a creative yet faithful gist of what the speakers said.

These arguments cannot *prove* that the speeches are true. Logically, it does not ineluctably follow that because Acts's speeches are, for example, short in comparison to Greco-Roman histories, they are genuine. The arguments are suggestive, not of the precise formal-logic type, which cannot, in any case, be used to demonstrate the truth of an ancient document. The best we can attempt by means of argument is probability.

This raises a question, especially for those who like myself hold to a high view of Scripture: Do I believe that the speeches in Acts are true because I can establish their historical probability, or do I believe they are true because they are part of Holy Scripture? In attempting to answer this question it is first necessary to understand what we mean by *true* in the context of the Acts of the Apostles. Given my conclusions about the practice of speech reporting in the ancient world and how Luke fits into it, *true* refers to an essential fit between the speech in the historical situation and the reporting of the speech in the historical work. *Furthermore, true* refers to the belief that what Luke affirmed through the speakers ultimately corresponds to the way that God ordains reality.[53] This is the concept of truth with respect to the speeches that I am working with.[54] If, then, we say that

---

[53]Much more elegantly stated by Nicholas Lash, *Theology on the Way to Emmaus* (London: SCM Press, 1986), 14, who speaks of God and reality in the following way: "The God whom we seek, the God whose truth sustains and infinitely transcends all projects and all imaginings is, in fact, the incomprehensible ground and goal of all reality and all significance."

[54]There may be, and are, those who conclude from their research of the ancient data that historians were not expected to be faithful to what the speakers said, but rather to the character of the speaker and the situation. This is their conclusion, in clean conscience, of the ancient material. Therefore, for them *true* refers to a fit between speech on the one hand and character of speaker and situation on the other. *True* for the speeches, therefore, is not linked primarily to what the speakers actually said. It is my opinion that

we believe that the speeches are true to the extent that we can establish
their historical plausibility, I believe we find ourselves in a similar situation
to that of historical Jesus research. That is, the real Jesus is not the one who
is portrayed in the Gospels, but rather the one that we can plausibly reconstruct through methods such as the criteria of multiple attestation, embarrassment and so on. Essentially, we create a fifth gospel that can pass the
test of modern philosophical and historical standards. I am willing to believe in Jesus to the extent that I can historically establish the plausibility
of his words and deeds. The Jesus that emerges from this filter, *that* is the
one in which I believe, not the one mediated by the Evangelists. Similarly,
we could say that we believe that the speeches of Peter or Paul reported in
Acts are true to the extent that we can validate their probability by historical methods. We test them through a number of criteria, and only the
amount that passes the criteria can we say is genuine.

I think there are a number of problems with this mindset for those who
hold to a high view of the Bible. The most significant problem is that this
mindset puts my own sense of possibility—whether historical, theological
or philosophical—above Scripture. I will only believe those things that can
pass through the sieves of my worldview. In the classic stance of theological
liberalism, I detach myself from faith in order to dare think independently.
I take myself out of the orbit of the Christian faith to look at the world
autonomously. I have thus ceased to submit to Scripture. If I accept the
speeches as true only to the extent they can be proved, I am making faith
in the Word of God dependent on human historical reconstruction.

The second option is to say that I believe the speeches to be true because
they are part of Holy Scripture. I do not need the consent of historians and
theologians to believe them. Thus I do not need proof to believe them. I
believe that the speeches are true because, being part of Scripture, the Holy
Spirit has persuaded me that they are genuine.

I believe that while the second option is the correct one for the Christian,
we still must do the historical work of examining the content of the

---

this does *not* compromise a high view of Scripture, since it is primarily a generic—or subgeneric—issue.
I am assuming, however, that these scholars would also take the next step to say that what Luke *affirms*
through the speeches is true. If this is refused, then there *is* a compromise with a high view of Scripture.

speeches in their context of the ancient world—*but not to prove that they are true, but rather to strengthen the faith of the believers and to defend and dialogue with those on the outside.* This assumes that believing the speeches is not a fideistic move or a retreat into mysticism. Although we cannot *prove* that they are true, we can offer reasons to believe. But can historical work *disprove* the veracity of the speeches? To say that this is impossible would indeed be a retreat into fideism, a posture that the Bible itself rejects. We must remain open to the possibility of falsification through historical research even if we believe by faith—reasonable faith—that this will not be the case. Should problems arise with the truth of the speeches—and they have—we continue in faith to do the research in order to find plausible answers. In that way we practice "faith seeking understanding." I realize that this is something of a simplification of an issue that is far more complex, but I think it is nevertheless helpful.

Let us now turn in the following chapter to the theology of the speeches.

five

THE SPEECHES IN ACTS (PART TWO)

The Theology of the Speeches

THE TITLE OF THIS CHAPTER must be emphasized. We are not dealing here with a theology of Acts as a whole. That would take not a chapter but an entire volume![1] We are dealing with the theology of the speeches. What does that mean? And is it not bound to be reductionist to look only to the speeches, thereby mutilating the theological body of Acts?

First, what does this mean? To answer this question we must start with assumptions; at least two come to mind. First, Luke, although not writing a theological treatise, nevertheless is a theologian. Writing in narrative form does not disqualify him from theological formulation. To think that it does is absurd, and the result of Enlightenment-based Western European epistemology and theology. The idea has in any case been debunked.[2] Luke is a historian-theologian. The second assumption, arising from readings of Acts, is that Luke's thought is coherent and sufficiently systematic to speak

---

[1] Well-known works on the theology of Luke-Acts include Hans Conzelmann, *The Theology of St. Luke* (New York: Harper & Row, 1960); J. C. O'Neill, *The Theology of Acts in Its Historical Setting*, 2nd ed. (London: SPCK, 1970); H. C. Kee, *Good News to the Ends of the Earth: The Theology of Acts* (London: SCM Press, 1990); Jacob Jervell, *The Theology of the Acts of the Apostles* (Cambridge: Cambridge University Press, 1996); I. Howard Marshall and David Peterson, eds., *Witness to the Gospel: The Theology of Acts* (Grand Rapids: Eerdmans, 1998). Most recently, see Darrell Bock, *A Theology of Luke and Acts: God's Promised Program, Realized for All Nations* (Grand Rapids: Zondervan, 2012).

[2] See Hans Frei, *The Eclipse of Biblical Narrative: A Study in Eighteenth and Nineteenth Century Hermeneutics* (New Haven, CT: Yale University Press, 1974). It has been the merit of a number of postliberal theologians to reemphasize the importance of narrative for theology: e.g., William Placher, Stanley Hauerwas and, of course, Frei himself. On this see further in chapter six.

of connected theological themes being advanced in his narrative. What we mean, then, when speaking of examining the theology of the speeches is the observation, description and explanation of themes that are marshaled in the speeches. The attempt is to link together salient motifs and explain them in connection to one another.

Second, it may be argued that by focusing *only* on the speeches we are impoverishing the theology of Acts. Is not the theology of Acts inextricably tied to its *narrative*? And does not a concentration on the speeches reveal a preference for direct speech—that is, discourse (and therefore not narrative)—as a channel for theology? There is certainly some validity in these observations. However, it may be mitigated by remembering that *to understand the meaning of the speeches it is necessary to read them in conjunction with their respective narratives*. Luke has so crafted his work that the reader must engage in a dialectic of speech and narrative to better understand *both* the speech and the narrative. When approaching the speeches this way, therefore, we do not leave the narrative behind, abandoned in a hermeneutical ditch. Rather, the narrative and speech ride together.

In what follows we will look at the main speeches in Acts. I have based the assessment of their importance on length and strategic placing by Luke. We will thus look at the following speeches: Pentecost, Stephen, Cornelius, Areopagus and Agrippa.

THE SPEECH OF PETER AT PENTECOST (ACTS 2:1-41)

Both at the end of Luke's Gospel (Lk 24:48-49) and the beginning of Acts (Acts 1:4-8), the disciples are commanded to remain in Jerusalem for the reception of the Spirit, who will empower them to be witnesses. The Spirit is poured on the disciples on the day of Pentecost. Luke uses a cluster of terms that show he wants his readers to think of the event in terms of a theophany: *from heaven, sound, rush of a violent wind* and *fire*. The echoes of God's visit to Israel at Mount Sinai are unmistakable (Ex 19:16-19). The coming of the Spirit is thus the coming of God to visit his people. With the sound of the Spirit's arrival and the speaking in tongues of the disciples, a crowd gathers. There are two different reactions on the part of the crowd. On the one hand, there are those who are "bewildered," "amazed" and "astonished." The terms used to describe their reaction do not necessarily carry a negative sense. They simply show that the crowd is at a loss to explain what has just happened; they want an answer: "What does this mean?" (Acts 2:12). On the other hand, there are those who are prepared to reach a judgment on the state of the disciples: "They are filled with new wine" (Acts 2:13).[3] The table is set for the speech of Peter, which will give an explanation of what just has happened.

The speech. It is fascinating to look at the way that Luke introduces the speech of Peter. He, along with the Eleven, lifted his voice and "addressed" the crowd. The term translated "addressed" is not the regular one used in Acts for a response.[4] Instead, Luke employs the less usual ἀποφθέγγομαι.[5] The verb appears only three times in the New Testament, all in the Lukan corpus. In the Septuagint it is often used of prophetic speech, sometimes of genuine prophets (1 Chron 25:1) and other times of false prophets (Ezra 13:9; Zech 10:2; Mic 5:11). Outside the Bible, the verb can be used of oracular speech, or simply of bold speech (see LSJ, 226.). It is tempting to understand the verb here as just a solemn way of introducing Peter's speech. That is, given the situation, Peter is about to deliver a powerful and grave sermon that demands a solemn term.[6] However, given that the verb was already used in the same context with reference to the Holy Spirit in Acts 2:4 ("All of them were filled with the Holy Spirit and began to speak in other languages, as the Spirit gave them ability [ἀποφθέγγεσθαι]"), it is better to understand the verb with the nuance of prophetic speech. That is, with his use in Acts 2:4, Luke has conditioned our comprehension of the verb to understand it as referring to prophetic speech inspired by the Spirit.[7] We shall come back to this important issue at the conclusion of this section.

---

[3]Notice the emphatic periphrastic phrase γλεύκους μεμεστωμένοι εἰσίν. One is tempted to paraphrase with a modern idiom: "They are wasted!"

[4]I.e., εἶπεν, ἀπεκρίνατο.

[5]Note that Codex Bezae uses the simpler εἶπεν.

[6]See similarly Acts 26:25.

[7]See especially Daniel Marguerat, Les Actes des Apôtres 1-12 (Genève: Labor et Fides, 2007), 86-87. Similarly Jacob Jervell, Die Apostelgeschichte, KEK 3 (Göttingen: Vandenhoeck und Ruprecht, 1998), 141-42: "Seine Rede ist Geistesrede, prophetische Rede, was hier ἀποφθέγγομαι zeigt" ("His speech is Spirit-speech, prophetic speech, as ἀποφθέγγομαι here shows").

The observation above is important to understand one of Luke's main points in this passage. For what Peter will do in this speech is to *explain* the theophanic phenomena that has attracted the attention of the crowd. Thus in Acts 2:16 he will employ the phrase "this is that" to introduce his explanation. More than likely Luke is using the Jewish explanatory technique of *pesher*, used abundantly in the Dead Sea Scrolls. The interpreter, assuming that his community was living in the last days, would take a contemporary event and provide an explanation of it drawn from Scripture, especially the prophets. This is what Peter is doing with his citation of Joel's prophecy in Acts 2:17-21.[8] Yet, since Luke has used prophetic terminology to introduce Peter's own words, he wants to make sure that the reader understands the speech as *authoritative pesher*.[9] We thus have a prophecy within a prophecy.

The quotation is from Joel 2:28-32 (LXX 3:1-5). Luke clearly uses the Septuagint version. The prophecy from Joel encapsulates several motifs of the Old Testament Day of the Lord. These include portents, prophesying, the Holy Spirit and salvation. By explaining the theophanic event through Joel's prophecy, Peter is announcing that the long-awaited eschatological day has finally arrived. But what has triggered the dawn of this wonderful event?

Acts 2:22-36 shifts from emphasis on the Spirit to emphasis on Christology. The syntax of the initial verses attempts to capture Peter's urgency in introducing Jesus as the agent responsible for triggering the Day of the Lord. It is actually a periodic sentence that catches the pathos of the speech.[10] Peter communicates two things here: that Jesus was certainly appointed by God (as demonstrated by his powerful deeds), and the hearers' guilt in killing him. The effect is powerful, showing the enormity of their guilt. Peter is basically saying: "You killed no less than the man who

---

[8]See F. F. Bruce, *Biblical Exegesis in the Qumran Texts* (Grand Rapids: Eerdmans, 1960), 76. On Peter's speech as *pesher*, see esp. R. P. Menzies, *Empowered for Witness: The Spirit in Luke-Acts* (London: T&T Clark, 2004), 176-79.

[9]This may sound redundant, since *pesher* exegesis was by nature authoritative. My point is that in the context of competitive claims about who are the people of God, Luke wants the readers to understand that the followers of Jesus *really* are the people of God.

[10]Note how Jesus is introduced immediately with the accusative Ἰησοῦν τὸν Ναζωραῖον. The main verb comes much later, at the end of Acts 2:23: ἀνείλατε.

had been appointed by God for your own benefit!" But in the history of Israel there had been other men (prophets) who had performed signs among the people and who also had been murdered. What is so special about Jesus of Nazareth?

Peter now moves to the resurrection, which will occupy the remainder of the speech. He will provide two proofs for the resurrection of Jesus: Scripture and personal testimony. Three Scriptures are given, all from the Psalms: Psalms 16:8-11; 132:11; 110:1. Peter makes clear that the psalmist was not speaking of himself but rather of the Messiah. Note the following sentences: "For David says *concerning him*" (Acts 2:25); "Since he was a prophet, he knew that God had sworn with an oath to him that he would put one of his descendants on his throne. Foreseeing this, *David spoke of the resurrection of the Messiah*" (Acts 2:30-31); "For David did not ascend into the heavens" (Acts 2:34). Bruce succinctly presents Peter's line of argument:

> The argument is that the words of the Psalm cannot refer to David . . . since his soul did go to Hades and his body did undergo corruption; they must therefore have been uttered by prophetic inspiration, with reference to the promised son of David . . . in whose name they were spoken. These words, it is argued, were fulfilled in Jesus of Nazareth, and in no other; therefore Jesus must be the expected messiah of David's line.[11]

Recall that Luke is presenting Peter as speaking with prophetic authority. Therefore his arguments from prophecy are meant to carry the utmost weight.

The second corroboration for Jesus' resurrection is that of personal witness. This begins in Acts 2:32 with a reemphasizing of Jesus of Nazareth as the one who was raised. Note the almost identical phraseology of Acts 2:24, 32: "whom God raised" (ὃν ὁ θεὸς ἀνέστησεν); "This Jesus God raised" (τοῦτον τὸν Ἰησοῦν ἀνέστησεν ὁ θεός). The point is that it is *this Jesus of Nazareth and no other* whom God has raised as the Davidic Messiah. How else do we know this to be true? Peter declares that the Twelve are witnesses of this event: "All of us are witnesses" (Acts 2:32). We thus have a back-and-forth argument when it comes to corroborating the resurrection

---

[11]F. F. Bruce, *The Book of the Acts*, rev. ed., NICNT (Grand Rapids: Eerdmans, 1988), 124.

of Jesus: the Scriptures promised that the Messiah would be raised; we have seen Jesus of Nazareth raised; this leads us back to Scripture, which then leads us back to the resurrection, and so on.

Recall that Peter began the speech by referencing to the supernatural event that had just happened. He stated that their ability to speak in other tongues should not be confused with drunkenness, for it was the outpouring of the Spirit. Notice the οὖν ("therefore") of Acts 2:33, which is resumptive: "Being therefore exalted at the right hand of God, and having received from the Father the promise of the Holy Spirit, he has poured out this that you both see and hear." Peter finally answers the question of why the Day of the Lord has dawned: it is because Jesus of Nazareth, God's Messiah, has been exalted and therefore has poured out the Holy Spirit. Peter has now come full circle. The structure of the speech should thus be understood in the following manner:

Pentecost → Old Testament prophecy → Christology (supported by Old Testament prophecy) → Pentecost

We can therefore speak of an A B B' A' pattern for this speech.[12] The phenomena that have just occurred on the day of Pentecost, Peter is saying, should be understood in light of the Joel prophecy concerning the Day of the Lord. What has *triggered* the dawn of the Day of the Lord is the resurrection of Jesus of Nazareth. This was foretold by David in Scripture, who spoke not of himself but of the exaltation of the future Messiah. This exalted Jesus, having himself received the Spirit, possesses the authority to pour him out on the disciples, which explains the phenomena at Pentecost.

The speech is concluded in Acts 2:36, as the final οὖν suggests. In this conclusion we find the thesis of the speech expressed in a comprehensive fashion. In addition, the adverb ἀσφαλῶς ("with certainty," cf. Lk 1:4) is employed, thereby injecting the preceding arguments with confidence. The goal is to move the hearers to accept the speech as worthy of belief, and consequently to repent.

---

[12]For other chiastic possibilities, see Craig Keener, *Acts: An Exegetical Commentary* (Grand Rapids: Baker, 2012–2014), 1:863-65.

Theological reflections. *Authoritative speech and canon.* We noted above that one of the striking features of the speech of Peter was the manner in which Luke introduced it. He did not simply say that Peter "spoke"; he implied that Peter spoke *with prophetic authority*—that is, as guided by the Holy Spirit. I suggest that the speech of Peter is programmatic for the rest of Acts; that is, when the Twelve, their followers and Paul speak, they do so with the same authority of the Spirit as Peter's.[13] This is reinforced in the following passages.

In Acts 4:8, as Peter is about to preach to the Sanhedrin, Luke states: "Then Peter, *filled with the Holy Spirit...*" Peter then provides a brief version of the kerygma. In Acts 4:23, Peter and John, having been released by the Sanhedrin, return to "theirs" (NRSV "their friends"). After praying, Luke concludes: "*They were all filled with the Holy Spirit* and spoke the word of God with boldness" (Acts 4:31). Note the use of the imperfect ἐλάλουν, probably iterative, suggesting that the result of being filled with the Spirit was constant proclamation of the word by the apostles and the circle around them. The point here is that the filling of the Spirit is linked to preaching.

Another example is Stephen. In introducing him to the readers, Luke has the interesting aside: "a man full of faith *and the Holy Spirit*" (Acts 6:5). Furthermore, after his speech to the Sanhedrin, Luke adds: "But *filled with the Holy Spirit*" (Acts 7:55). This implies that Stephen's speech—a panoramic explanation of the Old Testament in light of Jesus—was Spirit-led speech.

Another one of the Seven, Philip, is presented as clearly being guided by the Spirit in the episode with the Ethiopian eunuch. The Spirit directly tells Philip: "Go over to this chariot and join it" (Acts 8:29). Intriguingly, Philip will do the same thing Peter did at Pentecost (and Paul will do at Antioch Pisidia): he will preach Jesus from the Old Testament text. Other examples could be given. When the Twelve, their disciples and Paul preach the word of God, therefore, they are doing so with the authority of the Spirit.

I suggest that in this Luke has a contribution to make to our understanding of authoritative speech from God: *it is the apostles and the circle around them who have the authority to speak the word of God.* Why? Luke presents several reasons.

---

[13]See also Marguerat, *Les Actes des Apôtres*, 86-87; Keener, *Acts*, 1:872-73.

First, they were taught by Jesus himself how to interpret the Scriptures christologically. Consider Luke 24:44-48:

> Then he said to them, "These are my words that I spoke to you while I was still with you—that everything written about me in the law of Moses, the prophets, and the psalms must be fulfilled." Then he opened their minds to understand the scriptures, and he said to them, "Thus it is written, that the Messiah is to suffer and to rise from the dead on the third day, and that repentance and forgiveness of sins is to be proclaimed in his name to all nations, beginning from Jerusalem. You are witnesses of these things."

Here we see Jesus as not only the central content of revelation, but also as the one who can authoritatively *explain* that revelation.[14] He passes that task to the Twelve.

Second, notice the emphasis on the Twelve being witnesses of the resurrection. Their position of witness is one condition to their speaking the word with God's authority. This is one of the most important themes in Luke-Acts.[15]

Third, the exalted Christ has poured out the Spirit on the disciples, who will enable them to be witnesses until the ends of the earth (Acts 1:8).

We have, therefore, three "media" for the conferring of authority. One we may call *scholastic*. That is, the Twelve, primarily, are taught by Jesus himself, and they in turn preserve the teachings of Jesus. They are the link between Jesus and the early church. That is why it is so important that they devote themselves to the teaching ministry of the word (Acts 6:1-4). We can speak of a "*collegium* of the apostles," similar to the rabbinic and Hellenistic schools.[16]

The second medium we may call *ocular*. By being given the privilege to behold the resurrected Christ, the Twelve and their circle are given an authority to speak for God that others do not possess.

The third medium for conferring the authority of divine speech on the

---

[14]We will come back to this important observation in chapter six.

[15]See Lk 24:44-48; Acts 1:22; 10:41.

[16]On which, see especially Loveday Alexander, "Memory and Tradition in the Hellenistic Schools," in *Jesus in Memory: Traditions in Oral and Scribal Perspectives*, ed. W. H. Kelber and S. Byrskog (Waco, TX: Baylor University Press, 2009), 113-53.

apostles we may call *pneumatic*. That is, they can speak authoritatively for God because the Spirit has been poured out on them. We thus have a uniting of the historical with the suprahistorical. The scholastic and ocular ground the authority to speak for God on historical events and thereby guard against gnosticism. The pneumatic guards against historicism.

All this raises the question of New Testament canon, understanding that the final canonical product is the result of a complex process of foundational figures, communication between communities, reception and so on. One may pose the following question concerning the contribution of Acts to the early church's canonical process: Does the authoritative locus of Acts—namely, apostles and close followers—serve as a model for the early church's understanding of the canon? That is, only those works that were thought to be composed by apostles and close companions of the apostles can be taken as authoritative and therefore canonical?[17] Or was it the case that already, even during the period of composition of Acts in the late 60s, there was a canonical sense in the early church that led Luke to present his material the way he did—with apostles and their companions at the head? A third option, which I think more probable, is that Luke's presentation of divine speech in Acts affected the reflections of the churches on canon, *but that Acts itself had been shaped by the churches' germinating thoughts on divine speech and the canon.*

To sum up, Acts contributes to the ultimate shape of the New Testament canon while itself being influenced by the "precanonical" considerations of the early church. The central contribution of Acts to authoritative—and hence canonical—speech from God is the place of the apostles and their companions as the source of legitimate narration and explanation of the life, death and resurrection of Jesus.

Trinitarian nudges. From the speech of Peter and its surrounding context we may also speak of *trinitarian nudges.* I phrase the concept in this manner because the New Testament does not present a notion of the Trinity with the amount of nuance and technicality that one finds later in Nicaea.

---

[17]On this see, for example, Irenaeus, *Against Heresies* 3.1.1, who links Mark with Peter and Luke with Paul in order to show that their Gospels (Mark's and Luke's) have apostolic authority behind them. See chapter one.

Nevertheless, the New Testament already demonstrates a seminal trinitarian core that encourages further theological reflection and formulation. Acts has a contribution to make in this respect.

There is a beautiful trinitarian nudge in Acts 2:33: "Therefore, having been exalted at the right hand of God, and having received the promise of the Holy Spirit from the Father, he has poured out that which you see and hear" (my translation). The Father is presented as the ultimate source of the Spirit in the act of salvation. Jesus, as the exalted Lord who has been raised and sits at God's right hand, is the intermediary between the Father and the disciples. He has the authority to pour out the Holy Spirit on his disciples, thereby fulfilling the prophecy of John the Baptist (Lk 3:16; Acts 1:5). The Spirit, with his coming on the day of Pentecost, inaugurates the eschatological age of salvation.

There is further development on the identity of the Holy Spirit in Acts 2:1-4. By means of intertextuality, Luke is able to link the phenomena caused by God when he descends on Mount Sinai (Ex 19:16-19) to the coming of the Spirit. Since the Spirit causes the same phenomena when he falls on the disciples as God caused when he came to Sinai, the reader is left to conclude that the Spirit can be identified with God. Luke does not break into the narrative and say: "The Holy Spirit is God." Through intertextuality, however, he nudges the reader in that direction.

"To all the nations." Another important theological theme that emerges from the speech of Peter and its context is the spread of the word to all nations. Already from Luke 24:47-49 and Acts 1:8 the reader has been prepared for this move. In both of these passages the coming of the Spirit has been tied to witnessing to all nations. Luke 24:47 has the phrase "to all nations" (εἰς πάντα τὰ ἔθνη), while Acts 1:8 has "to the ends of the earth" (ἕως ἐσχάτου τῆς γῆς). But the preaching to the nations can only happen when the Spirit has come down to empower the disciples. This is what is described as happening in Acts 2:1-4.

The theme of tongues is essential to this text. We are told that on the disciples there appeared "tongues, as of fire," which rested upon each one (Acts 2:3). The meaning of this phenomenon is disclosed in Acts 2:5-11. Once, as third-person narrator, Luke calls attention to the wonder of the crowd "because each one heard them speaking in the native language of each" (Acts 2:6). Three times Luke allows the reader to hear the comments of the crowd with respect to languages: "Are not all these who are speaking [οἱ λαλοῦντες] Galileans?" (Acts 2:7); "And how is it that we hear, each of us, in our own native language?" (Acts 2:8); "In our own languages [ταῖς ἡμετέραις γλώσσαις] we hear them speaking about God's deeds of power" (Acts 2:11). Clearly, then, Luke wants to connect the visual phenomenon of the tongues of fire with foreign languages. The international emphasis is further clarified by the so-called Table of Nations introduced, somewhat abruptly, into Acts 2:9-11. There has thus been a progression in Acts 2:1-11. The visual tongues are *described*. Then some explanation is given as to their meaning: they refer to foreign languages. This *itself* is then explained as a declaration of God's powerful deeds of salvation for all the nations. For what those from the many nations assembled at Jerusalem hear are τὰ μεγαλεῖα τοῦ θεοῦ: the great deeds of God. As C. K. Barrett has shown, the phrase refers to the deeds of God's salvation for his people.[18] The coming of the Holy Spirit, who empowers the disciples for witness, is the great inaugural act that commences God's eschatological day of salvation for all the nations.

We should add that there is a proleptic element in this section, a looking toward the future. For, while certainly there are people from "all" the nations gathered at Jerusalem on that day of Pentecost, nevertheless they are all *Jews*. However, with the mention of so many nations and the remainder of the Gentile mission described in Acts, it is difficult not to conclude that Luke is anticipating salvation for those who do not belong to Israel.[19] There is double-level meaning here: while Peter and the disciples can only see Jews as the object of God's eschatological deliverance, the readers of Acts can see a prefiguring of salvation for the Gentiles.

THE SPEECH OF STEPHEN (ACTS 7:1-53)

This is the longest speech in Acts, and, in some ways, the strangest. The reason for this is that the speech does not seem to address the issue at hand.

---

[18]C. K. Barrett, *The Acts of the Apostles*, ICC (London: T&T Clark, 1994–1998), 1:124. He cites the following passages: Deut 11:2; Pss 70:19; 104:1; 105:21. From the Dead Sea Scrolls, 1QS 1.21.

[19]See esp. Keener, *Acts*, 1:834.

Stephen is accused of speaking against the temple and the law (Acts 6:11-14). Yet, he appears never to counter these charges directly. Rather, almost the entire speech is given to a rehearsal of Israel's history. Only at the end does Stephen confront his audience, accusing them of gross disobedience and murder. But *confrontation* appears to be precisely what is not called for; rather, we would expect an apologia, a defense against serious charges that Luke informs the reader were false (Acts 6:13). In short, the speech does not appear to fit the situation.

Scholars have responded to this anomaly in various ways. Ernst Haenchen held that the speech was originally independent and that Luke forced it into the context.[20] Barrett, although not believing that the speech was originally delivered in a trial, nevertheless thought that it reflects the views of Diaspora Jews such as Stephen.[21] Bruce held that Luke preserved the extemporaneous nature of the speech, which would explain why it does not seem to counter the charges with the precision we would expect.[22] Todd Penner believes that the speech is an invention of Luke that is actually an invective against Stephen's opponents and as such does not address the charges in the narrative.[23] Craig Keener believes that the speech does actually respond to the charges—but by using "the conventional rhetorical technique of returning their charges against them."[24] So there is an adequate response, Keener suggests, but not in the way modern readers might have expected.

All of the suggestions above are possible, although Haenchen's seems the least likely. Keener's proposal may be the most plausible; but the fact that the putting of the charges on the heads of the enemies does not come until the very end of the speech causes some hesitation. Perhaps it may be better to say that although the speech contains an

---

[20]Ernst Haenchen, *The Acts of the Apostles: A Commentary*, trans. R. M. Wilson (Philadelphia: Westminster, 1971), 286-89.

[21]Barrett, *Acts*, 1:339.

[22]Bruce, *Book of the Acts*, 167.

[23]Todd Penner, *In Praise of Christian Origins: Stephen and the Hellenists in Lukan Apologetic Historiography* (New York: T&T Clark, 2004), 262-330. Although there is much with which I disagree in this work, it is one of the most learned monographs on the speech of Stephen and the surrounding historical, rhetorical and ideological questions.

[24]Keener, *Acts*, 2:1329, 1332-34.

element of the counteraccusation genre, it does not belong cleanly to any one rhetorical type.

To sum up, the suggestions of scholars like Haenchen, who opines that the speech does not at all respond to the charges and is therefore inauthentic, are not well founded.[25] The speech, as we shall see below, does respond to the accusations, although this is done with subtlety. Nevertheless, ancient hearers probably would have picked up on this, as the strategy of counteraccusation was well known. The other strategy used in the speech—namely, the use of a summary of Israelite history to confront an audience—appears in both Old Testament texts and Second Temple literature.[26] It is now time to look at Stephen's response in more detail.

The speech. In his speech Stephen puts forth three main points as answers to his accusers. The arguments are interwoven and often made concurrently. For the sake of clarity I put them in the following order.

1. Stephen argues that some of the most important figures in Israel's history were not permanent residents in the Promised Land. Abraham, although the "father" of the nation (Acts 7:2) and the recipient of the great covenants (Acts 7:3, 6-8), nevertheless had no inheritance in the land to enjoy personally. In fact, he possessed "not even a foot's length" (Acts 7:5). Joseph was used mightily by God—*in Egypt.* Although he was in Egypt, "God was with him" (Acts 7:9; cf. Gen 39:2, 21, 23). God's presence with him triggered the blessings he received: deliverance, favor before Pharaoh, rule over Egypt (Acts 7:10-11). Here was a godly man who was blessed and used by God *outside* the Promised Land.

2. Stephen argues that God cannot be tied to Jerusalem and the temple. This emerges clearly in Acts 7:48-50. After saying that it was Solomon, not David, who built a house for God, Stephen immediately adds: "Yet the Most High does not dwell in houses made with human hands." This is followed with a quotation from the powerful passage of Isaiah 66:1-2:

> Heaven is my throne,
> and the earth is my footstool.

---

[25]For other scholars with similar views along with a competent refutation, see Martin H. Scharlemann, *Stephen: A Singular Saint,* AnBib 34 (Rome: Pontifical Biblical Institute, 1968), 6-7, 22-30.

[26]E.g., Josh 24:1-15; 1 Sam 12:1-18; 4 *Ezra* 3:1-36; Judith 5:6-19 (I owe these last two references to Keener).

What kind of house will you build for me, says the Lord,
or what is the place of my rest?
Did not my hand make all these things?

With this point and the previous, therefore, Stephen is "answering" the temple accusation. He is basically confessing: "This is what I have been saying about the temple. The temple cannot be used as an amulet to control God's presence. God cannot be tethered to the Jerusalem temple. In fact, I am in the company of the prophets in affirming this."

3. Stephen argues that the Sanhedrin does not possess the moral integrity to judge him. He advances this point by demonstrating from Scripture that the majority of Jews throughout their history have mistreated God's messengers. Stephen shows this in a particularly powerful way with reference to Moses in Acts 7:20-43. Moses was "pleasing" before God (Acts 7:20, my translation); he was educated in the ancient and venerable wisdom of the Egyptians (Acts 7:22); he was mighty in word and deed (Acts 7:22); he received a special call to rescue God's people (Acts 7:25); in fact, he had a unique vision of God and attendant call (Acts 7:30-35). With all of this Stephen's audience would have heartily agreed. And yet, Stephen will now point out that their fathers rejected this very man Moses! The emotion reaches a climax in Acts 7:35: It was *this* Moses (τοῦτον τὸν Μωϋσην) whom they rejected. *This* (οὗτος) Moses whom God had sent as liberator (Acts 7:35b). *This* (οὗτος) Moses who led them out of Egypt with wonders and signs (Acts 7:36). *This* (οὗτος) Moses who promised the raising of a future prophet of God (Acts 7:37). *This* (οὗτος) Moses who spoke with the angel of the Lord and received the living oracles (λόγια ζῶντα) of God (Acts 7:38). And yet, it was this same Moses to whom the fathers refused obedience; instead they "pushed him aside, and in their hearts they turned back to Egypt" (Acts 7:39). But does this apply to Stephen's present audience? Yes, says Stephen, for now they even murdered Jesus: "You stiff-necked people, uncircumcised in heart and ears, you are forever opposing the Holy Spirit, just as your ancestors used to do. Which of the prophets did your ancestors not persecute? They killed those who foretold the coming of the Righteous One,

and now you [νῦν ὑμεῖς] have become his betrayers and murderers" (Acts 7:51-52).

In this final point of the speech, therefore, Stephen has taken an offensive rather than defensive approach. His basic thesis is that they have never properly heard the Lord. How, then, could they be trusted in determining the truthfulness of Stephen's preaching? The argument is ad hominem. Stephen basically tells them that they are spiritually blind. He is saying: "You have no right to judge me. You have shown yourselves to be murderers, just like your fathers. You are not worthy of a straightforward defense. You would not understand it, for you are blind!" Stephen is consequently martyred.

Theological reflections. *A christological historiography.* Why did Luke grant so much space to the speech of Stephen? Scholars of Acts have long been preoccupied with this. Whatever our ultimate answer, if length of speech is a clue to those things that are important to Luke, then it is fair to say that the speech is of great value to him. This is all the more reason to get at the meaning of this speech. But discovering what Luke is doing with the speech has turned out to be puzzling. Why, in this the longest speech, is there no talk about Christ, salvation or missions? Is this not what Acts is supposed to be about? Yet, considerable space is given to a speech that appears to be nothing more than a survey of Old Testament history! What is going on here?

I suggest that one of the reasons why Luke devotes so much space to the speech of Stephen is that it represented the understanding of Scripture of the early Christians. Specifically, he wanted to put before his readers how the early Christians demonstrated through Scripture the sad tendency of Israel's leaders to disobey God's word. Historically, this manner of arguing did not emerge in a vacuum; it grew and developed and was honed in the context of apologetics with the Jewish synagogue. While fundamentally stemming from Jesus himself (Lk 24:44-50), it was refined in argument with unbelieving Jews.[27] The key to this approach to Scripture was whether it showed Jesus to be the fulfillment of Scripture or not. The

---

[27]See Justin Martyr's *Dialogue with Trypho* for an excellent example.

unbelieving Jews said no; the Christians said yes. And this yes is seen in the rest of the New Testament documents with their presentation of Jesus as the promised Christ. Whether it be Matthew with his fulfillment formulas, or Paul with his arguments showing that the crucified was the Messiah, or Hebrews with its typology, the New Testament documents represent at a macro level what Stephen is doing at a micro level. In a word, it was incumbent on Luke to demonstrate to Theophilus that the Christian reading of Scripture was the best one. And the reason it was the best one is that it showed how the Scriptures of Israel truly found their ultimate goal, telos, in Jesus of Nazareth, the one who had been raised, as the apostles had witnessed.

To say, therefore, that the speech of Stephen is *merely* a recapitulation of the Old Testament ignores the christological framework of the early Christians' reading of the Old Testament. In other words, to read the Scriptures was *necessarily* a christological exercise, for God was moving the sacred history of Israel—recorded in the Scriptures—to be fulfilled in Jesus Christ. Without Jesus Christ the Old Testament was like a story with no ending. This hermeneutic, itself already profoundly theological, was seen in Peter's Pentecost address, applied particularly to the resurrection, and will resurface in Paul's speech at Pisidia Antioch. It is also present in the speech of Stephen. Consequently, although the speech concentrates on Moses, one of its main points is christological. Stephen passionately argues that in the same way that Moses and the prophets were rejected, so now the Jews have rejected Jesus. *With the conviction that God so ordained history that the fate of the prophets (Moses being the main one) would be repeated in the Righteous One* (Acts 7:52), Stephen leads his readers to conclude that Jesus is the Messiah. Like Moses and the prophets, he too has been rejected and killed. This is the divine pattern, which can only happen if God is in control of history.[28]

---

[28]This has significant repercussions for how we read the Old and New Testament and our assessment of their unity. Richard Hays helpfully states: "The one Lord confessed in Israel's *Shema* is the same God actively at work in the death and resurrection of Jesus Christ. Apart from the truth of that claim, any talk of the unity of the OT and the NT is simply nonsense. There is only one reason why christological interpretation of the OT is not a matter of stealing or twisting Israel's sacred texts: the God to whom the Gospels bear witness, the God incarnate in Jesus, is the same as the God of Abraham, Isaac and Jacob.

To sum up, the long recapitulation of the Old Testament in the speech of Stephen has, among other things, a christological aim. The purpose is to show the readers that the Jews' rejection of Jesus (and Stephen!), far from negating his messianic status, actually confirms it. For it is part of a sovereign pattern, so ordered by God himself (Acts 2:23), that God's righteous servants be rejected by their people. This reaches a climax in Jesus, thereby simultaneously showing the guilt of the people as well as the messianic identity of Jesus. The speech is given so much space because this is the way that Luke wishes his readers to interpret the Old Testament—for so the great pillars of the early church did.

The decentralization of Jerusalem. Both the content of the speech of Stephen as well as the result from it indicate movement away from Jerusalem and hence Judaism. As to what Stephen says, the statement in Acts 7:48 coupled with the quotation of Isaiah 66:1-2 show that the temple does not have—and never had—an absolute claim on God's presence. Stephen is not criticizing the temple per se, but rather, in prophetic tradition, attacking the belief that God could be somehow roped to the temple.[29] God can be encountered anywhere, just as Abraham experienced in Mesopotamia (Acts 7:2) and Joseph in Egypt (Acts 7:9). Therefore the central theme of salvation beyond (but *from!*) Jerusalem is once again highlighted by Luke.

This transition of the locus of God's blessing from Jerusalem to all the nations is also communicated in the *result* of the Stephen speech. The speech cost Stephen his life (Acts 7:54-60); it also triggered persecution

---

Either that is true, or it is not" (*Reading Backwards: Figural Christology and the Fourfold Gospel Witness* [Waco, TX: Baylor University Press, 2014], 109).

[29]Contrast Penner, *In Praise of Christian Origins*, 308-18, who sees Luke as presenting a totally negative view of the Solomonic temple. According to Penner, David followed the Mosaic pattern in the tent of worship, but Solomon did not. Solomon's "devolution" of the original pattern was not sanctioned by God: "That the building of the temple for all intents and purposes is referred to as an act of idolatry seems fairly evident from the context" (316). Actually, Luke's conception of the temple is much more nuanced. To be sure, in view of Jesus' foretelling of the temple's destruction (Lk 21:5-9), the reader knows that it will not be permanent. Yet, the disciples initially attend the temple (Acts 2:46), pray at the temple (Acts 3:1) and continually meet at the temple (Acts 5:12). Paul accompanied into the temple men who had taken a Nazirite vow and paid for their expenses (Acts 21:22-26). Steve Walton's suggestion that the temple is presented as a place of transition from centralized to global worship seems to me to be persuasive ("A Tale of Two Perspectives? The Place of the Temple in Acts," in *Heaven on Earth: The Temple in Biblical Theology,* ed. T. D. Alexander and S. J. Gathercole [Carlisle, UK: Paternoster, 2004], 135-49).

on the church: "That day a severe persecution began against the church in Jerusalem, and all except the apostles were scattered throughout the countryside of Judea and Samaria" (Acts 8:1). The persecution caused by the speech of Stephen, however, was used by God to move the preaching of the word to other ethnic groups, this time by means of Philip, another one of the Seven. Keener states it well:

> Thus, having focused on Stephen in 6:8–7:60, Luke now turns to the second of the seven ministers he listed in 6:5, showing how Philip took the gospel across cultural and ethnic boundaries. If Stephen taught that God was not bound to the sacred land or the temple, Philip now implements the vision by evangelizing Samaritans and the first fully Gentile convert, an African official.[30]

What was found in proleptic fashion in the Pentecost event is now shown in concrete form. The gospel is going from Jerusalem to Samaria and as far as Africa. The speech event of Stephen is the beginning of this transition. Through it Luke shows the truth that the gospel is being rejected by many Jews and accepted more and more among the Gentiles. In fact, the aggressive attitude shown by the leaders of Jerusalem will be repeated, as others, mainly Paul, preach to Jews across the Mediterranean. Although, to be sure, the gospel finds a home in Jews of diverse places (e.g., Acts 14:1; 17:12; 20:24), the tendency becomes clear that the bulk of the people of God is no longer found in ethnic Israel.

THE SPEECH AT THE HOME OF CORNELIUS (ACTS 10:34-48)

The events surrounding the conversion of this Roman centurion were of such importance to Luke that he dedicates the modern equivalent of almost two chapters to it. If one wants to know what is important theologically for Luke, then surely the Cornelius episode is one place to search! The message of the episode is very clear, as it is repeated several times in Acts 10–11. "The circumcised believers who had come with Peter were astounded *that the gift of the Holy Spirit had been poured out even on the Gentiles*" (Acts 10:45); "Then Peter said, 'Can anyone withhold the water for

---

[30]Keener, *Acts*, 2:1464.

baptizing *these people who have received the Holy Spirit just as we have?'"* (Acts 10:46-47); "the Holy Spirit fell upon them *just as it had upon us at the beginning"* (Acts 11:15); "if then *God gave them the same gift that he gave us when we believed in the Lord Jesus Christ,* who was I that I could hinder God?" (Acts 11:17); "Then God has given even to the Gentiles the repentance that leads to life" (Acts 11:18). Three different voices in the narrative make the affirmations above: the narrator, Peter, and the apostles and brothers from Judea. Luke certainly wants these words to be carved in the readers' minds. And what is the message? Uncircumcised Gentiles have received the Holy Spirit by faith in Jesus Christ and therefore are in equal standing as the Jewish believers.[31] All these key concepts concerning salvation are intertwined. If we were to disentangle them, we could speak of (1) theodicy (Acts 10:34-35), (2) Christology (Acts 10:36-43) and (3) pneumatology (Acts 10:44-48).[32]

The speech. A helpful way to proceed with the speech is in commentary fashion, highlighting the principal portions. Once this is completed I will put forth some theological reflections.

- *Acts 10:33 Therefore I sent for you immediately, and you have been kind enough to come. So now all of us are here in the presence of God to listen to all that the Lord has commanded you to say.* These words of Cornelius are a beautiful setup for the speech of Peter. They tell the readers that what they are about to hear from the mouth of Peter is a message from God, and therefore authoritative.[33]

- *Acts 10:34 Then Peter began to speak to them.* This rendering of the NRSV obscures Luke's point at the beginning of Peter's speech. The Greek text should be translated: "And having opened his mouth, Peter said."[34] The statement adds a sense of solemnity to the scene,

---

[31]Cornelius is not a proselyte—that is, a Gentile who had submitted to circumcision in obedience to Torah (and so no longer a Gentile). Luke uses the phrase εὐσεβὴς καὶ φοβούμενος τὸν θεὸν (cf. Acts 13:16, 26), which refers to Gentiles who were favorable to Judaism but were not proselytes. See the same arguments of Barrett, *Acts,* 1:499-501. We will come back to this important point under "Theological Reflections" at the end of this section.

[32]Marguerat, *Les Actes des Apôtres,* 388, speaks of two concentrations in the text: Christology and universality.

[33]On this see our previous examination of Peter's speech in Acts 2 earlier in this chapter.

[34]ἀνοίξας δὲ Πέτρος τὸ στόμα εἶπεν.

suggesting that what is about to be said is of grave importance.[35]

I truly understand that God shows no partiality. An interesting term is employed here: προσωπολήμπτης. The term occurs only here in the entire Greek Bible, and it means "to raise up the face" and hence "to show favor."[36] It is a common concept in the Old Testament that God shows no favoritism (e.g., Deut 10:17; 2 Chron 19:7). As Barrett indicates, the concept is taken up in the New Testament and used in a negative fashion—that is, "to show favour *unfairly*."[37] Peter begins the sermon with this reflection and thereby introduces the theme of salvation under the category of theodicy. His point is that in judgment God does not take into account a person's race. This was important in the face of some strands of Judaism that believed that descent from Abraham would be meritorious in final judgment. Luke, through Peter, says no; even an uncircumcised Roman soldier like Cornelius is acceptable if he fears God and does justice.[38] It should be clear that Luke is not saying that there is salvific action in this. If that were the case, why would Peter be sent to preach to Cornelius in the first place? It is through belief in Jesus that salvation is received. Therefore, after this initial reflection, Peter jumps right into the kerygma.

• *Acts 10:36 You know the message he sent to the people of Israel, preaching peace by Jesus Christ.* The subject of the first clause of this verse is God. He sends the "message" (λόγος) to the children of Israel.[39] This message is clarified as "preaching peace" (εὐαγγελιζόμενος εἰρήνην). This phrase

---

[35]See also Marion Soards, *The Speeches in Acts: Their Content, Context, and Concerns* (Louisville, KY: Westminster John Knox, 1994), 72.

[36]The cognates προσωπολημπτέω and προσωπολημψία are found in James (Jas 2:1, 9) and Paul (Rom 2:11; Eph 6:9; Col 3:25).

[37]Barrett, *Acts*, 1:519; emphasis added.

[38]The acts of justice envisioned by Luke refer back to Acts 10:2—namely, prayer and almsgiving. Both of these are characteristic Jewish acts of piety. On prayer, see the tractate *mishnah Berakoth*. On giving to the poor, see *mishnah Peah* 8.7 with comments by David Instone-Brewer, *Prayer and Agriculture* in *Traditions of the Rabbis from the Era of the New Testament* (Grand Rapids: Eerdmans, 2004), 1:158-61. It is probable that Cornelius gave to a Jewish poor fund that distributed meals, etc., to the poor. On prayer and almsgiving together, see Tobit 12:8.

[39]On λόγος as used in Acts to refer to the message of salvation, see A. J. Thompson, *The Acts of the Risen Lord Jesus: Luke's Account of God's Unfolding Plan*, NSBT 27 (Downers Grove, IL: InterVarsity Press, 2011), 100-101. "Children of Israel" is an intertextual echo of Pss 107:20; 147:18-19 (LXX 147:7-8).

is a clear echo of Isaiah 52:7: "How beautiful upon the mountains are the feet of the messenger who announces peace [εὐαγγελιζομένου . . . εἰρήνης], who brings good news [εὐαγγελιζόμενος ἀγαθά]." The instrument of this proclamation, Luke clarifies, is Jesus Christ. Jesus is thus presented as the proclaimer of eschatological peace to Israel.[40] In a powerful aside, Peter fuses Jesus the servant with "the Lord of all" (οὗτός ἐστιν πάντων κύριος).[41] The phrase resonates with Old Testament statements about God's rule and sovereignty over all the earth.[42] In this context of Gentile inclusion, it emphasizes that Jesus Christ is the Lord also of non-Jews.[43]

- *Acts 10:37-39 That message spread throughout Judea, beginning in Galilee after the baptism that John announced. . . .* Peter now moves to a brief narration of the work of Jesus culminating in his crucifixion. It is essentially an outline of the Gospel of Luke. Jesus is presented as one whom God anointed with the Holy Spirit (Lk 3:22; 4:18-21). As a result of this,[44] he went around "doing good and healing all who were oppressed by the devil." By linking the unction of the Spirit with his deliverance of those oppressed by Satan, Luke is clearly thinking of Isaiah 61:1. Again, Jesus is related to the Isaianic Servant. Despite his acts of benevolence, nevertheless, Jesus was killed by being hung on a tree.

- *Acts 10:40-42 But God raised him on the third day. . . .* As has been the case in other examples of kerygmatic preaching (e.g., Acts 2:24; 3:15; 4:10; 5:30), so here the resurrection of Christ is highlighted. The unique part here is the expression "on the third day." There follows a statement of proof: " . . . and allowed him to appear, not to all the people but to us who were chosen by God as witnesses, and who ate and drank with him after he rose from the dead." The terminology employed opens up a court or judicial context.[45] The apostles along with their close companions

---

[40]Paul uses the same passage from Isaiah to refer to preachers of the gospel (Rom 10:15).

[41]Or this may be Luke's parenthetical aside, similar to Acts 1:18-19.

[42]See Keener, *Acts*, 2:1800.

[43]Thus also Jervell, *Die Apostelgeschichte*, 311.

[44]This is not explicit, but is probably what Luke means.

[45]ἔδωκεν αὐτὸν ἐμφανῆ γενέσθαι is quite similar to ἔσασθαι ἐμφανῆ τῷ Σαραπίωνος ἀρχιδικαστοῦ βήματι of Papyrus Oxyrhynchus II.260 (dated c.a. 59 CE), translated by the editors as "I will appear at the court of

witnessed the resurrected Jesus; in fact, they ate and drank with him after the resurrection. Therefore they are now witnesses *for* the resurrection of Jesus, a duty to which they were commanded (Acts 10:42).

- *Acts 10:43 All the prophets testify about him that everyone who believes in him receives forgiveness of sins through his name.* The apostles are not the only ones who testify on behalf of Jesus: the prophets (shorthand for all of Scripture) also bear witness. As we have said previously in this chapter, the proof of the kerygma in Acts is always a combination of witnessing the risen Jesus (the ocular) and scriptural interpretation (the scholastic). What is it that the prophets testify to? It is forgiveness of sins to "everyone who believes . . . through his name." The phrase is almost identical to Paul's preaching as recorded in Acts 13:39 and to the statement of the risen Jesus to Paul in Acts 26:18.[46] Surely the use of such a phrase in the preaching of the gospel is part of the earliest tradition of the kerygma.[47] Thus Peter declares that *everyone*—Jew and Gentile—can be forgiven by belief in Jesus Christ. This was good news indeed to his Gentile audience! Even while Peter is still speaking they have believed in their hearts. This is shown by their speaking in tongues, which is proof that they have received the Holy Spirit and are therefore saved and part of the people of God. Consequently, they are baptized (Acts 10:44-48).

Theological reflections. The main theological point of this speech is, of course, Gentile inclusion: Gentiles can be saved and thus become full citizens in the people of God by faith in Christ without needing to become Jews first. There are other themes, on which we reflect below.

The gospel comes from Jerusalem. In truth, the first Gentile convert recorded in Acts was not Cornelius but the Ethiopian eunuch (Acts 8:26-40).

---

the chief justice Serapion" (MM, 208). For the expression in the classical period, which is often used with τεκμήριον (Acts 1:3) see LSJ, 1768. Along with the term μάρτυσιν of Acts 10:41, the context is certainly judicial.

[46]Acts 13:38-39: διὰ τούτου ὑμῖν ἄφεσις ἁμαρτιῶν καταγγέλεται . . . ἐν τούτῳ πᾶς ὁ πιστεύων δικαιοῦται. Acts 26:18: τοῦ λαβεῖν αὐτοὺς ἄφεσιν ἁμαρτιῶν . . . πίστει τῇ εἰς ἐμέ.

[47]See especially G. Stanton, *Jesus of Nazareth in New Testament Preaching*, SNTSMS 27 (Cambridge: Cambridge University Press, 1974), 67-85, with particular attention to the use of Scripture in the speech of Cornelius.

Yet, when we ask Bible readers who the first Gentile was to convert to Christianity, usually the answer is Cornelius. This means that Luke has done his work well! The beautiful narrative of Cornelius's conversion along with the repetition in Acts 11 has grabbed our attention so powerfully that this seems as the first Gentile conversion. If, in fact, Cornelius was the *second* Gentile convert, why has Luke crowned this narrative as epoch-making? I suggest the following: although the Ethiopian eunuch was the first Gentile convert, his messenger was Philip. In the case of Cornelius, it was Peter; that was Philip, this is *Peter*! That is to say, in order for the early church to accept such a momentous step—namely, forgiveness of sins solely through belief in Jesus and not the observance of Torah—it was necessary that the principal apostle would vouchsafe for its truth.[48] If Peter, himself an observant Jew (Acts 10:9-15!) and the *vox* of the apostles, testified that Gentiles were saved by faith in Christ alone, then it should be accepted by the mother church in Jerusalem. Although a faction within that church still resisted (cf. Acts 15:1-5), Luke wanted Theophilus and his readers to see that Gentile conversion was legitimate, since the chief apostle had put his stamp of approval on it.

Peter and Paul preach the same gospel. One of the most interesting things to observe in this passage is how much like Paul Peter sounds. To be sure, this was to be expected to a certain extent, since ancient historians would summarize speeches using their own words (see previous chapter). Yet, the closeness of vocabulary does stand out. Both of the apostles were one in the following: (1) forgiveness is on the basis of Jesus Christ, who was crucified and raised; (2) the Scriptures bear witness to this; (3) *all* can be saved by belief in Jesus. The apostle to the Jews and the apostle to the Gentiles preach to all, everywhere, that salvation is given by God, through belief, on the basis of Jesus, who was crucified and raised: "There is salvation in no one else, for there is no other name under heaven given among mortals by which we must be saved" (Acts 4:12). Luke saturates his audience with this kerygma, encouraging them to believe that this is how it was and hence how it should be.

---

[48]See similarly with the Samaritans in Acts 8:14-25.

Cornelius and "anonymous faith." The concept of the "anonymous Christian" or "anonymous faith" was generated and developed with considerable power by Karl Rahner.[49] Rahner suggests that even without conscious reflection of the work of Christ, certain individuals can be saved. He states: "We are theologically justified in our definition of saving faith if we take into consideration that the teaching of the Church allows a man a chance of being saved as long as he does not grievously offend his conscience by his actions, even if he does not come in the course of his life to an explicit acceptance of the Christian message in faith."[50] Rahner adds the dynamic of "searching after the true God" into his formulation. Nevertheless, in the final analysis this does not negate the possibility of true salvation. Thus he says, "There can exist 'anonymous faith' which carries with it an intrinsic dynamism and therefore an obligation to find full realisation in explicit faith, but which is nonetheless sufficient for salvation even if a man does not achieve this fulfilment during his lifetime, as long as he is not to blame for this."[51] Is Cornelius, prior to his encounter with Peter, an example of this?

Although not explicitly drawing on Rahner, Clark Pinnock has seen in the story of Cornelius something very similar to the anonymous Christian. Recall that even before Peter preaches to Cornelius, the text indicates that he was "a devout man who feared God" (Acts 10:2). For Pinnock, therefore, "Cornelius is the pagan saint *par excellence* of the New Testament, a believer in God before he became a Christian."[52] Like Rahner, Pinnock says that salvation rests ontologically on the work of Christ even if existentially the individual is unconscious of this work. In the case of Cornelius, Pinnock makes the analogy with Old Testament saints, whom he believes were saved by the "faith principle"—namely, fearing God and working

---

[49] Among many of his writings, I have found his explanation of the concept to be particularly clear in Karl Rahner, "Anonymous and Explicit Faith," in *Theological Investigations* (New York: Crossroad, 1979), 16:52-60.
[50] Ibid., 53.
[51] Ibid., 54. See further the explanation of the concept by J. H. Fletcher, "Rahner and Religious Diversity," in *The Cambridge Companion to Karl Rahner*, ed. D. Marmion and M. E. Hines (Cambridge: Cambridge University Press, 2005), 235-48.
[52] Clark Pinnock, *A Wideness in God's Mercy: The Finality of Jesus Christ in a World of Religions* (Grand Rapids: Zondervan, 1992), 165.

righteousness.[53] Cornelius, according to Pinnock, provides the strongest support for the inclusivist view of the unevangelized. Similarly, John Sanders argues that Cornelius is a great example of inclusivism: "I believe it would be better to understand the text as indicating that Cornelius was 'saved' in the modern evangelical sense before Peter arrived and that he received salvation in its *fullness* when he heard about Jesus."[54]

The concept of anonymous faith is a very difficult subject that demands profound reflection in areas of philosophy and theology such as ontology, determinism, freedom, eschatology and more. Clearly, we cannot do justice to the topic here. However, we can ask whether Cornelius can in fact serve as support for inclusivism. And in my opinion the answer is no.

A reading of this passage that is not attuned to the relations between Jews and Gentiles in the New Testament period can lead to an overestimation of Cornelius. The modern reader hears phrases such as "a devout man who feared God" and "he gave alms generously to the people and prayed constantly to God" (Acts 10:2) and the words of the angel, "Your prayers and your alms have ascended as a memorial before God" (Acts 10:4), and can think of Cornelius as a saint. To be sure, Luke does show a high estimation of Cornelius; *but the language he uses was common language for God-fearers.*

In the context of Jewish-Gentile relations, there were probably two designations for Gentiles who sought the God of Israel: proselytes and God-fearers.[55] The former were those Gentiles who not only expressed admiration for Jewish things but went ahead and (in the case of males) submitted to circumcision and thereby a commitment to obey Torah.[56] Luke uses the term προσήλυτος at Acts 2:11; 6:5; 13:43 to refer to these. The God-fearers (or

---

[53]Ibid., 98. For an excellent explanation of this aspect of Pinnock (and much more), see Daniel Strange, *The Possibility of Salvation Among the Unevangelised: An Analysis of Inclusivism in Recent Evangelical Theology* (Carlisle, UK: Paternoster, 2001), 109-36.

[54]John Sanders, *No Other Name: An Investigation into the Destiny of the Unevangelized* (Grand Rapids: Eerdmans, 1992), 66.

[55]Shaye J. D. Cohen, *The Beginnings of Jewishness: Boundaries, Varieties, Uncertainties* (Berkeley: University of California Press, 1999), avoids dependence on particular terms and instead classifies "seven forms of behavior by which a gentile demonstrates respect or affection for Judaism" (140).

[56]This is category 7 in Cohen's classification (156-62).

better, "venerators of God"[57]) did not commit as far as circumcision. They could straddle a number of categories, such as friendliness to Jews, practice of some Jewish rituals and veneration of the Jewish God.[58] The terminology used of them by some Jews could be very positive. For example, the Aphrodisias inscription, which lumps together venerators of God with Jews and proselytes, speaks of them as θεοσεβής ("God-fearer," "God-venerator") and includes them with those who παντευλογων, "those who wholly praise (the Lord)" or "those who constantly recite benedictions."[59] Intriguingly, in the text of Acts Cornelius is called εὐσεβής; of his actions he is said to "pray to God constantly" (δεόμενος τοῦ θεοῦ διὰ παντός). J. Reynolds and R. Tannenbaum suggest that the participle παντευλογων in the Aphrodisias inscription "could be an equivalent of διὰ παντός."[60] The venerators of God thus in some sense were attached to the synagogue, prayed to God and generally were pious. Cornelius was such a venerator of God.

If the analysis above is correct, there emerge two details about Cornelius that challenge the views of Pinnock and Sanders. First, as a venerator of God (and not a proselyte), he had not submitted to circumcision. If Cornelius was as devoted as Pinnock and Sanders make him out to be, one would think that he would follow the core command of circumcision (see Gen 17). By not submitting to circumcision, Cornelius was breaking a fundamental command of the Old Testament! Second, Luke notes that Cornelius was a centurion in the Italian cohort (Acts 10:1). As Irina Levinskaya has noted, being a Roman official demanded certain duties of Cornelius: "Because of his official duties and despite his belief in one God, [he] has to demonstrate publicly his polytheism."[61] He had to worship the Roman gods publicly in order to maintain his position. Levinskaya is thus blunt: "He is an idolater, participating in offerings to pagan gods."[62] Pinnock's portrait of Cornelius as an Old Testament saint looks more and more

---

[57]The phrase is Cohen's.

[58]Cohen's categories 3-5. For the last one Cohen adds "denying or ignoring all other gods" (171). I have left this phrase out because I am not convinced that venerators of God were not syncretists. See above.

[59]This translation is from J. Reynolds and R. Tannenbaum, *Jews and Godfearers at Aphrodisias: Greek Inscriptions with Commentary* (Cambridge: Cambridge University Press, 1987), 35-36.

[60]Ibid., 35.

[61]Irina Levinskaya, *The Book of Acts in Its Diaspora Setting* (Grand Rapids: Eerdmans, 1996), 121.

[62]Ibid.

deformed. In fact, only at the expense of shoddy or no historical work at all can one say that Cornelius was a saint or that he was already saved. The ancient reader of Acts, on the other hand, despite the positive comments of Luke, would have understood the dynamics of a God-venerator like Cornelius. The reader would have understood that although Cornelius did some good things, he nevertheless was an idolater who needed to hear the gospel of Christ to be saved.[63] The portrait of Cornelius as an Old Testament saint is thus no more than a caricature.

THE SPEECH AT ATHENS (ACTS 17:16-31)

This is one of the most famous speeches in the Acts of the Apostles. As such, it has been the object of mountainous research.[64] Our focus here is on the theology that Luke is communicating through the speech. In order to have a better understanding of this, it is as necessary to study the narrative framework of the speech as the speech itself.

Two important observations need to be made about the narrative portion of this section. First, we need to pay attention to the narrative characterization of Athens by Luke. He accomplishes this both directly and indirectly. Directly, by using the verb παροξύνω in Acts 17:16 Luke is focalizing on Paul by describing his inner feelings. He does this to allow us to see his reaction to the city of Athens. As Paul waits for Silas and Timothy, the narrator tells us that Paul's spirit "was deeply distressed." The verb παροξύνω is tricky to translate. While it may communicate a sense of disappointment on the person who undergoes the emotion, there is a question on whether this disappointment is accompanied by pity or by anger. Thus Richard Pervo states that in Acts 17:16 the verb could mean "anger or pity for the failings of polytheism."[65] Jervell is more certain when

---

[63] I find it interesting that Petronius, who did not obey Caligula's mandate to erect a statue in the temple, is described by Philo as possessing εὐσεβείας due in part perhaps to previous Jewish learning. But Petronius was certainly a pagan! (*Embassy to Gaius* 245). Luke's description of Cornelius is similar.

[64] Although a bit dated now, Bertil Gärtner, *The Areopagus Speech and Natural Revelation*, ASNU 21 (Lund: Gleerup, 1955), 37-44, is still a good place to start on the history of research. Two recent and thoughtful articles are C. Kavin Rowe, "The Grammar of Life: The Areopagus Speech and Pagan Tradition," *NTS* 57 (2011): 31-50; Joshua Jipp, "Paul's Areopagus Speech of Acts 17:16-34 as *Both* Critique and Propaganda," *JBL* 131 (2012): 567-88.

[65] Richard Pervo, *Acts: A Commentary*, Hermeneia (Minneapolis: Fortress, 2009), 436.

he says that "Paul is seized with wrath."[66] The verb is used in Isaiah 63:10 to explain God's feeling toward the idolatry of his people. The πνεῦμα of Yahweh is "grieved" or "upset." It is probably the case that Paul feels both a sense of indignant anger as he sees the image of God deformed by idols, and mercy as he views the Athenians' ignorance. This description of Paul's feelings toward the idolatry of Athens will guide the reader in the assessment of the introduction of the speech, particularly Paul's use of δεισιδαίμων in Acts 17:22. It is with this in view that we approach the use of the superlative in Acts 17:22. Although this verse is part of the speech proper, it is so important to understand Luke's strategy that we may comment ahead.

The term δεισιδαίμων can have the positive sense of "pious" or "religious" (LSJ, 375); but it is often used negatively of those who go to ridiculous lengths to obtain protection (or to avoid punishment) from the gods. In this sense the term can be translated as "superstitious."[67]

So what is Paul's sense here? Is he congratulating the Athenians on their *pietas*? Or does he come out firing from the beginning, calling them a superstitious bunch? It is probably the case, as often happens in Acts, that we are dealing with double-layered meaning, dramatic irony. At the level of the historical event, given that Paul is delivering an apologia (as we shall see below, Paul is on some sort of trial), it is probable that the term is not meant to be heard as an outright indictment. The rhetorical strategy of *insinuatio* is recommended to a speaker when facing a critical audience.[68] The *reader* of Acts, on the other hand, knowing how Paul feels about Athenian religiosity from Acts 17:16 (it is idolatry!) hears in the term the negative sense of "superstitious." A possible praise in the historical moment

---

[66]Jervell, *Die Apostelgeschichte*, 443: "Paulus wird vom Zorn erfasst."

[67]Probably the work that gives the modern reader the best insight into the sense of "superstitious" is found in Theophrastus's *Characters*, probably written in the third century BCE. The book gives sketches of the daily lives of characters in the city of Athens. One of those characters is the one controlled by "superstition" (δεισιδαιμονία): "He is apt to purify his house frequently, claiming Hekate has bewitched it. If owls hoot as he passes by he becomes agitated, and says 'mighty Athena!' before he goes on. He refuses to step on a gravestone, view a corpse or visit a woman who has given birth, and says it's the best policy for him not to incur pollution" (16). The superlative δεισιδαιμονεστέρος is used negatively in Lucian, *Defense of the Portrait Study* 27; Diogenes Laertius, *Lives of Eminent Philosophers* 2.132.

[68]See Karl Olav Sandnes, "Paul and Socrates: The Aim of Paul's Areopagus Speech," *JSNT* 50 (1993): 13-26.

is a censure in the moment of reading.[69] Understanding the discourse as incorporating dramatic irony is important for our overall assessment of the speech, for a flat reading obscures the complexity of the encounter between Christianity and paganism that Luke is portraying. In other words, it is not as simple as "Luke is positive toward the Athenians and thereby acknowledges the contribution of pagan philosophers to our knowledge of God"; or "Luke is wholly negative, completely rejecting the possibility of natural theology."

Luke also does direct narration in Acts 17:21 by an unusual editorial comment: "Now all the Athenians and the foreigners living there would spend their time in nothing but telling or hearing something new." This sort of indictment communicated directly to the reader is rare in Acts. The sentiment of unhealthy Athenian curiosity is found in much ancient literature.[70] Luke joins in to express his displeasure.

Last, there is indirect characterization by allowing the reader to overhear what some of the philosophers were saying about Paul: "Some said: 'What does this babbler want to say?'" (Acts 17:18). Paul is called a σπερμολόγος— that is, he is like the lazy men who hung around the agora and lived off the fruits that fell from freights. So is Paul as a philosopher. He lacks *paideia*, and so he picks up bits and pieces of philosophy from different places without really knowing what he is talking about.[71] From the perspective of Luke and his readers, this is insulting and plainly false!

So the Athenians are characterized by Luke as idolaters, ravenously curious of the latest fad, and as doing character assassination of none other than Paul! The reader's appraisal of Paul's statements in the speech that follows must be affected by the characterization provided in the previous verses.

The second important observation prior to the examination of the speech is Luke's clear enriching of the text by the inclusion of echoes from

---

[69]See also Rowe, "Grammar of Life," 39-40, for the view that dramatic irony plays an important part in the Areopagus speech.

[70]See, e.g., Thucydides 3.38.5; Chariton, *Callirhoe* 1.11; Lucian, *Icaromenippus or the Sky-man* 24. Some of these citations I owe to Pervo, *Acts*, 429n42.

[71]On σπερμολόγος and its strongly pejorative sense, see Demosthenes, *On the Crown* 127.3; Dionysius of Halicarnassus, *Roman Antiquities* 19.5.2; Suetonius, περὶ βλασφήμων καὶ πόθεν ἑσκάτη (*Scientific Investigation of Swearwords*) 6.15; Harpocration, *Lexicon of the Ten Orators* 278.1-5.

the Socratic tradition. This can be heard in several places. In Acts 17:17 there is the statement about Paul arguing (διελέγετο) in the "marketplace (ἀγορᾷ) with those" who were passing by (παρατυγχάνοντας; compare to Plato, *Apology* 1.17; Xenophon, *Apology* 1.11; Diogenes, *Lives* 2.21). In Acts 17:18 the philosophers opine that Paul is a "proclaimer of foreign divinities [ξένων δαιμονίων]" (compare to Xenophon, *Memorabilia* 1.1). In Acts 17:20 at the Areopagus, the council states that Paul is "introducing strange things to our ears" (ξενίζοντα . . . τίνα εἰσφέρεις, my translation; compare to Xenophon, *Memorabilia* 1.1; *Apology* 1.10). And last, of course, is Acts 17:22 with ἄνδρες Ἀθηναῖοι; we cannot fail to hear the echo of Socrates before the Athenian court.[72]

The Socratic echoes produce at least three results. First, they imbue the narrative with suspense: everyone knows what happened to Socrates in Athens. Will the same fate await Paul? Second, the echoes invite the reader to understand the event at the Areopagus as a "trial." The Socratic parallel would make little sense if Paul's interaction with the Areopagus was just benign philosophical dialogue. To be sure, it is probable that, being ultimately under Rome, the Areopagus council lacked the authority to dish out the penalty of death without further ado. But it must be remembered that powerful Athenian citizens sat on the council (see *OCD*, 151-52, Areopagus), and they could have used their influence to precipitate a trial.[73] Interestingly, in another occasion where Paul is clearly on trial—namely, before Felix (Acts 24)—he also uses a *captatio benevolentiae*. Since Paul also here begins with a *captatio*, we are encouraged to view the event as a trial also.[74] Third, the Socratic echoes provoke us once again to ask the

---

[72]Some of these texts I owe to Sandnes, "Paul and Socrates," 20-22.

[73]It is worth remembering that although Rome technically had final word on the affairs of a polis, it depended heavily on the cooperation of the city's elite for anything from collecting taxes to keeping the peace. In return, these elites could put pressure on the Roman representative to do some things as they wished. This might have been especially the case in a city like Athens, which had received so many favors from Rome. The situation is perhaps not dissimilar to the dynamics between the Sanhedrin and Pilate in Jerusalem. For the dynamics of rule between Rome and the provinces, see helpfully Martin Goodman, *The Roman World 44 BC–AD 180* (London: Routledge, 1997), 100-112.

[74]Important in viewing the scene as a trial is the use of ἐπιλαβόμενοι in Acts 17:19. The term is not always negative in Luke-Acts (e.g., Lk 9:47; Acts 9:27; 23:19). Since the term is used along with ἄγω in this verse, I performed a *TLG* search on the combination. The combination appears quite a bit. For our purposes, two passages are worth noting: Plato, *Gorgias* 527A1; and Dionysius of Halicarnassus, *Roman Antiquities* 7.25.3. Both texts appear in a judicial context, and both use the combination of ἐπιλαμβάνω and ἄγω clearly

question of the relationship between Christianity and paganism. That is, is the use of Socrates simply a communicative device to help the reader understand just what is happening at Athens? Or is the echo also meant to sweep in with it the philosophy of Socrates or other philosophers? Is the use of Socrates simply an illustration not to be pursued further? Or is it the tip of the iceberg of a rapprochement between Christianity and at least some illuminated philosophers? We shall come back to this under the "Theological Reflections" section.

The speech. There are three main movements in this speech. First, there is the *captatio benevolentiae* in Acts 17:22-23. Here, without going to servile extremes, Paul attempts to secure the goodwill of the council. He also uses the example of the inscription "to the unknown god" as a point of departure.

The second movement runs from Acts 17:24-29 and is held together by the verb ποιέω used in Acts 17:24, 26.[75] The God whom Paul would proclaim to the Athenians is the God who created all things, heaven and earth. Although some philosophers would have agreed with this conception of God to some extent (e.g., Euripides, *Fragments* 968; Epictetus 4.7.6), the thought is primarily biblical (e.g., Gen 1:1; 1 Kings 8:27; Is 42:5; 66:1; cf. also Wis 9:1-9). Being the Lord of heaven and earth implies that his habitation cannot be confined to temples made by men. Again, the thought is primarily biblical (1 Kings 8:27; Is 66:1), although it shares enough at a superficial level with what some philosophers said that communication with those outside the biblical heritage is made possible.[76] God's creation of heaven and earth has another corollary for the dynamics of worship (Acts 17:24b-25). He is not in need of any service by human hands.[77] On the contrary, it is humans who are in need of "life and breath and everything," which God provides for them. As Joshua Jipp has shown, there is a powerful echo here of Isaiah 42:5.[78]

---

to denote a "taking" for trial and judgment. For further (to my mind) persuasive arguments for the Areopagus scene as a trial, see T. D. Barnes, "An Apostle on Trial," *JTS* 20 (1969): 407-19.

[75]Cf. Barrett, *Acts*, 2:841.

[76]On gods not dwelling in human-made temples, see Plutarch, *On Stoic Self-Contradictions 6*.

[77]Some philosophers expressed a similar thought. See Euripides, *Heracles* 1345-46; Plato, *Euthyphro* 14-15; Seneca, *Epistles* 95.47. For χειροποίητος used negatively in the Old Testament, see Jipp, "Paul's Areopagus Speech," 579, drawing on Isaiah, where the term is used negatively against idolatry.

[78]Jipp, "Paul's Areopagus Speech," 579.

God's transcendence and aseity thus have repercussions for worship: he cannot be contained by a temple, and he is not in need of continuous looking after as if otherwise he would perish. On both accounts the Athenians come out badly. Athens, as the narrator has told us and as is corroborated by ancient sources, was chock-full of temples and idols.[79] The thought of creation continues in Acts 17:26 (ἐποίησέν). There is a shift to humanity proper with the statement: "From one ancestor he made all nations." The reference is clearly to Adam—and thereby a biblical narrative framework moving from creation to judgment is employed.[80]

Paul makes two main points about the creation of humans. First, God created them with a benevolent purpose: "To inhabit the whole earth, and he allotted the times of their existence and the boundaries of the places where they would live" (Acts 17:26). There is a sense of magnanimity here.[81] God's good creation is given to humans without any begrudging (probably recalling Gen 1:28-30). This is not contradicted by the mention of boundaries, which is to be understood as an expression of God's paternal care.[82] The second point Paul (Luke) makes about human creation has to do with purpose: "So that they would search [ζητεῖν as an infinitive of purpose] for God and perhaps grope for him and find him—though indeed he is not far from each one of us" (Acts 17:27). God's benevolence in creation is meant to provoke humans to search after him.[83] The success of that search is portrayed in not-very-optimistic fashion, as both the lexical choice (ψυλαφάω) and the grammatical construction with the optative show.[84] But God is not to be blamed for this failure. For, Paul adds, drawing on two poets, God is near us. In fact, "we are his offspring."[85] Or, in biblical language, we are made in his image.

Paul brings the second movement of the speech to a conclusion in Acts 17:30 (οὖν). If it is *humans* who bear the image of God, it follows that the

---

[79]See Pausanias, *Description of Greece* 1.17.1; Strabo, *Geography* 9.1.16.

[80]On this, see especially Rowe, "Grammar of Life," 43-44.

[81]The sense here is probably the same as the other speech to non-Jews at Lystra—namely, Acts 14:17.

[82]See Deut 32:8; Ps 74:17.

[83]The thought is thus quite similar to Rom 2:4.

[84]See Bruce, *Book of the Acts*, 338n73; Barrett, *Acts*, 2:844-6.

[85]The second quotation is from Aratus's *Phaenomena*, a tremendously popular poem in the Hellenistic period (see OCD, 136-37).

crafting of idols in gold, silver and stone is a perversion of the truth.[86] The reader is probably to think of the concept of the human as the "idol" who represents God, as this is seen in Genesis 1.[87]

To sum up the second movement of the speech: Paul has been explaining who this "unknown god" is whom he has introduced into Athens. He is the transcendent, self-sufficient, benevolent Creator of the universe and humans. He created humans to seek after him. Even though he is actually not far from them, they have groped about blindly after him. The fact that humans have attempted to represent this God by ingenious (or is it foolish?) crafting of material images demonstrates that they have failed in their search for God. And given that Athens is a place especially filled with all kinds of images of the gods (they even have an altar to the unknown god!), it has failed perhaps more spectacularly than anyone else. Far from being the leading light of truth, the apogee of human intellectual achievement, Athens is presented as the enclave of idolatrous fools. Is there any hope for them?

The third and final movement of the speech is found in Acts 17:30-31. God has "overlooked the times of human ignorance."[88] He now "commands all people everywhere to repent."[89] The reason why repentance is ordered is that God will bring eschatological judgment on a set day against those who have not repented (Acts 17:31). Luke does not mention Jesus directly here, but the phrase "by a man whom he has appointed" clearly refers to him. The evidence (πίστις) that through Jesus God will one day judge the world with justice has been granted by raising Jesus from the dead. Here the speech ends, and Luke records a varied response in Acts 17:32. On the one hand, some were "mocking" Paul on account of his teaching the resurrection of the dead. On the other, some gesture that they would like to hear Paul again. Yet, Luke states that there was initial success to the speech, as some joined themselves to him. Two people are specified:

---

[86]For somewhat similar thoughts see Seneca, *Epistles* 31.11; Plutarch, *On Superstition* 6; Strabo, *Geography* 16.2.35 ("paraphrasing" Moses); Dio Chrysostom, *Orations* 12.80-83.

[87]See C. H. T. Fletcher-Louis, "God's Image, His Cosmic Temple and the High Priest: Towards an Historical and Theological Account of the Incarnation," in Alexander and Gathercole, *Heaven on Earth*, 81-99.

[88]ἀγνοία in this verse links up with ἀγνοοῦντες of Acts 17:23, thus forming a sort of *inclusio*.

[89]The translation above is an attempt to capture the alliteration ἀνθρώποις πάντας πανταχοῦ.

Dionysius the Areopagite and Damaris (Acts 17:34). Thus Paul has won converts to the faith while avoiding any further prosecution from the Areopagus council.

Theological reflections. Paul and the Greek philosophers: Collusion or collision? Since the Areopagus speech is the only place in Acts where there is explicit interaction with Greek philosophy, theologians from as far back as the second century have been examining it for any yield of what the Bible says about pagan knowledge of God.[90] Most often the answer has been positive. Clement of Alexandria serves as an example: "It is evident that by employing poetic examples from the *Phaenomena* of Aratus, [Paul] approves of the well-spoken words of the Greeks and discloses that through the 'unknown God' the creator God was in a roundabout way honored by the Greeks."[91] This line of thinking has been followed by numerous scholars in their interpretation of Acts 17. For example, most recently Loveday Alexander can write the following about the Areopagus speech: "The whole tone of the sermon, though uncompromising in its condemnation of the practice of 'idolatry' (17.29), tends towards the recognition that the Zeus of the Greek poets and philosophers is the same as the creator whom Paul proclaims (17.24-28)."[92]

C. Kavin Rowe, on the other hand, sees in the Areopagus speech not a collusion with Greek philosophers but a *collision* against them. Paul is not attempting to translate the Christian message into pagan philosophical terms: "Rather than positing conceptual equivalence between the former and the latter—the sine qua non for 'same-saying' or translation—the Areopagus discourse articulates a rival conceptual scheme. For Luke, pagan philosophy is not Christian discourse in a different language."[93]

I think Rowe's reading is more persuasive for at least two reasons. One is explicated by Rowe; the other I add. First, Rowe notes that although Paul quotes or alludes to pagan philosophers, he does this within the biblical

---

[90]See Rowe, "Grammar of Life," 31-35.

[91]Clement of Alexandria, *Stromata* 1.19. I owe this quotation to Rowe, "Grammar of Life," 35.

[92]Loveday Alexander, *Acts in Its Ancient Literary Context: A Classicist Looks at the Acts of the Apostles*, LNTS 289 (T&T Clark, 2005), 197.

[93]C. Kavin Rowe, *World Upside Down: Reading Acts in the Graeco-Roman Age* (New York: Oxford University Press, 2009), 40.

narrative framework that he has superimposed on the speech from Acts 17:24 onward. "In the Areopagus speech the line from Aratus's *Phaenomena* and other allusions are removed from their original interpretive frameworks and embedded within a different framework, one that stretches from Gen 1 through the resurrection of Jesus to the last day."[94] This is decisive. By extracting the Greek philosophical statements from their original contexts, Paul has, as it were, taken out the poison from pagan thinking. Only when put in contexts do words have the vitality to mean and persuade. By using a biblical framework Luke has taken the words of the poets and put them in a different context. Thereby the pagan philosophical baggage that came with the words has been cut off. Now placed within the biblical movement from creation to consummation, the phrases of the Greek poets can serve as communicative bridges for Paul, without sliding into affirmation or equivalence with Greek thought. In short, Paul is practicing ad-hoc apologetics.[95]

Second, in order to answer the question of collusion or collision, we must link the Areopagus speech with the other speeches in Acts.[96] And herein lies the frustration. For the speeches in Acts are addressed to those whose theological framework was built on the Old Testament, and hence this is the main corpus of intertextuality. There is, however, one more speech besides the Areopagus that is addressed to a pagan crowd, and that is at Lystra (Acts 14:8-18). Can this speech shed light on the Areopagus speech (and vice versa), particularly on the matter of collusion or collision? In fact, the speech at Lystra is strikingly similar to the Areopagus. Both share the following elements: (1) a call to repentance (Acts 14:15); (2) an emphasis on God as the benevolent Creator (Acts 14:15); (3) God's permitting the nations to go their own way (Acts 14:16); (4) yet not leaving himself without a witness (Acts 14:17). The main difference is that at Lystra Paul does not quote or allude to Greek philosophers. Why not?

---

[94]Ibid.

[95]Rowe himself does not reach this conclusion. As Jipp, "Paul's Areopagus Speech," 567-68n2 indicates, Rowe does not provide a robust answer as to *why* Paul uses the pagan tradition to the extent that he does. In my opinion, the reasons are theological, missional and political.

[96]It is the merit of Marion Soards, *Speeches*, to note the interpretive currency gained by mirroring one speech to another.

The answer may seem simple: because the Athenians were educated and these Lycaonians were unsophisticated and rustic (cf. Acts 14:11). But surely some of the Greek myths had penetrated even into this group.[97] Why does Paul, an educated man, not attempt at least some accommodation in preaching to this group? Instead, the language is saturated with Old Testament expressions.[98] But, in fact, this is only half the story. As is best seen in Pervo's commentary, there are a number of terms and concepts that call to mind Greek philosophy, especially the Stoics.[99] Yet, the speech at Lystra is not usually employed to argue for Luke's collusion with Greek philosophy. The Areopagus speech we are happy to use, but not the Lystra speech.

I believe the reason for this is that we have allowed the Aratus quotation in Acts 17 to fool us into giving undue emphasis to the Greek elements in the speech. But we must remember that the Aratus poem was so well known in the Hellenistic period that we may call some of its lines cliché— the man on the street could have quoted from it easily.[100] Thus quoting from Aratus does not entail collusion with the author's Stoic philosophy. To argue for this would be like saying that when the person on the street today tries to explain their actions by appealing to the subconscious, they are a Freudian. What I am suggesting, therefore, is that the speech at Athens is *not* as full of Greek philosophy at the deeper layer as is often thought. It is much like the speech at Lystra, possessing a clear biblical framework, with the exception that at Lystra there are no quotations from Greek poets. Keeping this in mind may shield us from an overemphasis on Paul's supposed rapprochement with pagan philosophy in the Areopagus speech. There is simply not enough in this text to build a case for Luke's or Paul's understanding of metaphysics, natural theology and so on, from it.

"God does not dwell in temples made by hands." The speech of Stephen in Acts 7 and the Areopagus speech link up on the theme of temples, thereby

---

[97]E.g., the apparition of Jupiter disguised as a human as found in Ovid's *Metamorphoses*.

[98]See Martin Dibelius, *Book of Acts: Form, Style, and Theology* (Minneapolis: Fortress Press, 2004), 196-97.

[99]Pervo, *Acts*, 356-58.

[100]Says G. J. Toomer about the poem: "The *Phaenomena* achieved immediate fame . . . and lasting popularity beyond the circles of the learned poets: it became the most widely read poem, after the *Iliad* and *Odyssey*, in the ancient world" (*OCD*, 136-37, Aratus).

further disclosing for the reader Luke's understanding of the subject. There are three visible links between the two speeches. First, both use Isaiah 66:1 as an intertext to critique a skewed understanding of temple structures (Acts 7:48-50; 17:24). Second, they use strikingly similar vocabulary in their critique:

- οὐχ ὁ ὕψιστος ἐν χειροποιήτοις κατοικεῖ (Acts 7:48)

- οὐκ ἐν χειροποιήτοις ναοῖς κατοικεῖ (Acts 17:24)

Last, both texts connect God's creation of, and transcendence over, the universe to argue that God cannot possibly be contained by a structure made by human hands.

At least two conclusions could be drawn from the above. First, Luke makes it absolutely clear for his readers that the plan of God was moving in a direction where the temple could no longer function as a meeting place between God and his people. To be sure, there are examples of the apostles praying and preaching at the temple (Acts 2:46; 3:1-26; 5:13, 20, 42; 21:22-26). Yet, in light of the speeches of Stephen and Paul at the Areopagus (not to mention Jesus' prophecy of the destruction of the temple in Lk 21:5-36), the reader understands that the temple is no locus to meet with God.[101] Second, by using the same intertexts, terminology and theological logic for *both* the Jerusalem temple and pagan temples, Luke has relativized the importance of the former. He wants his readers to move forward with worship that is centered on Christ.

Repentance for all. The *peroratio* of the speech comes in Acts 17:30 with a call (done indirectly) to repentance. God has been patient for a long time with the idolatry of the peoples; but now he makes a universal call to repentance (μετανοεῖν). The term as well as the concept of repentance is very common in Acts, particularly in the context of proclamation (Acts 2:38; 3:19-20; 5:31; 8:22; 11:18). As at Acts 3:19-20 and Acts 8:22, so here repentance is linked with the avoidance of judgment. All must repent "because" (καθότι) God has set a day for judgment of the world (Acts 17:31). If one is to avoid an unfavorable verdict at this final judgment, it is necessary

---

[101]If Acts was written post–70 CE, the point would also be that the prophecies of Jesus concerning the temple were fulfilled.

to "turn ... to the living God" (Acts 14:15) in brokenness and a desire to follow the ways of God. Whether the audience be Jewish as in Acts 2, a Samaritan as in Acts 8, or educated Athenians as in this chapter, the call is repentance for all.

The man who will judge is the one who was raised. As Paul has been moving to the telos of biblical narrative, a shift from the universal to the particular can be observed. In the words of Rowe, when Paul finally reaches the stage of judgment, this particularity becomes the strongest: "At this point, the radical particularity of the Christian message erupts from the universalizing scope of Paul's speech heretofore: there is a particular man (ἀνήρ) upon whom and a particular day (ἡμέρα) upon which the relation of God to the entirety of the world depends."[102] But on what authority does Paul say this? What is the corroboration that this "man" (the readers of course know it is Jesus) has the right and power to judge the world? The answer is the resurrection. God "has given assurance [πίστιν] to all" by raising Jesus from the dead.

The resurrection of Jesus is central to the kerygma in Acts. It has been emphasized, however, that the raised Jesus appeared only to the apostles and their circle (e.g., Acts 2:32; 3:15; 10:41; 13:31). Because they saw Jesus resurrected (indeed, they ate and conversed with him for numerous days), they can speak with authority. The "proof" of Jesus' resurrection is found in the testimony of the apostles. Access, therefore, to the proof of the resurrection is mediated through apostolic testimony.[103] Not so here. "Proof" is given to all (πᾶσιν). In previous chapters proof is given to the apostles only; in this chapter proof is provided for all. How are we to understand this verse, which is striking in view of the previous passages? A plausible explanation must take into account the universal thrust of this entire speech: the term πᾶς occurs no less than seven times in Acts 17:22-31.[104] It is probably the case that this universal thrust leads Paul (Luke) to stress the accessibility of the proof of the resurrection for all. We shall come back to this matter in the following chapter.

---

[102]Rowe, *World Upside Down,* 39.

[103]On this see further chapter six.

[104]See further Gärtner, *Areopagus Speech,* 229-41, on the universal thrust of the speech.

THE SPEECH BEFORE AGRIPPA (ACTS 26:1-32)

Starting with Acts 13, the spotlight has shined almost exclusively on Paul, and in particular on his role as missionary. Two currents flow from this and run into each other. First, Luke's narration has been about the carrying out of the gospel to the different regions of the Mediterranean. Whether at homes, synagogues, markets or trials, Luke presents the power of the word of the Lord to win converts to faith in Jesus. The second current that must ineluctably go with the first (Acts 14:22) is the clashes that occur when the gospel confronts the world. The preaching of the gospel has thus provoked a stoning, beatings, accusations, trials and even imprisonments, all of which force the reader to ask a question: Can what Paul is doing with the preaching of Jesus be considered seditious behavior by the Romans? Is the message of Paul, therefore, a direct challenge to the concept of the *pax romana*, and therefore a candidate to be quashed immediately? How is the reader to understand the constant trouble that has accompanied Paul almost everywhere he goes? And what is the real reason he is being tried and indeed detained?

I suggest that beginning in Acts 18 Luke has been giving his readers a consistent answer: Paul's troubles have to do *not* with Roman law per se, but with intra-Jewish disputes, with Jewish ζητήματα. The speech before Agrippa, one of the longest in Acts and therefore of great importance for Luke, will bring his answer to a climax.

The speech. We offer an explanation of this speech by making the following six observations:

1. Luke characterizes the speech as a "defense." The verb ἀπολογέομαι is used as an *inclusio* in Acts 26:1, 24 (see also Acts 26:2). Some scholars assert that this is not a judicial defense but rather preaching of the gospel or proclamation.[105] To be sure, we do not find in this speech a technical defense. Since Luke provided such a direct defense in Acts 24:10-21, and since Paul had already appealed to Caesar (Acts 25:11-12), Luke can afford to provide only an indirect defense. And this indirect defense is carried out by framing

---

[105]See, e.g., Beverly Gaventa, *The Acts of the Apostles*, ANTC (Nashville: Abingdon, 2003), 338-39. Bruce, *Book of the Acts*, 461, calls it "a defense of the gospel."

the case in theological terms. Yet, it is a defense, as Luke insists by his use of the term ἀπολογέομαι. The heavy use of theological language is actually part of the strategy; for the point of the speech, as we shall see, is that Paul's case is a matter of theological dispute, not breaking of Roman law. This is something that Kavin Rowe captures well:

> Theology here *is* politics. Paul's appeal in the *captatio*, that is, attempts to frame the charges against him in terms of a shared theological horizon as a way to enable Agrippa to understand the political configuration of those who follow the Jewish Messiah. If Agrippa listens patiently, Paul intimates, he will hear in Paul's *apologia* the answer to Festus's political conundrum.[106]

2. As we said above, the charges and defense have to do with issues of Jewish laws and disputes (Acts 26:3). In other words, this is intra-Jewish argumentation. Luke has been making this point since Acts 18 when Paul came before Gallio (Acts 18:12-15), with Claudius Lysias (Acts 23:25-30) and in the conversation between Festus and Agrippa (Acts 25:19). The point is clear: *Paul has not been guilty of breaking Roman law.*

3. Paul thus asserts that the real issue at hand is the resurrection from the dead (Acts 26:6-8). The fact that this is the true reason he is on trial he finds absurd. It is not as if by the preaching of the resurrection he is proclaiming some novelty. After all, he is a Pharisee (everyone knows that [Acts 26:5]), and the resurrection from the dead as the future hope is exactly what Pharisees preach. Is preaching the resurrection a crime among our people? Absurd, answers Paul. In fact, the twelve tribes strain day and night in perseverance of this hope (Acts 26:7). But what does Jesus have to do with this? Everything!

4. Now, before Paul talks about his life as a Christian, he wants to make clear that in his conversion to Jesus he has not deluded himself. That is why in Acts 26:9-11 he describes for Agrippa in detail how much harm he tried to do to the name of Jesus and his followers. He imprisoned many, gave a nod when they were being killed, tortured them in the synagogues so they would blaspheme and even followed them to other cities outside Jerusalem. As he says, he was "enraged" (ἐμμαινόμενος) in his persecution

---

[106]Rowe, *World Upside Down*, 85.

against them (Acts 26:11). He did not want to convert to Christ!

5. But something extraordinary happened that changed all that (Acts 26:13-18). As he was traveling to apprehend more Christians, a light, brighter than the sun at midday, shined around him and his companions. Humiliated to the ground, a voice in the Hebrew language spoke to him: "Saul, Saul, why do you persecute me? It is hard for you to kick against the goads." And Paul said: "Who are you, Lord?" And the Lord said: "I am Jesus, the one you are persecuting." The exalted Jesus then commissioned Paul. He was to go to the Jews and Gentiles "to open their eyes so that they may turn from darkness to light and from the power of Satan to God, so that they may receive forgiveness of sins and a place among those who are sanctified by faith in me."

6. So that was it. Paul believed that the promise of the hope, the promise of resurrection proclaimed in the prophets and Moses, had been fulfilled in the resurrection of Jesus of Nazareth. How could he disobey the commission to preach this message (Acts 26:19)? On the contrary, with God's help he has been preaching to both small and great "that the Messiah must suffer, and that, by being the first to rise from the dead, he would proclaim light both to our people and to the Gentiles" (Acts 26:22-23).

And so the speech ends (or rather, is interrupted). After a brief interchange in which Paul, accused of madness, tries to convert Agrippa himself (Acts 26:24-29), Luke allows the reader to hear the verdict of the expert Agrippa and his *consilium*: "This man is doing nothing to deserve death or imprisonment." Agrippa then says to Festus, "This man could have been set free if he had not appealed to the emperor" (Acts 26:31-32).

Theological reflections. *Salvation: Repentance, faith, forgiveness of sins.* In the words of the risen Jesus to Paul we have a concise yet packed statement of Lukan soteriology. A number of themes appear that are interlinked to other speeches in Acts. First, there is the theme of repentance, which we have seen before (Acts 2:38; 3:19-20; 5:31; 8:22; 11:18; 17:30). Here what repentance means is expanded. Paul is "to open their [Gentiles and Jews] eyes so that they may turn from darkness to light and from the power of Satan to God" (Acts 26:18). This section of the text is suffused with Isaianic echoes (Is 31:6; 44:22; 45:22; 49:6). In that context repentance is presented in both intellectual and moral terms: our worldview is shattered as God permits us to perceive our failure to honor him as the Lord who created the heavens and the earth. The goal/result of this is a "turning" (ἐπιστρέψαι) presented first metaphorically ("from darkness to light") and then from a transcendental perspective ("from the power of Satan to God"). The person who repents, therefore, is transferred from one domain to another. Repentance is Luke's message to both Jews and Gentiles (Acts 14:15; 17:30).

The second soteriological theme from this text is that of faith. The risen Christ speaks of those who repent as receiving a "place among those who are sanctified by faith in me [πίστει τῇ εἰς ἐμέ]." Already in Acts we have seen the connection between salvation and belief or faith in Jesus Christ (Acts 10:43, πάντα τὸν πιστεύοντα εἰς αὐτόν; Acts 13:39 ἐν τούτῳ [i.e., Christ] πᾶς ὁ πιστεύων δικαιοῦται; Acts 20:21, διαμαρτυρόμενος Ἰουδαίοις τε καὶ Ἕλλεσιν τὴν εἰς θεὸν μετάνοιαν καὶ πίστιν εἰς τὸν κύριον ἡμῶν Ἰησοῦν). There is a remarkable consistency in Luke's emphasis that salvation is by faith in Christ. For that message has been proclaimed in the contexts of both Gentiles and Jews.

The last element is that of forgiveness of sins. Those who repent and believe receive ἄφεσιν ἁμαρτιῶν. There is a strong echo here of Isaiah 55:4-7. Faithful Israel (presented as David) has been placed by God as a witness among the nations (μαρτύριον ἐν ἔθνεσιν) to proclaim to the wicked that if they should repent, he would forgive their sins (ἀφήσει τὰς ἁμαρτίας ὑμῶν). Forgiveness of sins as a result of faith in Christ is also a major theme in Acts (Acts 2:38; 10:43; 13:38).

"Nothing but what the prophets and Moses said. . . ." With respect to the promises of the Old Testament, Luke's concentrated effort throughout both of his volumes has been to show that the Scriptures of Israel are most persuasively fulfilled in the life, death and resurrection of Jesus. If the book of Acts in particular is a dramatization of the debates going on between the followers of Jesus and other Jews,[107] Luke, as it were, stands before the court presenting his arguments in favor of Jesus as the legitimate Messiah of Israel. Not only is this accomplished by the dense intertextuality

---

[107]See Alexander, *Acts in Its Ancient Literary Context,* 183-206.

observable in his work, but it is also definitively stated by Jesus in Luke 24:44-49: he is the Messiah who suffered, was raised and is to be proclaimed, all according to Moses, the prophets and the Psalms. This statement has been repeated—if with more hermeneutical and exegetical detail—by his followers since the time they received the Holy Spirit. In the same way, Paul's repetition of the words of the exalted Christ to him represent an endpoint in the book. After this, Paul will not be heard again in direct speech giving apologetic arguments in favor of Jesus. It is as if, with the powerful plea before Agrippa, Luke has rested his case. All the more reason for us to pay attention to this speech, since final arguments are of course important.

If I may summarize: the suffering and resurrection of Jesus fulfills everything that is written in Moses and the prophets. Furthermore, Paul's own suffering is part of the fulfillment of the Scriptures. For the fate of Isaiah's servants is the same as that of the Servant. Just as he suffered, they (and in this case Paul) suffer. In fact, they are one. When in Acts 26:23 Paul says that first the Christ, from his resurrection, would proclaim light to the people and Gentiles (Is 49:6), he is describing what all the apostles, including Paul and Silas (Acts 13:47), have been doing since being empowered by the Holy Spirit (Acts 1:8).[108]

In view of this, we could say that for Luke there is an unbreakable continuity between the Old Testament and Jesus. In fact, only those who have believed in Jesus can rightly understand—and live—the Scriptures of Israel.

Conversion, not revolution. But.... As we indicated above, in the second half of his narrative Luke has been carefully weaving a message that may genuinely be called political. He has been saying, especially through the mouths of politically well-positioned non-Christians, that the Christian message is not seditious. We would say that Luke's message is that Christianity is not a politically revolutionary movement. Its object is not the overturning of the government. Does it cause friction, complaints and even the occasional uproar in the public arena? Yes. But this is not the intention of the message. When disturbances have been caused it is because

---

[108]See helpfully Peter Mallen, *The Reading and Transformation of Isaiah in Luke-Acts*, LNTS 367 (London: T&T Clark, 2008), 92-93.

the message has challenged some unsavory individuals: exploiters of a young mantic girl (Philippi), greedy craftsmen who used religion to become rich (Ephesus), irrational crowds that everyone knew easily rioted (Ephesus and Jerusalem). These were already villainous elements in society. The fault lays with them, not the message. This is not to say that Luke's perspective is aristocratic. That is, it is not as if he thumbs his nose down on "popular" sins of the masses while turning a blind eye to the more "refined" sins of the intellectuals or *honestiores*. To the contrary, the Athenians, for all their supposed intellectual refinement, are idolaters. Luke denounces Felix as an immoral, greedy and self-seeking governor (Acts 24:24-27), Festus also as a self-seeking hypocrite (Acts 25:6-12), and Agrippa and his wife, Bernice, as pompous (Acts 25:23). As to those disorders that have occurred with the Jews, these have stemmed from disputations about the interpretation of their Scriptures—hardly a crime in Roman eyes (see Gallio). The Christian message challenges society, but it does not—and should not—foment insurrection. As Kavin Rowe has argued, Luke presents Paul vis-à-vis Roman law as δίκαιος, *iustus*.[109]

On the other hand, it is undeniable that the effect of the Christian mission has been the unraveling, or at least destabilization, of some of the fundamental aspects of pagan culture, such as religion and economics.[110] Furthermore, a number of claims from the Christians were ultimately irreconcilable, not only with strands of Greco-Roman culture, but also with Roman political declarations. In particular, it is clear that if a Christian were to be challenged on his or her ultimate loyalty, he or she would have to say that it belonged to κύριος Ἰησοῦς rather than κύριος Καίσαρ (cf. Acts 4:19). The time would come when this would be put to the test.

There is therefore a tension in the book of Acts: the Christian movement is not responsible for creating sedition; yet, it does create tensions in most places it goes. Furthermore, some of its claims, if taken to their logical end (which Luke does not), would set up an irreconcilable dichotomy between King Jesus and King Caesar (cf. Acts 17:1-9). Is this tension or dialectic ever solved in Acts? My sense is that it is not. Luke, it seems to me,

---

[109]Rowe, *World Upside Down*, 53-89.
[110]On this again see the excellent account in ibid., 17-51.

is saying the following to his Christian audience: "Be prepared for anything. We have seen cases where some Roman proconsuls and governors have clearly stated that our movement is not seditious. Let us take heart from this. Yet, remember that Paul was imprisoned for a long time! Some of the Romans will judge in our favor and leave us in peace; others, even while ruling in our favor, may leave us in jail. Keep preaching the word whatever the circumstance!"

SUMMARY AND CONCLUSIONS

This chapter has been an attempt to sketch Acts's salient theological themes by drawing on the speeches. That the speeches can serve as an important source for Lukan theology is something that few scholars would dispute. By paying close attention to the narrative within which each speech is contained, the hope has been for a more holistic approach. We conclude the chapter by providing a more systematic summary of the theology of the speeches.

   God. Luke did not intend Acts to be a comprehensive metaphysical presentation of God! The person of God is not presented in abstraction; he is shown concretely by being narrativized into the story of Acts, a story that is about the salvific movement of the word from Jerusalem to the ends of the earth (Acts 1:8). As such, it may not be surprising that the God of Acts is a *universal* God. He is the one God who created the heavens and the earth. He transcends the universe and is completely satisfied in himself. That is why he cannot be confined to temples (Acts 17:24-25), even that temple that served as a meeting place between himself and his people (Acts 7:47-50). Neither can he be represented by images of silver or gold, for that is a profound misrepresentation of who he is. The God of Acts is the same God who speaks against idolatry in the Old Testament. This God created all of humanity with a benevolent purpose: that they might enjoy his bountiful provision and seek after him (Acts 17:26-28). Although God is Creator of all and does not show favoritism by being partial (Acts 10:34-35), nevertheless humans cannot approach him by their own specific religious expressions. Rather, God has set a specific man, Jesus Christ, through whom he can be encountered (Acts 17:31).

Christology. Jesus Christ is the Lord and Messiah whom God has appointed as the object of belief (Acts 2:36). It is very important for Luke that Jesus be understood as human. Yes, he is Lord (κύριος) of all (Acts 10:36), and as such he is God. But he is the God who is Jesus of Nazareth, who was in the midst of the people (Acts 2:22) doing good to the people by healing and delivering them from satanic oppression (Acts 10:38). He suffered and was crucified (Acts 2:23; 7:52; 10:39; 26:23). But God did not allow his body to see corruption (Acts 2:31); he exalted him by raising him and sitting him at his right hand (Acts 2:33). As the exalted Messiah he has been given the authority to grant the Holy Spirit to all who believe (Acts 2:33; 11:17-18). It is he who will judge the living and the dead (Acts 10:42; 17:30).

All of this concerning Jesus Christ happened as a fulfillment of the Scriptures (Acts 2:25-36; 26:22-23), thereby showing that he is the Messiah.[111] His suffering was not random; in fact, God had determined all of sacred history to climax in the death of the Righteous One. The suffering of the prophets at the hands of the fathers was a divine pattern that would reach its zenith in the passion of Jesus (Acts 7:51-52). The sufferings of Jesus, therefore, do not at all disqualify him from being the Messiah, but confirm him. In his sufferings there is a meeting of God's sovereignty, Christology and eschatology.

Pneumatology. Lukan theology is theology of the Spirit. Since Acts is about the gospel reaching the ends of the earth, and since this can only happen when the witnesses are empowered by the Holy Spirit, the Spirit plays a foundational role in Acts.[112] It is with the coming of the Spirit in Acts 2, an advent that is likened to the coming of the Holy One to Sinai, that the mission to all nations begins. In fact, the pouring out of the Spirit on the disciples is both a climax and a beginning in salvation history. It is a climax in that it is the long-awaited fulfillment of the Day of the Lord; it is a beginning in that the pouring of the Spirit signifies a fresh movement of God's salvation to all the nations (Acts 2:17-21).

Reception of the Spirit is inextricably linked to Jesus Christ. Only those who repent and are baptized in his name can receive the Holy Spirit (Acts

---

[111]See here the excellent work of Bock, *Theology of Luke and Acts*, chaps. 6-8.
[112]See ibid., 219-25.

2:38-39; 11:17; cf. Acts 19:1-7). The reception of the Holy Spirit by faith in Christ marks the recipients as the cleansed people of God, whatever their ethnic background (Acts 10:9-48; 11:17-18). The Spirit thus eradicates religious and ethnic backgrounds to create a new people of God, made up of Jews and Gentiles. The Holy Spirit thus holds together the ecclesiological, eschatological and soteriological horizons of Acts.

Soteriology. Salvation is to be found solely in Jesus Christ, apart from any works of the law (Acts 10:43; 13:38-41; 15:8-11). The human responsibility is to repent and believe (Acts 2:38; 16:31). And yet, when salvation is presented solely under the category of repentance, it is presented as a gift of God: "God exalted him at his right hand as Leader and Savior that he might *give* repentance to Israel and forgiveness of sins" (Acts 5:31); "Then God has *given* even to the Gentiles the repentance that leads to life" (Acts 11:18).

What is salvation in Acts? It is a multifaceted work of God presented from multiple perspectives. It is to be delivered from coming judgment (Acts 2:40; 3:19-20; 17:30). It is to have our sins forgiven (Acts 2:38; 10:43; 26:18). It is to be justified before God (Acts 13:38). It is to be liberated from the power of Satan to serve the living God (Acts 26:18). It is to be granted an inheritance with the saints in God's kingdom (Acts 2:47; 26:18). All of this is based on the suffering and exaltation of Jesus; all of this is from God.

six

THE JUSTIFICATION
OF TRUTH-CLAIMS IN ACTS

A Conversation with Postliberalism

IF NEW TESTAMENT EXEGESIS, both in the interpretive process and in its ultimate goal, is not done in the matrix of theology, it is less than Christian exegesis. At different points in the exegetical work the interpreter should bring to bear scriptural insights into the broader discourse of God, canon, Christology and so on. To be sure, the movement is not unilateral, as if during the exegetical process the interpreter is not in some way being partially driven by theology. Exegesis and theology must go together because in Christian theology the Bible should have a dominant voice and because the Bible itself is theological—that is, its ultimate subject is God in Jesus Christ. Furthermore, Christian proclamation must provide for its hearers theological grounding on which they can walk the faith both in the ecclesial context and outside.

It is with this in mind that this chapter is offered. To be sure, our previous chapter on the theology of the speeches was just that: an exegesis of the main speeches that sought to link together the different theological themes of Acts. Nevertheless, the concentration was only on Acts. The conversation, we can say, was between the different chapters of Acts. To the extent that Acts is one corpus (in two volumes), it was more a soliloquy than a true conversation. In this chapter the conversation seeks to go beyond Acts to an outside partner.

This chapter, then, is a sustained dialogue between Acts—as I understand it—and a theological movement that has come to be known as postliberalism. In particular, the chapter is an attempt to allow some of the main proposals of postliberalism to help explore the following question: On what basis, if any, does Acts justify its truth-claims about Jesus Christ? At the same time, we hope to shed light on this aspect of postliberalism by subjecting it to questions from the biblical text. The goal is therefore a dialogue. Postliberalism is an appropriate conversation partner with Acts in the matter of justification of truth-claims for at least three reasons.

First, postliberalism has been an attempt to move beyond the liberal theology of the eighteenth to twentieth centuries. And the liberal theology of this period is nothing if not an attempt to justify the truth of Christianity as it was constructed by liberal theologians. Liberal theology has therefore been primarily *apologetic* in nature. It seeks to prove to society and academy that Christianity—as *it* understands it—is true. At the risk of exaggerating, the heart of postliberal theology, by contrast, is to suggest, from *within* faith, that the way liberalism went about trying to justify its assertions is illegitimate. Can postliberal theology shed light on the way Acts seeks to prove Christianity in the public square? And can Acts help sharpen postliberal theology in this respect?

Second, postliberal theology has highly emphasized the place of the biblical narrative—both the entire canonical story and particular narrative books—as constitutive of the character of Christianity. The role of propositional content in the use of theology has given way to narrative. Ronald Thiemann, for example, attempts a project on the subject of prevenience that, *because* it is postliberal, engages closely with a narrative book of the New Testament—namely, the Gospel of Matthew.[1] It may be enriching to read the narrative of Acts in light of postliberalism to see how the two can possibly benefit each other. To my knowledge, Acts has not been employed in such heuristic manner with postliberal theology.

Last, postliberalism is a significant movement in theology today. Contrary

---

[1] Ronald Thiemann, *Revelation and Theology: The Gospel as Narrated Promise* (Notre Dame: University of Notre Dame Press, 1985).

to the opinion that postliberalism is on the decline,[2] the recent flow of publications shows quite the contrary.[3] I fervently believe that postliberalism has a future in the Christian church, particularly in North America among evangelicals. Evangelicals have been in an apologetic posture for almost a century now. I sense, however, in the younger generation of evangelicals a certain fatigue with the apologetic task. It is not that they view the task as having failed (although some do); or that apologetics should no longer be part of the agenda. Rather, many younger evangelicals want to move beyond apologetic battles to a concentration on the text of the Bible as such and on theology. And this is precisely what postliberalism offers. Postliberalism is attractive because it says: let's get on with the task of reading the Bible and describing how it can shape the Christian church; enough of the apologetic task! In fact, already in the so-called postconservative movement we are seeing the fruits of postliberalism.[4] This is all the more reason for us to understand postliberalism better and allow Scripture to shed light on it. For it may be that, as attractive as postliberalism is and as many qualities as it surely possesses, there are deficiencies that may cause us to pause.

The task at hand, then, is the following: to survey the theology of postliberalism and then to move to the more particular question of the justification of truth-claims. More specifically, given the confession of these theologians that Jesus Christ is the Messiah, how do they go about defending this claim in the public arena? The answers will then be brought

---

[2]For example, Paul J. DeHart, *The Trial of the Witnesses: The Rise and Decline of Postliberal Theology* (Malden, MA: Blackwell, 2006).

[3]Consider the following: David Kamitsuka, *Theology and Contemporary Culture: Liberation, Postliberal and Revisionary Perspectives* (Cambridge: Cambridge University Press, 1999); Jeffrey C. K. Goh, *Christian Tradition Today: A Postliberal Vision of Church and World* (Louvain: Peeters, 2000); Mike Higton, *Christ, Providence & History: Hans W. Frei's Public Theology* (London: T&T Clark, 2004); C. C. Pecknold, *Transforming Postliberal Theology: George Lindbeck, Pragmatism and Scripture* (London: T&T Clark, 2005); Robert Andrew Cathey, *God in Postliberal Perspective: Between Realism and Non-Realism* (Surrey, UK: Ashgate, 2009); Jason Springs, *Toward a Generous Orthodoxy: Prospects for Hans Frei's Postliberal Theology* (Oxford: Oxford University Press, 2010); Peter Ochs, *Another Reformation: Postliberal Christianity and the Jews* (Grand Rapids: Baker, 2011); John Allan Knight, *Liberalism Versus Postliberalism: The Great Divide in Twentieth-Century Theology* (New York: Oxford University Press, 2013).

[4]See my essay "Postconservative Theologians and the Authority of Scripture," in *"My Words Shall Never Pass Away": The Enduring Authority of the Christian Scriptures*, ed. D. A. Carson (Grand Rapids: Eerdmans, 2016).

into conversation with the way Acts justifies its central truth-claim, that
Jesus of Nazareth is the promised Messiah.

POSTLIBERALISM: A SKETCH

Postliberalism is hardly a monolithic movement. Suggestions like the
"Yale school" or "narrative theology" are eventually unhelpful because
they are reductionist. The movement is complex, and the different players
can at times disagree with one another on some significant issues. There
is, however, a cluster of beliefs that are broadly shared. We shall come to
these presently.

The two foundational figures of postliberalism are George Lindbeck and
Hans Frei. While Lindbeck coined the label postliberal, he himself suggested that Frei be viewed as the chief figure of the movement.[5] Although,
to be sure, Lindbeck was displaying modesty in this assertion, nevertheless
those who carried the movement forward immediately after Frei and
Lindbeck worked on projects that seemed more sympathetic to Frei's particular interests.[6] By contrast, many of the "third generation" postliberals,
probably because their concentration is more on the epistemology of the
movement, have appropriated (and developed) more from Lindbeck.[7]

Theology as a descriptive enterprise for the church. It would be difficult
to understand the agenda of postliberal theologians without some famil-
iarity with modern theology, especially of the eighteenth and nineteenth
centuries.[8] As diagnosed by Karl Barth and many others, one of the main
problems of modern theology was its excessive preoccupation with apologetics. That is, there was an insistence to explain theology—and revelation
in particular—for the purpose of showing its coherence with the prin-
ciples of modernity (primarily philosophy). The intentions were often
noble, but the results were disastrous for theology.

---

[5]See George Lindbeck, "A Panel Discussion: Lindbeck, Hunsinger, McGrath & Fackre," in *The Nature of Confession: Evangelicals & Postliberals in Conversation,* ed. Timothy R. Phillips and Dennis L. Okholm (Downers Grove, IL: InterVarsity Press, 1996), 247.

[6]For example, Thiemann and Placher.

[7]For example, Pecknold and Ochs.

[8]To my mind, Karl Barth's *Protestant Theology in the Nineteenth Century: Its Background and History,* trans. Brian Cozens and John Bowden (London: SCM Press, 1972), remains the most illuminating account. See also Thiemann, *Revelation and Theology,* 9-46.

For seeking to do theology primarily from an apologetic standpoint led to the dissolution of the unique message of Christian revelation. The main way that modern theology went about fulfilling its apologetic vision was by trying to find a vantage point *outside* the Christian faith in order to justify its truthfulness and relevance for modern man. Whether it was John Locke or Friedrich Schleiermacher, both depended on a form of foundationalism to justify the truth of revelation.[9] Thiemann helpfully summarizes: "The key theological task becomes the devising of a category which will be congenial to a general epistemology and yet establish the uniqueness of the process of religious knowing."[10]

Barth shows another path of which the following observation is crucial for postliberal theology, especially as carried forward by Frei. Barth insists with all his powers that *revelation*, as found and disclosed by the Holy Spirit in the Bible, should be our starting point. No philosophical system or human experience is revelatory, for they are ultimately anthropologically based. Revelation, on the other hand, because it is God himself giving himself to us, cannot be devised or grasped by mere human intellect. Modern theology, with its apologetic goal that depends on philosophy, ends up domesticating—or trying to domesticate—transcendence.[11]

Postliberal theology, when taking its cue from Frei, depends on and further works out Barth's theological vision; when it draws more from Lindbeck, the influences are Thomas Aquinas and Martin Luther theologically, while philosophically the work of Ludwig Wittgenstein is more significant.[12] Whatever the inspiration, postliberal theology views its work as primarily descriptive for ecclesial communities. Lindbeck's cultural-linguistic proposal to doctrine is an attempt to move beyond "cognitive propositional" (which is foundationalist) approaches and "experiential-expressive" (which is "logically and empirically vacuous")

---

[9] Foundationalism is a misunderstood and misrepresented concept to which we will come back later in this chapter.

[10] Thiemann, *Revelation and Theology*, 43.

[11] See the excellent introduction to Barth by John Webster, *Karl Barth*, 2nd ed. (London: Continuum, 2004). In particular, see Barth's comments in relation to Prolegomena: *CD* I.1, pp. 25-44, 288-92.

[12] See George Hunsinger, "Postliberal Theology," in *The Cambridge Companion to Postmodern Theology*, ed. Kevin Vanhoozer (Cambridge: Cambridge University Press, 2003), 42-45.

approaches.[13] He suggests that we begin with the Christian tradition to provide the framework to apprehend the world. In his now-famous words: "Intratextual [postliberal] theology resdescribes reality within the scriptural framework rather than translating Scripture into extra-scriptural categories. It is the text, so to speak, which absorbs the world, rather than the world the text."[14]

Frei, profoundly influenced by Barth,[15] was concerned that theology should not be explanatory or apologetic in nature. Theology should be de-scriptive and christocentric. He thus suggested that we begin with the Gospels' account(s) of Jesus. The attempt should be to study the Gospels, not so we could use them to find some universally accepted philosophy that would cohere with them and thus validate theology, but in order to describe the identity of God in Jesus Christ.[16] Subjects like philosophy and literary criticism should be used only formally and on an ad hoc basis lest they over-power the literal meaning of the biblical text.[17] William Placher, a strong voice in postliberal theology, agrees. "If my arguments have been correct, then Christian theology needs to take the form that Frei sees in Barth: a description of the world as seen from a Christian perspective that draws what persuasive power it has from the coherence and richness of the whole."[18]

To sum up: postliberals insist that if theology is going to be true to its nature and continue to have a voice in the future, it must view its purpose as providing for the academy and the church a portrait of the identity of Jesus Christ. Drawing from the portrait of Christ found in the narrative of Scripture, it provides for ecclesial communities a theology that shows them a pattern that they should learn and practice as members of the

---

[13]George Lindbeck, *The Nature of Doctrine: Religion and Theology in a Postliberal Age* (Philadelphia: West-minster, 1985), 32.

[14]Ibid., 118.

[15]His dissertation under Richard Niebuhr at Yale was a massive work on Barth. See Hans Frei, *Theology and Narrative: Selected Essays*, ed. George Hunsinger and William Placher (Oxford: Oxford University Press, 1993), 5. Yet, as Bruce McCormack, *Orthodox and Modern: Studies in the Theology of Karl Barth* (Grand Rapids: Baker, 2008), 113-27, has to my mind convincingly shown, Frei incorrectly minimized the extent to which Barth's theological statements could adequately refer to God.

[16]Frei, *Theology and Narrative*, 27-30; idem, *Types of Christian Theology* (New Haven, CT: Yale University Press, 1992), 38-46, 78-83.

[17]Frei, *Theology and Narrative*, 31-36.

[18]William Placher, *Unapologetic Theology: A Christian Voice in a Pluralistic Conversation* (Louisville, KY: Westminster John Knox, 1989), 135.

church. This view of theology comes in stark contrast to the modern one, where theology—at least as practiced in the academy—was an enterprise that primarily sought to provide universal validity and acceptance for its truth and existence. The way it went about this was by ultimately subordinating revelation to philosophy and thereby starting from outside faith. Instead of "faith seeking understanding," it was "faith seeking foundation."[19] While postliberals are not in principle against philosophy, they view its place in theology as no more than an occasional tool to help sharpen conceptuality.[20]

Theology that is not foundational. From the comments above we could describe postliberalism as a movement that has been fighting to take off the philosophical straitjacket in which theology was put by modernity. The epistemological account that postliberals see as dominant in modernity is what has come to be known as foundationalism. Since modern theology was construed on this epistemological base (and we know how disastrous this was to theology), postliberals vigorously reject it. In most postliberal work, foundationalism is presented as the ultimate deceiver, the false guide who took theology to the deep woods and abandoned it there.

Foundationalism, as explained by Ronald Thiemann, comprises the following elements.[21] (1) Knowledge is grounded on self-evident beliefs that serve as a foundation for all subsequent knowledge. (2) There exists a clear distinction between the foundations and the propositions inferred from those foundations. (3) The foundational beliefs do not need justification but are immediate and direct. (4) There is a strong dependence on mental intuitions. (5) There is "an assertion of correspondence between the self-evident beliefs and the language independent world."[22] Thiemann is clear

---

[19] The helpful phrase is Thiemann's, *Revelation and Theology*, 16-46.

[20] Higton, *Christ, Providence & History*, 199, explains Frei's vision of theologians vis-à-vis philosophy this way: "[They] will make all sorts of uses of philosophy, but they are likely to see philosophy more as a set of intellectual skills, practices of rigour, and well-honed concepts than as a comprehensive criteriology, let alone a comprehensive worldview or a discipline that has its own distinct subject matter." And yet, as I will suggest in a number of places, postliberals too often end up subordinating Scripture to philosophy, particularly of a Wittgensteinian type (as *they* understand Wittgenstein!).

[21] I choose Thiemann because his theological project as found in *Revelation and Theology* is an explicit attempt to ground prevenience in a nonfoundational epistemology. He thus interacts closely with foundationalism from a postliberal perspective.

[22] Thiemann, *Revelation and Theology*, 158-59 n. 20; 165-66 n. 40.

that it was the use of this type of foundationalist epistemology that has undone modern theology and, more specifically, the doctrine of prevenience. "The causal explanation model has become influential in modern theology both because of its long theological history and because it has seemed an appropriate means of providing explicit theoretical justification for belief in God's prevenience. But the adoption of that model is . . . the very move which undermines that defense."[23] According to Thiemann, if we are to move from this failure in the doctrine of revelation, it is necessary to adopt a nonfoundational account. Thiemann's specific account is a form of holist or coherentist justification.[24]

William Placher, in his well-known *Unapologetic Theology*, also wants to move away from a theory of epistemology that he views as now defunct. Theologians who operate from foundationalism are "trying to do something that our best philosophers tell us is impossible—not merely for religious beliefs but for any beliefs whatsoever."[25] To be sure, Placher makes what seems like a foundationalist claim when he says that "as a Christian I believe that the central claims of Christian faith are true—not merely 'true for Christians' or 'true within the context of the Christian tradition' but in a strong sense just plain true."[26] But the issue is that of *justification*. Yes, Christians should make the claim that Christianity is true, Placher says; but that is different from saying that the assertion is justified. Like Thiemann (but much less systematically), Placher rejects foundationalism and instead proposes a form of justification that has to do with an eschatological "emerging pattern" of the world that makes the best sense from a Christian point of view.[27]

One may ask whether postliberals' problems with foundationalism have to do with the fact that it was this specific epistemology that dominated the way that revelation was to be explained or justified and that in their opinion ruined theology. Or is the problem with *any* philosophy, since by definition philosophy works outside the realm of revelation? Evidently it

---

[23]Ibid., 44.
[24]Ibid., 72-91. The coherentism he adopts is the type inaugurated by W. V. O. Quine.
[25]Placher, *Unapologetic Theology*, 34.
[26]Ibid., 123.
[27]Ibid., 126-37.

is the former. Since foundationalism, as understood by many postliberals, makes universal claims of knowledge as well as an unbroken correspondence between language and the empirical world, and since we know that this is impossible, we must resolutely break with it. It should be noted that this spirited rejection of foundationalism is a move beyond Frei. The master was too circumspect to become heavily involved with philosophy as such in the theological project: "Theology cannot even invest so much in the foundational/anti-foundational debate as to come out (qua theology) in principle on the anti-foundational side."[28]

Narrative as the preferred method for doing theology. One of the, if not the most important, contributions of postliberalism to Christian theology has been its revitalization of narrative for the project of theology.[29] In this respect Hans Frei's *Eclipse of Biblical Narrative* is of great importance and hence needs some unpacking if we are to understand postliberalism.

Frei argues in this book that beginning in the eighteenth century theologians broke with the traditional way of reading biblical narrative. Prior to this, the church read biblical narratives literally. That is, for them the texts simply meant what they said. When reading narrative, even if the ultimate interpretation was spiritual or figural, precritical interpreters first paid their respects to the narrative as such. According to Frei, therefore, the church of this period operated with a strong sense of the realistic nature of biblical narrative.[30] In the eighteenth century, however, with the rise of biblical criticism based on philosophy, a new way of interpreting biblical narrative emerged.

Whereas pre-Enlightenment thought viewed the world in the Bible and the world outside the Bible as commensurate, Enlightenment thought viewed them as separate entities: there was a reality independent of that found in the Bible. No longer could one assume that the world outside the Bible was part of the biblical world continuum. Instead of seeing the contemporary world as in *continuity* with the biblical world, Enlightenment

---

[28]Frei, as quoted by Springs, *Toward a Generous Orthodoxy*, 122.

[29]See the helpful essays in *Scriptural Authority and Narrative Interpretation*, ed. Garrett Green (Philadelphia: Fortress, 1987).

[30]Hans Frei, *The Eclipse of Biblical Narrative: A Study in Eighteenth and Nineteenth Century Hermeneutics* (New Haven, CT: Yale University Press, 1974), 1-3.

thinkers saw it as discontinuous—another entity.[31] What effect did this have on the hermeneutics of biblical narrative? Frei suggests that interpreters no longer read the narrative literally. More specifically, they began to collapse the *meaning* of the story with its *external reference*. At first sight this might not seem at all different from the precritical period: in both accounts the narrative refers to the world. The significant difference, however, is that in the critical period "the world" is one that is *independent* of the biblical world. Thus the modern joining of the meaning of the narrative with its external reference is with an externality that is *separate* from the cosmos of Scripture. This type of new equality between the meaning of the narrative and its reference is, according to Frei, a mistake of category. He says about this: "This coincidence of the story's literal or realistic depiction with its meaning has been taken to be the same thing as the claim that the depiction is an accurate report of actual historical facts. This identification of two different things is a classic instance of a category error."[32]

As a result of this category mistake, the biblical narrative was no longer read for its literal meaning. Conservative interpreters viewed the meaning of the Gospel narratives as the positive, factual affirmation that Jesus was the crucified and raised Messiah.[33] In other words, the narrative did not mean, unless it was first shown that Jesus *really* had been crucified and raised. Liberal interpreters also equated meaning with reference. To be sure, they may have said that what the narrative portrays is "true": yes, Jesus was crucified and raised. But since certain things, according to the liberal mindset, no longer obtained in our world, one must interpret the resurrection of Jesus in a way that is not literal. Thus "Jesus as raised" may be interpreted in an existential manner so that it refers, say, to my weakness one day being turned into power. Or "Jesus as raised" may be a way of saying that evil will not have the final word; and so on. Whatever existential or universal repacking, the meaning of the narrative is *not* its literal sense. The narrative instead becomes an apologetic to support my theological

---

[31]Ibid., 3-8.

[32]Hans Frei, *The Identity of Jesus Christ* (Eugene, OR: Wipf & Stock, 1997), 60.

[33]Henceforth we will focus primarily on the Gospels, since this was the corpus that Frei interacted with mostly.

worldview, whether that be conservative or liberal. I believe this is what Frei means with the following words: "With regard to the gospel narratives, the apologetical impulse from left to right meant that they could finally be interpreted only in two ways. Either their explicative and applicative meaning . . . is that of reference to Jesus as the messiah is historical fact, or . . . this is only their mythological form, their substance being something else."[34] In either case, "Interpretation was a matter of fitting the biblical story into another world with another story rather than incorporating that world into the biblical story."[35] In Frei's opinion, this way of interpreting the Gospels remained until the time he wrote in the twentieth century: biblical narrative had been eclipsed.[36]

How are we to recover biblical narrative? How are we to practice a hermeneutic of the narrative that takes its nature as narrative seriously? Here Frei partially builds on Erich Auerbach's monumental *Mimesis* by suggesting that we understand biblical narrative, the Gospels in particular, as belonging to the category of *realistic narrative*. Auerbach saw the three historical high points of realistic narrative as the Bible, Dante's *Divine Comedy* and the nineteenth-century novel.[37] Realistic narrative, as Frei reconstructs the genre, shares a number of traits: history-likeness, simplicity of style, lack of artificiality and lack of heroic elevation of characters. Its nature as realistic narrative—and this is something that Frei emphasized strongly—demands that it be interpreted literally. It is worth quoting Frei here: "By speaking of the narrative shape of these accounts, I suggest that what they are about and how they make sense are functions of the depiction or narrative rendering of the events constituting them—including their being rendered, at least partially, by the device of chronological sequence."[38] For Frei, the meaning of Jesus in the Gospels is irreducibly linked to its narrative rendering—and this takes us back to the cause of the eclipse of biblical narrative and Frei's solution.

If the Gospels are examples of realistic narrative, and if the meaning of

---

[34]Frei, *Eclipse*, 133. Cf. also 11.
[35]Ibid., 130.
[36]Ibid., 16.
[37]Ibid., 15.
[38]Ibid., 13.

realistic narrative is independent of the veracity of the external world it depicts, then we could move beyond the impasse erected by interpreters of the eighteenth century and beyond.[39] Realistic narrative is the key. The genre demands to be interpreted literally. If we understand (and accept) this, then we could go back to reading the Gospels as they were meant to be read: for their meaning, which is apart from their ostensive reference to the world. Frei's hope was that, irrespective of whether the Gospels' external reference was accurate, we could use them for the task of theology. Frei was saying: You don't have to be obsessed with the external world of the Gospels to do theology—that is, with whether their depiction is accurate or not. Look at what the Gospels communicate narratively about the identity of Jesus Christ. That is your task as a theologian. In other words, Frei wanted to move away from an apologetically driven theology (whether the defense was conservative or liberal) to one that focused on the identity of God in Christ.

POSTLIBERALISM AND THE QUESTION OF TRUTH-CLAIMS

Postliberalism is an attempt to move theology out of the labyrinth into which it was taken by modernity. The false turns that modern theology took were ultimately the cause of an adherence to the epistemology of the period—namely, foundationalism. Its dependence on foundationalism led theology to become above all things apologetic. The main goal of this type of theology was to defend the relevance of the Christian faith for modernity. It tried to do this by translating biblical categories into extrabiblical categories that could appeal to universal reasoning. This type of theology was concretized in both conservatives and liberals, for both fell on the same trap of trying to prove faith by categories external to revelation, especially philosophy. Postliberal theology presents itself as an account of doctrine that finds a third way beyond cognitive-propositional (as, e.g., Carl Henry) and experiential-expressive (as, e.g., Schleiermacher). Or, from the philosophical point of view, it is an attempt to move beyond modernity with its foundationalist epistemology.

---

[39]Note that the move is not *backward* to a precritical stage but forward. Why not? Because Frei accepts the bifurcation of the world of the Bible and the modern world.

How can this be done? Drawing inspiration from a number of theological and philosophical (!) figures like Karl Barth, Ludwig Wittgenstein and Clifford Geertz (anthropologist), postliberals have concluded that theology should be done from an exclusively Christian perspective. Theology is Christian self-description that provides for the church a vocabulary to express itself. It should not be translation of the Christian message but redescription. At its core, theology should be christocentric. It should read the Gospel narratives in a literal sense in order to discover the identity of Jesus Christ.

From the general observations above we must now move to the more particular question of truth-claims in postliberalism. More specifically, what type of justification do they offer for the assertions about the truth of Christian theology? What support do they provide for the strong claims they make concerning Christology, Scripture, church and so on?

Before turning to what postliberals themselves say, we must note here some of the criticisms they have received. To get straight to the point, there are many theologians who conclude that—given postliberals' views on the nature of doctrine, epistemology and narrative—they simply cannot provide the type of justification that engages with those outside the Christian faith. The way they envision theology, it is said, is in principle inadequate for connecting with others on external, objective criteria of corroboration. Thus Sheila Davaney thinks that postliberalism is internal-looking and isolationist. She explains: "A number of postliberals are responding to this charge by calling for an ad hoc apologetics—unsystematic and occasional conversations with other perspectives. . . . Yet postliberals have no basis within their approach for entering these conversations, or, once there, for making them much more than show and tell."[40] Francis Watson, concentrating on Hans Frei's approach to narrative vis-à-vis external reference, also offers a number of criticisms. As Watson sees it, part of Frei's problem stems from his understanding of the Gospels as realistic narrative. In describing this genre, Frei speaks above all of its irreducibility. That is, realistic narrative is from be-

---

[40]Sheila Davaney, "Mapping Theologies," in *Changing Conversations: Religious Reflection and Cultural Analysis*, ed. Dwight N. Hopkins and Sheila Davaney (New York: Routledge, 1996), 30-31. I owe this quotation to Springs, *Toward a Generous Orthodoxy*, 133.

ginning to end *narrative*; it is "history-like," to be sure, but what it is about is the literary depiction of the identity of Jesus Christ.[41] Frei's aversion to the external correspondence of the text lands him in a difficult position when theological questions are posed. Watson suggests that ultimately Frei is not able to show how the literary observation that Jesus is portrayed as raised in the Gospels can transition to faith. And this is a significant problem, for it isolates the text and theology from reality:

> Frei's self-contained text is a privileged space in which one unsubstitutable individual (the reader) encounters another (Jesus). In its largely justified emphasis on the important tautology that narrative is narrative, this herme-neutic of self-containment proves unable to achieve an adequate correlation of the text with the church and the world. Indeed, the perceived need to protect the text from the world may stem from the failure adequately to address the church's proper concern with the fundamental truth of the bib-lical story of salvation: for if, and only if, this story is true, then all worldly reality must be understood in light of it.[42]

It is worth exploring a bit further these perceived shortcomings of postlib-eralism from the three foci of the movement sketched in the previous pages.

First, recall that for postliberals the primary purpose of doctrine is reg-ulative. That is, doctrine is like a grammar that regulates a language. The duty of grammar is to explain how a language works. It does not tell us why there is such a language, where it comes from, or whether it is "true." It exists within the world of the language, and it is not in its power to move beyond or outside language. Doctrine, according to Lindbeck and postlib-erals, is like that: "It is not primarily an array of beliefs about the true and the good (though it may involve these), or a symbolism expressive of basic attitudes, feelings, or sentiments. . . . Rather, it is similar to an idiom that makes possible the descriptions of realities, the formulation of beliefs, and the experiencing of inner attitudes, feelings, and sentiments."[43] The influence

---

[41]Francis Watson, *Text, Church and World: Biblical Interpretation in Theological Perspective* (Edinburgh: T&T Clark, 1994), 20-25.

[42]Ibid., 29.

[43]Lindbeck, *Nature of Doctrine*, 33. In the same paragraph he speaks tellingly of doctrine as similar to the Kantian a priori.

of Wittgenstein is clear here. For Wittgenstein could be called the anti-metaphysic philosopher. He views the work of philosophy not as trying to find "the ghost in the machine," but as descriptive of how things are. Similarly for Lindbeck, doctrine is not firstly about ontological claims but about regulating the life of worship of the church. For many theologians the problem with Lindbeck is what he does *not* say about the correlation of doctrine to ontology, reality.[44] Can Christian theology make justifiable claims that can be engaged in the world outside the church, outside its idiom?

Related to this, of course, is the question of the nature of truth. Lindbeck holds to a conception of truth as "self-involving."[45] In his "Excursus on Religion and Truth" he gives the example of the crusader who cries out "Christus est Dominus" as authorization to bash the skull of the infidel.[46] In this scenario, according to Lindbeck, the statement "Christ is Lord" is a false statement because it does not cohere with the Christian form of life—namely, suffering servanthood. In this account of truth right conduct (as the community construes it) appears to be logically prior to truth.[47] Hunsinger provides a clear explanation: "More precisely, *rightness* becomes a necessary condition for the possibility of *truth*, just because what corresponds to ultimate reality is the religious form of life as such, not minds or sentences independent of that form of life or in conflict with it."[48] Essentially, this immanent account of truth stems from a particular interpretation of Wittgenstein.

But this may be a misreading of Wittgenstein because, in the words of Christopher Insole, it is simultaneously "too Wittgensteinian in some respects, and not Wittgensteinian enough in others."[49] Philosophically,

---

[44]See, e.g., the critique of Miroslav Volf, "Theology, Meaning & Power: A Conversation with George Lindbeck on Theology and the Nature of Christian Difference," in *Nature of Confession*, 45-66.

[45]The phrase is from George Hunsinger, "Truth as Self-Involving: Barth and Lindbeck," in *Disruptive Grace: Studies in the Theology of Karl Barth* (Grand Rapids: Eerdmans, 2000), 305-18.

[46]Lindbeck, *Nature of Doctrine*, 63-69.

[47]Hunsinger, "Truth as Self-Involving," 308.

[48]Ibid. Hunsinger goes on to show in the remainder of this essay that there is on this point a fundamental divergence between Lindbeck and Barth, despite Barth sometimes sounding as if he would adhere to truth as self-involvement.

[49]Christopher Insole, "The Truth Behind Practices: Wittgenstein, Robinson Crusoe and Ecclesiology," *Studies in Christian Ethics* 20 (2007): 364-82.

postliberals like Lindbeck and Stanley Hauerwas tend to read Wittgenstein's account of truth and meaning as *immanent* to practices, in the sense that truth inheres in "the social activities of actual communities."[50] We could call this a metaphysically maximalist interpretation of Wittgenstein. According to Insole, however, it is more correct exegetically to understand Wittgenstein's concentration on performance as a rejection of an empiricist theory of meaning than a positive formulation of the meaning of meaning. All Wittgenstein is saying is the following: "(i) we can use concepts meaningfully, and that (ii) the empiricist theory of meaning does not provide an explanatory account of how we do this."[51] The maximalist reading of Lindbeck that surfaces in the Crusade example takes Wittgenstein into directions that the philosopher probably never intended to go. It is not Wittgensteinian enough in that it does not sufficiently adhere to the nuances of the philosopher.

From a scriptural and theological perspective, it would seem that Lindbeck's account is also problematic because it works with an idealized and therefore flat eschatology. That is, it implies that truth—if I may put it this way—can only flow when the vessel is pure. Yet, we know that in a realistic, already/not yet eschatology, the statement "You are the Christ, the son of the living God," is true even if it comes from the mouth of one who cuts the ear of his enemy and denies with curses the Christ whom he swore to follow.[52]

Moving to the second plank (or circle, if you like) of postliberals, we must briefly discuss their understanding of foundationalism. Postliberals are persuaded that it is impossible to carry on the postliberal project if one operates within a foundationalist epistemology. That may well be true. But the question that needs to be asked is whether postliberals have properly understood foundationalism. For most of the descriptions of foundationalism that one finds in postliberals are really descriptions of *classical*

---

[50]Ibid., 365.

[51]Ibid., 369-70.

[52]Similarly, see ibid., 376: "If meaning, and so truth, are immanent to our practices, and practices are read as being performances of concrete communities, then communities will have complete access to that truth. The prevailing wind—whether we run with it or against it—will be towards an overrealized eschatology, and a triumphalist and separatist ecclesiology." He goes on (378-79) to critique this view by using the examples of the disciples in the Gospel of Mark, including the case of Peter as I have done above.

foundationalism.[53] In reality, in contemporary epistemology, it is more appropriate to speak of foundational*isms*. Postliberals fall into the trap of rejecting some theological positions because they find them to be foundationalist *simpliciter*. But this is not helpful and potentially misleading:

> To describe a position as "foundationalist" without further explanation is to plunge into a swamp of verbal vagueness. The range of positions called "foundationalism" has been expanding by leaps and bounds in recent years, so much so that the expansion is well on the way to the point where the shared property will be little more than *being an epistemological position of which the speaker disapproves*. To be called a "foundationalist" is like being called a "reactionary" in general society. One is not so much described as accused.[54]

This type of misunderstanding, or reductionism, concerning foundationalism leads to a host of theological views being labeled "foundationalists" and therefore being disposed of with disgust. I have found that both postliberals and postconservatives brand certain theologies as foundationalist because they may make the following propositions: there is such a thing as universal truth; I can formulate doctrine on the basis of Scripture; evangelism can be done with more than deeds of love (i.e., proclamation); language can refer truly to predicates about God; and so on. In truth, it seems that anything that is questioned by postmodernity is labeled foundationalist and easily dismissed. William Alston is correct:

> The term "foundationalism" has fallen on hard times, not only because the position is well nigh universally excoriated but also because the term itself is one of the most variously used, and abused, in epistemology. In the hands of one or another writer it is used to designate a commitment to absolute truths (truths not relative to some context, social group, orientation . . .), an uncritical acceptance of dogmas, a realist metaphysics of some sort, etc. etc.[55]

---

[53]See, e.g., Thiemann, Placher.

[54]Nicholas Wolterstorff, *Thomas Reid and the Story of Epistemology* (Cambridge: Cambridge University Press, 2009), 187.

[55]William Alston, *Beyond "Justification": Dimensions of Epistemic Evaluation* (Ithaca, NY: Cornell University Press, 2005), 230.

It is no wonder, then, that one detects a sense of "foundationalist paranoia" among postliberals that leads them to swear off any contact with foundationalism. In my opinion, it is this lack of distinction between classical foundationalism (which should indeed be rejected) and softer types of foundationalism that severely limits Thiemann's work on prevenience. He wants to salvage the doctrine by taking into account, on the one hand, radical pluralism, and, on the other, foundationalism. That is, given that this is now the state of affairs in postmodernity and that foundationalism cannot be used for justification, how could one still rescue prevenience? His solution is to resort to *another* epistemology—namely, a form of coherentism. Yet, it seems to me that Thiemann has gone beyond the ad hoc use of philosophy that his teacher Frei suggested to *basing* his project on a particular epistemology. It is not primarily that Thiemann saw in coherentism a way to *help* redescribe and justify prevenience; it is rather that coherentism is *not* foundationalism. And yet, jumping onto the coherentist bandwagon is no remedy for the justification of a belief. The sort of pure coherentism that Thiemann adopts cannot in the end produce warranted belief, because coherence in *itself* is not a source of warrant.[56] This is not to say that Thiemann had to become a classical foundationalist for his book to be more persuasive. There are other forms of coherentism, in which, for example, coherence can come in the form of relations between beliefs *and* experiences, not just other beliefs. Alvin Plantinga suggests as an example of this the work of F. H. Bradley.[57]

Another example, this time from the postconservative John Franke, shows that a lack of nuance on the different types of foundationalisms can lead to some serious theological problems. Franke believes that basing doctrine solely on Scripture is foundationalist because the movement of warrant goes from the superstructure (various doctrines) down to the foundations (the Bible).[58] And if there is some defect in the foundation (say, contradictions in the Gospel accounts), then all non-

---

[56]See especially Alvin Plantinga, *Warrant and Proper Function* (Oxford: Oxford University Press, 1993), 178-82.

[57]Ibid., 181.

[58]John Franke, *The Character of Theology: A Postconservative Evangelical Approach* (Grand Rapids: Baker, 2005), esp. chaps. 2-3.

foundational beliefs come crashing down. Franke suggests that Christian doctrine must adopt an epistemology of dialogue if it is to escape foundationalism. He thus envisions a conversation between Scripture, the church and culture as a way to formulate doctrine.[59] Each of these sources is to have equal authority in this conversation. If Franke means by this that as we interpret Scripture the church leans on its traditions and can also sometimes learn from culture, then we have no problem. However, if he means that each conversation partner has as much right as the other, then this is simply not Christian theology. To be sure, Franke adds that this must all be done "always in accordance with the normative witness to divine self-disclosure in Jesus Christ."[60] But which Jesus? The biblical, ecclesial or cultural? If Franke says the biblical, then he has fallen back on some form of foundationalism, given his flawed understanding of this epistemology.

It is, I believe, an urgent matter for postliberals and postconservatives to develop a more nuanced understanding of foundationalisms. Again, classical foundationalism has been shown to be fatally flawed because it "is self-referentially incoherent; it does not meet the conditions for justification that it lays down."[61] But it does not follow from this that I cannot base a belief on the merit of another; or that we all now must become coherentists; or even worse, that epistemology is dead or that truth does not exist.[62] Many philosophers and theologians have accepted a more modest form of foundationalism. There is, for example, what has been called Reidian foundationalism. In this form a belief can be basic even if it is not immediately intuited. A number of beliefs on Reidian foundationalism can be properly basic, including testimony.[63] In this form of foundationalism the basic beliefs do not have to be infallible, indubitable or incorrigible to serve as such.[64] In addition, the warrant connections between immediate and supported mediate beliefs can be probabilistic in nature by drawing

---

[59]Ibid., 79.
[60]Ibid., 79-80.
[61]Plantinga, *Warrant and Proper Function*, 182.
[62]Plantinga calls this "a whopping *non-sequitur*" (ibid.).
[63]See Wolterstorff, *Thomas Reid*, 163-84.
[64]See Alston, *Beyond "Justification,"* 232-33.

not only on logical deduction, but also on coherence between one mediate belief and another.[65]

One evangelical theologian who appears to me to be working with a soft model of foundationalism is Kevin Vanhoozer. In his *The Drama of Doctrine: A Canonical-Linguistic Approach to Christian Theology*, he wants to move beyond a purely propositionalist account and a cultural-linguistic one without throwing out some of the good insights of both traditions.[66] The first one can come too close to classical foundationalism; the second can become entirely community based and hence minimize *sola Scriptura* for the ultimate authority of doctrine (e.g., David Kelsey). While viewing the relation between Scripture and community in a more dynamic fashion than many have allowed, Vanhoozer wants at the end of the day to preserve *sola Scriptura* as the ultimate authority of doctrine. But is this not foundationalist? Is this not making the Bible, a document considered by many to be impossibly flawed, into a sort of basic or immediate incorrigible belief, thereby falling into the old trap of modern theology? Vanhoozer answers that this is not the case. In soft-foundationalist fashion he acknowledges the fallibility of his *own* understanding of Scripture; he acknowledges that his linkages of doctrine to Scripture can in fact be flawed; he acknowledges his own situatedness as interpreter. He thus removes the obstacle of classical foundationalism and quickly moves to a formulation of doctrine that stems from careful reflection on Scripture and tradition.[67]

My comments above should not be viewed as a defense of soft foundationalism; they are simply meant to show that there are other alternatives to classical foundationalism and coherentism than postliberals and postconservatives state.

Let us move to a brief exploration of the third concentration of postliberalism that I have sketched—namely, narrative. Frei, as we saw in relation to his groundbreaking *Eclipse of Biblical Narrative*, defended a view of the Gospels as realistic narratives. As such, the Gospels are not first about historicity or symbolism.

---

[65]Ibid., 233. Cf. also Wolterstorff, *Thomas Reid*, 190n2.

[66]Kevin Vanhoozer, *The Drama of Doctrine: A Canonical-Linguistic Approach to Christian Theology* (Louisville, KY: Westminster John Knox, 2005).

[67]Ibid., 291-94. See also idem, "Scripture and Tradition," in *Cambridge Companion to Postmodern Theology*, 162-69.

The Gospels are, quite simply, about what they say. And what they say cannot be separated from the *way* they say it. The Gospels are irreducibly *narrative*. This narrative is crucial for presenting the identity of Jesus Christ.[68] For the identity of an individual in realistic narratives is what the person does and what is done to him or her in temporal sequence: "Indeed, in and by these transpirings he [Jesus] becomes what he is."[69] If the goal of theology is the rendering of Jesus Christ from within Christian logic (not from philosophy), and if the person of Christ is depicted literally in the Gospels, then we can see how essential these narratives are for theology. Frei and postliberals believe that by concentrating on the identity of Christ by means of narrative, they have freed theologians from those shackles that had paralyzed modern theology—the identification of meaning with the external world of the text, whether the connection be historical or symbolic. Since this is not what the text is about, we can get back to doing theology beyond liberalism and conservatism.

But has Frei truly broken through the impasse? There remain some serious questions, the main one being, as I see it, the admittedly complicated correlation of the text to the world.[70] Frei admits that the precritical mindset, where the world of the Bible and ours was continuous, is no longer tenable. Frei accepts the modern split between the "holy" world of Scripture and ours. Our lives are not an unbroken continuation from the last page of an opened Bible that jumps out to today. The Bible is shut, and we live in another world. Are those two worlds to be brought together? Should the two be aligned? For Frei, as a postliberal, the biblical world (i.e., the text) absorbs the "secular" world. But is not the church, although "not of this world," still "*in* the world"? (Jn 17:15-19).[71] For the church to absorb

---

[68]Kevin Vanhoozer, *Biblical Narrative in the Philosophy of Paul Ricoeur: A Study in Hermeneutics and Theology* (Cambridge: Cambridge University Press, 1990), 162, helpfully explains: "What is lost in Ricoeur's account of biblical narrative is precisely what Frei values, namely, the literal specificity of the persons and events—the defining feature of realistic narratives."

[69]Frei, *Theology and Narrative*, 73-74. The echoes of Barth's actualistic ontology are clear here.

[70]This is intimately related to the question of genre. A serious problem with Frei's account is his identification of the Gospels as "realistic narratives." As we discussed in chapter two, it is much more defensible to view New Testament narratives as examples of history: in the case of the Gospels as ancient biographies (which overlap with history); in the case of Acts the historical monograph. Both genres seek to refer to the real world in a significantly stronger way than Frei's (anachronistic?) "realistic narrative."

[71]I take it that when postliberals speak about the text absorbing the world they mean the text of Scripture as embodied in the church: texts don't swallow things.

the world would mean that it is *itself* absorbed, since it lives *in* the world. But is there not here, again, a problem with eschatology? For if the church swallows the world, the "not yet" is finished and all is realized. I sense an eschatological naivete here that is problematic. I fear that Frei's deployment of narrative to go beyond modernity is perhaps a retreat into the conventicle. It has not, at the end of the day, provided a way for theology to engage the world with what it (the church) sees as reality.

And yet, postliberals would insist that they do attempt to engage the public with a nonfideistic presentation of the Christian faith. We conclude this section, therefore, with some examples of their defense. Since space is limited, I will focus my investigation to the two pillars of postliberalism, George Lindbeck and Hans Frei.

George Lindbeck. A generous reading of *The Nature of Doctrine* may lead to the conclusion that although Lindbeck would affirm the central doctrines of Christianity, he nevertheless does not view his goal as a defense of them, at least in this particular book. Rather, since his view of theology is that it is a second-order activity only, his job is to comment on and describe doctrine, not engage on the validity of first-order assertions.[72] A more pessimistic reading could conclude that at best Lindbeck is a Christian fideist, and at worst a religious relativist. Evangelicals have expressed concern about this: Would the real Lindbeck please stand up?

In the 1995 Wheaton Theology Conference, Lindbeck was asked in a rather straight manner by Alister McGrath about this: "Let me put it this way: What reasons might I give for saying to, for example, a Muslim, that I believe that the community, the narrative, within which I stand has merit over his or hers?"

After speaking about ad hoc apologetics, the need to know the specific background of the person asking the hypothetical question, and his belief that God calls people through the Holy Spirit in various ways, Lindbeck concluded: "We Christians think, look and argue from within

---

[72]See Lindbeck, *Nature of Doctrine*, 65. Cf. also Alister McGrath, "An Evangelical Evaluation of Postliberalism," in *Nature of Confession*, 35-39. On page 46 of *Nature of Doctrine* Lindbeck says this about his work: "It is not the business of a nontheological theory of religion to argue for or against the superiority of any one faith." Can there be such a thing as a "nontheological theory of religion"? Lindbeck sounds a lot like the modernist he is trying to correct!

the faith. There is no way of getting outside the faith to objectively compare different options. Why follow Christ rather than someone else? I find myself thinking very much along the epistemological lines of Alasdair MacIntyre."[73]

Lindbeck is referring to MacIntyre's tradition-based rationality, in which he argues that all forms of rationality are communal. One does not engage or argue with a different tradition from a completely neutral position but always from *within* one's communal context. This does not lead to total relativism or insularity, according to MacIntyre, for communities change and disagree and learn from other communities.[74] Thus Lindbeck's answer is basically a repetition of his argument in *The Nature of Doctrine*. Does he deny that Christians, by a gift of God's grace through his Spirit, have access to God's good news of salvation that, while necessarily contextualized differently in each culture, nevertheless is universally true because it is transcendent? It is difficult to answer. Yet, it is surely ironic that when Lindbeck is asked one of the most basic questions of the Christian faith he resorts to a philosopher, not to Scripture and church tradition.

Hans Frei. As has been indicated in the preceding pages, Frei was not afraid to uphold the central truth-claims of traditional Christianity. He was, however, very guarded on the defense of those claims. That is, he was circumspect in laying out a clear program on how those claims could be defended or suggested to the unbeliever.

An interesting encounter occurred at Yale in 1985 when Frei was asked for more clarity on this matter by Carl F. Henry. In the process of critiquing the "narrative theology" of Gabriel Fackre and Frei, Henry wanted to know whether Frei could affirm the reality of Christ's death and resurrection as a fact outside the text. Did the Gospels refer to an extratextual reality? Frei responded by saying that his concept of reference was not as clear as Henry's. He hints that to possess a very clear understanding of reference as a universal, contextual-free concept was

---

[73]Lindbeck, "Panel Discussion," 252.
[74]See Alasdair MacIntyre, *Whose Justice? Which Rationality?* (Notre Dame: University of Notre Dame Press, 1988).

more philosophical than Henry assumed.[75] Yet, Frei did acknowledge
belief in the historical reality of Christ's death and resurrection. He said:
"If I am asked to use the language of factuality, then I would say, yes, in
those terms I have to speak of an empty tomb. In those terms I have to
speak of the literal resurrection. But I think that those terms are not
privileged, theory-neutral, trans-cultural, an ingredient in the structure
of the human mind and of reality always and everywhere."[76] Thus Frei
was willing to confess the resurrection but was circumspect in just how
the biblical text referred to the external world in such a complicated
event as the resurrection of Jesus.[77] One detects here, perhaps, Frei's
hesitation before the potential specter of foundationalism. It appears
that, for him, to state that the concept of factuality was part of "the
structure of the human mind," thus making the concept universally identical, was to go too far in the foundationalist direction.

So Frei did recognize that the resurrection of Christ was a real event
outside the text. That is a truth-claim; but what about *defending* or *suggesting* that truth-claim to others? I find Frei's clearest reflection on this in
his lecture "Remarks in Connection with a Theological Proposal."[78] After
providing an overview of his theological program, which as we have seen
is inextricably linked to biblical narrative, Frei concludes with the question
of "the transition from the aesthetic, nonapologetic, understanding to the
truth-claim—historical, metaphysical, and existential."[79] To the believer,
he says, the gap between the aesthetic (i.e., the text) and the truth of the
text should present no problem. The Christian simply believes that what
the text says is true. And the nonbeliever? It is worth quoting Frei here: "To
the pilgrim—and who isn't?—the possibility of its truth is not often a
matter of the evidence for it, but of the surprising scramble in our understanding and life that this story unaccountably produces. Understanding
it aesthetically often entails the affirmation and existential commitment

---

[75]Frei, *Theology and Narrative*, 209-10.
[76]Ibid., 211.
[77]For further, persuasive evidence that Frei did believe in the external reference of the Gospels, see Springs, *Toward a Generous Orthodoxy*, 85-103.
[78]Frei, *Theology and Narrative*, 26-44.
[79]Ibid., 43.

that it appears to demand as part of its own storied pattern."[80] This is a fascinating statement, which for me irresistibly leads to comparing it to what happens when one is moved by a piece of art—whether a painting, sculpture, film and so on. The artifact is so powerful that it tears down presuppositions (for example) and provides a fresh way of seeing things. One is so seized by the beauty and profundity of the piece that one is simply changed. We consequently view life in a different way from previously. Whether the painting or literary piece actually depicts a factual event does not initially matter. What matters is that I am changed by the object; there is "a surprising scramble in our understanding and life that this story unaccountably produces." When my understanding surrenders to the story, I (unreflectively at first?) simply confess that the story is true.

I do not wish to simplify the possible account that Frei has put forth. But perhaps he is saying that in our engagement with the nonbeliever our duty is to "tell the story." We should not be concerned with giving evidence. We tell the story of Christ as found in the Gospels, perhaps adding a dash of "ad hoc apologetics" (a favorite phrase of Frei's), and allow the power of the narrative to overcome the individual. In my opinion, this account is better than Lindbeck's, although pneumatologically it is insufficiently robust. Where is the Holy Spirit in the "scrambling" of the individual's worldview? For, as we shall see shortly in Acts, it is the Spirit who has the power to "prick to the heart."

To sum up: given the three orientations—doctrinal, epistemological and methodological—of postliberalism that we have been describing above, it would seem that the positive suggestion and/or defense of the Christian gospel to those outside the church would figure minimally or not at all in its conception of the church. In other words, in view of the commitments they have made in these three areas, it is difficult to see how—logically—a robust postulation and apology for the statement that Jesus is the God incarnate, crucified and raised Lord, who is the only way to the Father in the entire world, could follow.

But perhaps this region of theology is one that postliberals have not

---

[80]Ibid., 43-44.

(yet?) viewed as a direct area of engagement. Perhaps postliberals would like to be viewed as simply a corrective movement in the church vis-à-vis the formulation of Christian doctrine, a doctrine that needed to be urgently rescued from the claws of modernity. And yet, it is difficult to view postliberalism as a mere corrective when its attempts are to remedy areas as fundamental as doctrine, epistemology and method. It would seem that by making such strong statements in these essential areas it must ipso facto be more than a corrective movement. Whether they like it or not, postliberals are in effect saying that this is the way that things should be as we move forward.

And this brings us back to the area of the justification of the truth-claims of the gospel in the public arena: Quite simply, is the postliberal vision (or lack of vision!) biblical? I do not mean, can we find a verse here and there isolated from its context that would prove or disprove in one fell swoop the postliberal way with evangelism? Rather, when viewed in the light of the scriptural current and logic—in short, the biblical worldview—is it biblical? Since this is a book on the Acts of the Apostles, the net cannot be cast very wide canonically. And yet, it would seem that a book that is a portrait of the church in the world would be an excellent place to assess how the church defends (or not) the truth of Jesus, and thereby throw some light on the issue. What we have learned from postliberalism may illuminate how we interpret certain parts of Acts; and Acts may show ways in which postliberalism is deficient.

THE JUSTIFICATION OF TRUTH-CLAIMS IN ACTS

The preface to Luke's Gospel, which as we saw in chapter three also applies to Acts, provides us with a statement of purpose for the two volumes. Luke tells Theophilus that the purpose of his writing is to provide ἀσφάλειαν ("assurance") concerning the things in which the latter has "been instructed" (κατηχήθης). More than likely, Theophilus and the community he represents are already Christians; they have been instructed in Christian teaching (cf. the almost identical vocabulary in Gal 6:6).[81] But now Luke

---

[81] See Loveday Alexander, *The Preface to Luke's Gospel: Literary Convention and Social Context in Luke 1.1-4 and Acts 1.1*, SNTSMS 78 (Cambridge: Cambridge University Press, 1993), 139-41.

wants to ground them further. Therefore he is composing the Gospel of Luke and, as we see from Acts 1:1, also the second volume, which has come to be known as the Acts of the Apostles.

How is Luke going to give Theophilus further assurance of the faith he has been taught? Although the answer to this question is not unequivocal, the emphasis in both volumes that the life, death and resurrection of Jesus as well as the preaching of the gospel to all nations are the fulfillment of Holy Scripture suggests that the assurance has something to do with the *legitimacy* of the Christian faith in the context of Judaism. The different sects within Judaism—Essenes, Sadducees, Pharisees and Christians—were all "religions of the book." They wished to base their legitimacy as the superior expression of Judaism on their reading of the Old Testament. That is, they each argued that the promises of the Old Testament were best seen as fulfilled in *their* movement; they claimed that the Scriptures referred to them. And to speak of "claims" and "arguments" is to introduce the concept of *apologetics* into the discussion.

In fact, the book of Acts has for a long period been viewed as in some sense an apologetic text. Precisely *who* the audience of Luke's apologia is has been vigorously debated. Nevertheless, we can with clean conscience speak of something of a consensus forming in the last twenty years or so. Expressed negatively, the proposal that Acts was written as a direct defense to Greeks or Romans has now collapsed.[82] On the other hand, readings that propose that Luke's defense is primarily to strengthen in some way those who *already* belong to the church have seemed more persuasive. Especially attractive has been the suggestion of Loveday Alexander, who has written that Acts is to be viewed as an apologia in the context of the early struggles between Christians and the synagogue. In her words: "Acts is a dramatized narrative on an intra-community debate, a plea for a fair

---

[82]Some of the scholars responsible for this have been Gregory Sterling, *Historiography and Self-Definition: Josephos, Luke-Acts and Apologetic Historiography*, NovTSup 64 (Leiden: Brill, 1992); Daniel Marguerat, *The First Christian Historian: Writing the "Acts of the Apostles,"* trans. Ken McKinney, Gregory Laughery and Richard Bauckham, SNTSMS 121 (Cambridge: Cambridge University Press, 2002); Loveday Alexander, *Acts in Its Ancient Literary Context: A Classicist Looks at the Acts of the Apostles*, LNTS 289 (London: T&T Clark, 2005). Most recently, see C. Kavin Rowe, *World Upside Down: Reading Acts in the Graeco-Roman Age* (New York: Oxford University Press, 2010).

hearing at the bar of the wider Jewish community in the Diaspora, perhaps especially in Rome."[83] It is worth exploring this proposal a bit further since it will have strong methodological implications for what we are doing in this chapter.

Alexander observes that it is the way of literary apologia such as is found in Acts to create a gap between the audience inscribed in the work and the audience *outside* the work.[84] So for example, while the inscribed audience may be the Jews in Jerusalem on the day of Pentecost (Acts 2) or the Athenians at the Areopagus (Acts 17), the *real* audience outside the work may be neither Jew nor Greek. The situation is similar to the ancient law-courts: there is a speaker who is responding to charges, and there is the tribunal to whom he is responding. But there is also an audience beyond the tribunal, a "public gallery" who is overhearing the speaker: "But the forensic scenario also allows for the presence of a wider 'public gallery' of supporters and spectators, to whom the defendant may covertly appeal."[85] Thus it is probably the case that the "supporters and spectators" outside the book of Acts are Christians, with Theophilus as their representative.[86] In this apologetic scenario, how is it that the characters inscribed in the book (e.g., Peter, Stephen, Paul) reach out to the audience outside the book—that is, the "supporters and spectators"? Alexander suggests that it is the bread and butter of this literary context to address the audience through the medium of *direct speech* from the main characters. The speeches in Acts, therefore, may be viewed as the privileged places where we can explore how Luke appeals to his readers on how to defend the faith before the public.[87]

I suggest, therefore, that when posing the question of how Acts defends the truth-claims concerning Jesus, we explore once again some of its speeches. There are four main audiences who receive speeches in Acts:

---

[83]Alexander, *Acts in Its Ancient Literary Context*, 183-206, at 205.

[84]Ibid., 187-88.

[85]Ibid., 187.

[86]It should be noted that this is my own extension of Alexander's argument, although there are hints in this direction in her work.

[87]Ibid., 190-200. See also Alexandru Neagoe, *The Trial of the Gospel: An Apologetic Reading of Luke's Trial Narratives*, SNTSMS 116 (Cambridge: Cambridge University Press, 2002), who makes a strong argument that especially in the trial narratives the gospel itself is being defended, thereby providing for Theophilus the assurance promised in Lk 1:4.

Jews, God-fearing Gentiles, Greeks, and Roman citizens who have a close connection to Judaism. I thus suggest that in answering the question of this chapter we look at the following speeches, which would comprehensively cover all the audiences: Pentecost (Acts 2), Cornelius (Acts 10), Athens (Acts 17) and Agrippa (Acts 26).

Pentecost. The entirety of the speech of Peter at Pentecost is summarized in Acts 2:36: "Therefore let the entire house of Israel know with certainty that God has made him both Lord and Messiah, this Jesus whom you crucified."[88] We can therefore say that the central thesis of the speech is christological: the Jesus whom they crucified is actually the Lord and the Messiah. With the use of ἀσφαλῶς (see Lk 1:4), Peter wants to lay as much emphasis as possible on this proposition. The question before us now is: How has he sought to argue for this truth-claim?

The answer would seem plain enough: the resurrection. But on closer inspection the matter turns out to be more complex. Recall that what created the possibility for the speech in the first place was the coming of the Spirit with the resultant speaking in tongues. The miracle of tongues triggered the questions of the people and Peter's subsequent explanation of the miracle. This explanation was scriptural (Joel and Psalms) and testimony-based (Acts 2:32). The defense for the assertion that Jesus is the Lord and Messiah is therefore intertwined in the following three areas.

First, there is the miracle. Its effect is succinctly described by the crowd itself: "Amazed and astonished, they asked, 'Are not all these who are speaking Galileans? And how is it that we hear, each of us, in our own native language? . . . In our own languages we hear them speaking about God's deeds of power'" (Acts 2:7-8, 11). But note that the miracle as such is not the proof that Jesus is the Messiah: the miracle needs to be explained christologically to serve as evidence.

Second, there is the scriptural interpretation, which as we saw in chapter five was an example of *pesher*. Thus Peter explains the miracle of tongues by appealing to the prophecy from Joel concerning the Day of the Lord.

---

[88]See Craig Keener, *Acts: An Exegetical Commentary* (Grand Rapids: Baker, 2012–2014), 1:963 (quoting approvingly Barnabas Lindars's *Apologetic*); Daniel Marguerat, *Les Actes des Apôtres (1-12)* (Genève: Labor et Fides, 2007), 94.

The contemporary miracle of speaking in tongues is demonstration that the prophecy has been fulfilled. But a Jewish audience knew that the Day of the Lord could not just come out of the blue without a decisive eschatological act of God. What has happened to activate this event? This leads to the third area of proof.

Jesus, the one crucified, has been raised, exalted to God's right hand, and *he* has poured out the Spirit, which is the fulfillment of the Day of the Lord (Acts 2:24, 32-33). The resurrection of Christ is thus at the bottom of everything that has happened at Pentecost. It is because he has been raised that the miracle of tongues has taken place, which therefore demonstrates that the Scriptures have been fulfilled, which in turn links back to the claim that Jesus is the Messiah. The resurrection of Christ as the fulfillment of Scripture is thus the main statement of evidence. To be noted here is that Peter does not ask the audience to accept the resurrection simply on the basis of the miracle or his interpretation of Scripture. He adds in Acts 2:32, "we are witnesses." The key term μάρτυς is used here, which, as A. A. Trites has persuasively argued, evokes a living metaphor—namely, that of the courtroom. The apostles, because they saw Jesus raised, are presented as witnesses for the resurrection before the public audience.[89]

To sum up: although the resurrection of Jesus is the corroboration for the declaration that he is the Lord and Messiah, it is intertwined with miracle, Scripture and witness. Perhaps one way to put it is that the resurrection *as such* is not offered as evidence for the messianic status of Jesus. *It is the biblically interpreted, testimony-based resurrection in the context of a miraculous deed that is offered as evidence.* Scriptural interpretation without event (i.e., the miracle of tongues) is not sufficient. Resurrection talk *without* the apostles' testimony is not sufficient. Miracle without a scriptural context or an objective correspondence is insufficient. The justification that Jesus of Nazareth is the Messiah is thus an intertwining of the scriptural, the apostolic and the pneumatological (miracle). The dissolution and therefore individuation of these falls short of the biblical model as found in Pentecost.

---

[89]Allison Trites, *The New Testament Concept of Witness*, SNTSMS 31 (Cambridge: Cambridge University Press, 1977), 128-53.

Cornelius. There are a number of significant truth-claims about Jesus offered by Peter in this account. They are the following:

1. Jesus is the medium through which God brings the good news of peace (Acts 10:36a).

2. Jesus is "Lord of all" (Acts 10:36b).

3. God anointed Jesus with the Holy Spirit and power (Acts 10:38a).

4. Jesus did good to all, and healed all those under the power of the devil (Acts 10:38b).

5. God was with Jesus (Acts 10:38c).

6. Jesus was crucified and raised on the third day (Acts 10:39-40a).

7. Jesus is the judge of the living and the dead (Acts 10:42).

8. As the prophets testify, through Jesus forgiveness of sins is given to all who believe (Acts 10:43).

At least two comments can be made from the predicates about Jesus made above. First, although there is no sentence in the indicative saying, "Jesus is the Messiah," clearly this is the sense of Peter's kerygma. To be sure, χριστός is used in apposition to Ἰησοῦ in Acts 10:36, and in Acts 10:38 it is said that God "anointed" (ἔχρισεν) Jesus. So in those senses Jesus is presented as the Messiah. Yet, we find a lot more than a simple appellation: Jesus is *described* as the Messiah, and a Messiah who, while in continuity with Jewish expectations, certainly bursts beyond them. The climax is found in Acts 10:36: "He is Lord of all."

Second, behind the description of Jesus there is a whole catena of Scripture. We had occasion to comment on this in chapter five, so now we simply enumerate them: Deuteronomy 21:22 (cf. Gal 3:13); Psalm 107:20; Isaiah 52:7; 53:4-6; 58:8; 61:1. Thus Peter is making a truth-claim about Jesus before Cornelius that is clothed in the garb of scriptural echoes. According to Luke, how was this claim defended by Peter, and therefore is also to be defended by Luke's present readers?

We should remember, first, that as in the speech at Pentecost so here the wheels are set into motion by a supernatural event. An angel from God appears to Cornelius, instructing him to ask for Simon called Peter who is a guest at the home of Simon the tanner in Joppa.[90] Cornelius sends messengers, and it turns out exactly as the angel predicted. The fulfillment of the angelic words paves the way for Cornelius's acceptance of Peter's message. In fact, when Peter finally enters the home, Cornelius falls and worships him. The act is rejected, of course, but it dramatically shows how persuaded Cornelius is about the divine source of the message he is about to hear. So he tells Peter: "Now we all are here before God [ἐνώποιν τοῦ θεοῦ] to hear all that has been ordered to you by the Lord [ὑπὸ τοῦ κυρίου]" (Acts 10:33, my translation).[91]

Second, just as in Acts 2:33, the combination of resurrection and witness (μάρτυσιν) is used in Acts 10:41. As we saw previously, a juridical metaphor is thus employed: Jesus is the Messiah, and his resurrection as witnessed by the apostles is corroboration of this. Interestingly, Peter adds that they ate and drank with Jesus after his resurrection, and that he commanded them to bear witness (διαμαρτύρασθαι) to the people concerning Jesus' status (Acts 10:41-42). For the readers of Luke-Acts this statement leads back irresistibly to Luke 24:28-49. As we have noted (see chapter three), this is a climactic scene in which the death and resurrection of Jesus are explained by him as the fulfillment of all that was written "in the law of Moses, the prophets, and the psalms" concerning himself as the Messiah (Lk 24:44). Luke adds that Christ "opened their minds to understand the scriptures" (Lk 24:45). Jesus then speaks further about his death and resurrection, and tells the disciples that they are to be witnesses once the Spirit comes on them (Lk 24:46-49). This lengthy scene is epitomized at the beginning of Acts (Acts 1:1-8). The portrait of the raised Jesus explaining Scriptures about himself to his disciples suggests that in order for them to understand the meaning of the resurrection, authoritative commentary on it by Jesus himself is absolutely necessary. Even though they see the raised Jesus, they think he is a ghost (Lk 24:36-41). Christ himself must open their minds (Lk 24:45) so that they could make sense of all that was happening.

---

[90]Some inferior manuscripts (69^mg, vg^cl) add "he will tell you what you must do." This effectively brings forward the statement from Acts 11:14.

[91]𝔓45, 𝔓74, 𝔓127 all read ἀπό, thereby bringing out the sense of source in a stronger way than ὑπό.

As his witnesses, the apostles *continue* the work of Jesus (cf. Acts 1:1, 8) by presenting themselves as witnesses of the *event* of the resurrection as well as explaining the *meaning* of the resurrection.

The third part of evidence in Cornelius's speech is found in Acts 10:43. Whereas in the previous verses Luke has not brought Scripture to the forefront, here he does: "All the prophets testify about him." Luke's choice of words here concerning the work of the prophets is the same he used to describe the work of the apostles: μαρτυροῦσιν. Thus the resurrection as beheld by the apostles testifies in favor of the status of Jesus as the Christ.

Is the work of the Holy Spirit as described in Acts 10:44 the fourth piece of evidence for the status of Jesus? We are told that while Peter was still speaking the Spirit fell on the ones who were listening. It could perhaps be argued that as the members of Cornelius's home were hearing the sermon, the Spirit empowered them to believe, which they did, and consequently spoke in tongues. This seems to be what David Peterson has recently argued: "Cornelius and his household had not yet openly professed faith in Jesus as Lord and Christ, but the Spirit enabled them to respond appropriately to the gospel."[92] Yet, this is not what the text says; there is no comment about the Spirit coming to enable these Gentiles to believe. What is emphasized is the surprising fact that they believed even before Peter encouraged them to do so (thus highlighting the initiative of God). Given the pattern that Luke has presented in Acts, *it is presupposed* that Cornelius and his family believed and *then* were baptized by the Holy Spirit.[93]

In conclusion, we note that there is a similar pattern of justification in the speeches at Pentecost and to Cornelius. An irruption of a transcendent being (the Holy Spirit at Pentecost and the angel to Cornelius) is part of the persuasion for the divine origin of the message to be heard. The resurrection forms a key component in the argument. The motif of the apostles as eyewitnesses is essential. Their witnessing of the resurrection forms the historical evidence of the messianic claims about Jesus. At the same time— and as we saw at Pentecost—the resurrection is a *scripturally mediated and apostolically interpreted* event, and so demands *faith*.

---

[92]David G. Peterson, *The Acts of the Apostles*, PNTC (Grand Rapids: Eerdmans, 2009), 339.
[93]Thus convincingly James Dunn, *Baptism in the Holy Spirit* (Philadelphia: SCM Press, 1970), 79–82.

The main difference between the two speeches is the following. At Pentecost, given that the audience is Jewish, there is a more overt use of Scripture, and the exegetical sophistication is sharper. In the speech to Cornelius the use of Scripture is more in the way of echoes. This is to be expected, since the second audience is composed of venerators of God who would not have much expertise in the use of Scripture.

Athens. We have examined this speech in detail in the previous chapter. Now we approach it with the specific question of evidence for truth-claims in mind. Paul makes a number of truth-claims in this speech (Acts 17:24-29) that are not ones we are concerned with. The reason for this is that these claims would have found broad agreement with his audience. Statements to the fact that God does not dwell in human temples, that he cannot be served by human hands, that in some sense we are his offspring, that he cannot be captured by the construction of images in silver and gold, and so on would all have been affirmed by the majority if not all the ones sitting at the Areopagus. Eckhard Schnabel helpfully speaks of these claims as "points of agreement" in missionary strategy.[94]

Beginning with Acts 17:30, however, Paul is going to make the type of truth-claims that are integral parts of the gospel and therefore would have been hard to accept by the unbelieving audience.[95] Paul now moves to proclamation of the gospel.[96] The principal truth-claim that he makes is the following: "because he has fixed a day on which he will have the world judged in righteousness by a man whom he has appointed" (Acts 17:31). How does Paul seek to prove the veracity of the startling statement—that is, all must repent because one day God will judge all through the man he has appointed?

---

[94]Eckhard Schnabel, *Paul the Missionary: Realities, Strategies and Methods* (Downers Grove, IL: InterVarsity Press, 2008), 171-74.

[95]See helpfully Keener, *Acts*, 3:2667-68, noting that it was rhetorically advisable to leave controversial points to the end of a speech when the audience was hostile. See also Beverly Gaventa, *Acts*, ANTC (Nashville: Abingdon, 2003), 252-3, stating that what comes from Acts 17:30 forward would find disagreement with Paul's audience.

[96]Jacob Jervell, *Die Apostelgeschichte*, KEK 3 (Göttingen: Vandenhoeck & Ruprecht, 1998), 450: "In dem letzten Abschnitt der Rede kommt die Konklusion. Der Stil zeigt, dass jetzt nicht mehr argumentiert, sondern verkündigt wird." ("In the final section of the speech comes the conclusion. The style shows that he is no longer arguing but will proclaim [the gospel].").

The answer is found in the second part of Acts 17:31 and is one of the clearest formulations of the place of the resurrection in the warrant of belief: "and of this he has given assurance to all by raising him from the dead." This is a difficult phrase both syntactically and conceptually. Syntactically, how does the aorist participle ἀναστήσας function in the sentence? It is probably an adverbial participle of means, although one would perhaps have expected it to be in the present tense. If it is a participle of means, we could translate: "giving proof to all *by raising* him from the dead." This would make sense with the use of πίστις here as "proof," rather than the more usual "faith."[97] Conceptually, what does Luke mean by granting proof to *all*? This is strange, since in Acts 10:41 it is specifically stated that when God raised Jesus from the dead he did not make him appear to "all the people, but to the witnesses who ate and drank with him." As we noted in chapter five, the use of πᾶς here is probably due to the universal thrust of the Areopagus speech as well as to alliteration with the start of the letter π in the phrase πίστιν παρασχὼν πᾶσιν. Theologically, the idea may be that proof is in principle available to all who wish to believe. Or the "all" of Acts 17:31 may be read in light of Acts 13:48, a Lukan editorial comment: "When the Gentiles heard this, they were glad and praised the word of the Lord; *and as many as had been destined for eternal life became believers.*"[98]

The speech at the Areopagus is similar in structure to the other speeches examined above. There is a messianic truth-claim, which is then corroborated by appeal to the resurrection of Jesus. At the same time, this speech is different. There is no overt use of Scripture; and although the resurrection is claimed as warrant, there is no mention of Paul or the apostles as privileged eyewitnesses who alone have the authority to explain the resurrection.[99] Instead, the resurrection as proof is in some sense available to "all."

Agrippa. As we saw already in the Areopagus speech, self-defense in Acts can slide almost imperceptibly into gospel preaching. This again is

---

[97] Codex Bezae (D) reads the infinitive παρασχεῖν, thus bringing the usual New Testament meaning of "faith" to πίστις. The translation would be: "*to give* faith to all by having raised Jesus from the dead." The more "difficult" reading should be accepted.

[98] This verse was brought to my attention by Kevin Vanhoozer. Cf. Barth's interesting comments on this verse in *CD* IV.2.804.

[99] Although as we saw in chapter five, Scripture is certainly simmering underneath the discourse.

certainly the case in the speech before Agrippa. As we saw in the previous chapter, the verb ἀπολογέομαι dominates Acts 26; and yet, we find that the bulk of the speech is not a juridical defense but Paul's testimony. To be sure, his testimony is in a sense a defense, for it highlights the resurrection as the issue at hand; and these sorts of ζητήματα were generally viewed by the Romans as having little to do with true breaking of the law. Nevertheless, the principal aim is not to mount a defense as such (which Paul already did in Acts 24:10-21).

Especially in this speech we must return to the insight with which we began this section—namely, that literary apologia is an appeal that goes *beyond* the inscribed audience (in this case Festus, Agrippa and his *consilium*) to the actual readers of the text. The defense to *this* group is that the Christian message is not some aberration that has nothing to do with the Scriptures of Israel. Rather, it is the long-awaited fulfillment that the twelve tribes have been waiting for with perseverance day and night—that is, the resurrection of the dead as promised by Moses and the prophets.

In this context the driving truth-claim is found in Acts 26:22-23: "To this day I have had help from God, and so I stand here, testifying to both small and great, saying nothing but what the prophets and Moses said would take place: that the Messiah must suffer, and that, by being the first to rise from the dead, he would proclaim light both to our people and to the Gentiles." This is a remarkable statement, for it is virtually identical to what Jesus said in Luke 24:44-49. The apostles, and now Paul in particular, are therefore simply *continuing* the message that their master preached. From Jesus to the apostles, the proclamation is that the Messiah, in accordance with the Scriptures, must suffer, be raised and be preached to all the nations, and that this Messiah is Jesus of Nazareth.

As in the speeches at Pentecost and Cornelius the resurrection is presented as evidence for the status of Jesus as the Messiah. However, whereas in the earlier speeches of Peter the evidence of the resurrection was given as a declarative statement: "he was raised from the dead and we are the witnesses," here Paul tells a *story* that elaborates the simple declaration that Jesus was raised and witnessed by the apostles. That is, inasmuch as Paul's testimony refers to an encounter with the living Christ, it serves as warrant for the truth-claim that Jesus is the Messiah who fulfilled the Scriptures by suffering and being raised.

Conclusion. We have discovered in the Acts of the Apostles a broad pattern. The apostles make the truth-claim that Jesus is the Christ, and this truth-claim is corroborated primarily by the declaration that the apostles were eyewitnesses of the resurrection of Jesus, as it (the resurrection) was promised in the Scriptures. We could thus say that the truth-claims were of two types: christological and eschatological. Christologically, the main claims had to do with the identity and work of Jesus: he is the exalted Messiah and Lord through whom forgiveness of sins is granted by faith to all who repent; and he is the one who will judge those who refuse to repent. Eschatologically, the main claims had to do with the dawn of the Day of the Lord by the giving of the Spirit. We could also say that the Messiah's forgiveness and judgment also belong with eschatology, since in Scripture Christology and eschatology are intertwined.

By way of evidence to the messianic truth-claim, we saw the following: miracles, fulfillment of Scripture and the resurrection of Christ. Miracles were powerful works of God that opened the door for proclamation from Scripture. The Scriptures were explained as finding their telos in the sufferings and resurrection of Jesus. Last, the resurrection as explained by Jesus and witnessed by the apostles was a constant line of justification for the message of the church.

Although the resurrection is scripturally and apostolically mediated and therefore more than concrete fact, emphasis is put on the reality that *the apostles were eyewitnesses of the resurrection*. They saw him. It is remarkable how in all the speeches examined (minus Areopagus) stress was laid on the apostles' not only seeing but also speaking and dining with Christ. Indeed, without this the kerygma is incomplete. And this is not just the case in Acts but also in Paul:

> For I handed on to you as of first importance what I in turn had received: that Christ died for our sins in accordance with the scriptures, and that he was buried, and that he was raised on the third day in accordance with the scriptures, and that he appeared to Cephas, then to the twelve. Then he appeared to more than five hundred brothers and sisters at one time, most

of whom are still alive, though some have died. Then he appeared to James, then to all the apostles. Last of all, as to one untimely born, he appeared also to me. (1 Cor 15:3-8)

The risen Christ as witnessed by the apostles and others is thus the "factual" piece of evidence for the universal truth-claim that Jesus is Lord and Messiah. Without this the kerygma would be irrational and fideistic.

Does this mean that in the kerygmatic presentation of Acts we have both a faith-based argument (the Scriptures) and an empirically based one (the apostles *saw* Jesus resurrected)? Is the logic of becoming a Christian one that operates with a "reasonable" mixture of revelation on the one hand and facts outside revelation on the other? I think that this would be a grave misreading of Acts. And the reason is the following: *the eyewitness encounters between the apostles and the risen Christ are all scripturally mediated.* The apostles simply cannot understand the meaning of the risen Christ. They even thought he was a ghost (Lk 24:37)! He had to open their eyes so that they could understand the Scriptures and thereby understand him (Lk 24:45). Their comprehension of the risen Christ is opened through that which is written in Moses, the prophets and the Psalms. What they see (the raised Christ) passes through the filter of Scripture with the result that their observation and understanding of Christ is not some neutral, "empirical" event outside of faith. Luke certainly affirms that the apostles in fact saw the corporeally raised Christ; but they do not "see" Christ from an independent, nonrevelatory perspective. We thus have a paradox or dialectic: yes, the resurrection of Jesus is a historical fact that the apostles appeal to in corroborating the truth-claim about Jesus as Messiah; but that fact is passed on to them by the risen Jesus through the lens of Scripture so that it is at the same time revelation. The result is an irreducible tension.[100]

CONCLUSIONS

To complete this chapter it is time to offer some concrete theses on the conversation between postliberals and Acts as it relates to the offering and

---

[100]For similar observations but with less emphasis on the facticity of the resurrection (although not a denial) see Watson, *Text, Church and World*, 288-93.

justification of evangelistic truth-claims. There will be two areas where Acts can provide a serious challenge to the postliberal program; there will be one area where thoughtful interaction with postliberalism can refine our understanding of Acts.

First, there is nothing innovative in saying that proclamation and defense of that proclamation is found on almost every page of Acts. Acts is about preaching the gospel, a kerygma that already incorporates within it an apologia for its truthfulness.[101] This is another way of saying that Lukan theology is at its core missional theology.[102] The good news that God through Jesus Christ is calling all nations, regardless of their previous rebellions, to repentance and forgiveness of sins is constitutive of the theology of Acts. Ultimately, missions is theological, and theology is missional, because it stems from the character of God:

> Theology too is missiological: its subject matter, nothing less than God's triune mission to the world; its goal, to enable Christians in any and every time or culture to participate fittingly in that same mission. *Christian mission and theology alike involve ministering the gospel to culture in words and acts of truth, love, and justice that correspond to, participate in, and render the prior triune mission.*[103]

A church, therefore, that is not missional is not a church. And as we have seen, inasmuch as mission involves the proclamation of the gospel, its defense is done with boldness, παρρησία (Acts 2:39; 4:12, 29).

This is missing in most representatives of postliberalism.[104] There is a timidity here that is evident in both Lindbeck's and Frei's work, and that, as far as I can see, has not been remedied in the new generation of postliberals. There is certainly in Lindbeck a concern with other faiths. But the farthest he goes is to speak about "dialogue." In fact, when he speaks of *solus*

---

[101]It is my opinion that C. H. Dodd, *The Apostolic Preaching and Its Development* (London: Hodder & Stoughton, 1936), minimized the apologetic dimension of the *kerygma*, often stating that this was part of the *teaching* of the church, not its gospel preaching.

[102]See Peter O'Brien, *Gospel and Mission in the Writings of Paul: An Exegetical and Theological Analysis* (Grand Rapids: Baker, 1995). On the New Testament as whole, see Jostein Ådna and Hans Kvalbein, eds., *The Mission of the Early Church to Jews and Gentiles*, WUNT 1.127 (Tübingen: Mohr Siebeck, 2000).

[103]Vanhoozer, *Drama of Doctrine*, 313.

[104]An exception is Douglas Harink, *Paul Among the Postliberals: Pauline Theology Beyond Christendom and Modernity* (Grand Rapids: Brazos, 2003), 255-60.

Christus, he speaks of this being the case in what he calls a prospective possibility of salvation. That is, once eschatological clarity occurs at the moment of death, the individual, in order to be saved, must approach God through Christ *alone.* The individual, according to Lindbeck, does not have to reach a decision in this life when there is such eschatological obscurity. When the veil is lifted at death, however, sufficient clarity is available for the person judiciously to choose Christ alone or not. It is with this firmly in mind that Lindbeck proposes we approach Christianity's relation with other faiths.[105]

I must confess that I find this proposal quite removed from Scripture, particularly as it relates to the biblical concept of faith. But we must add something else that is troubling with respect to Lindbeck. When speaking about interreligious dialogue he immediately frames the issue as *solus Christus* and those who have never heard. In other words, Lindbeck completely sidesteps (the much more common situation) where the gospel is *actually* preached to those who are not Christians (Hindus, Muslims, etc.), where the gospel is actually *heard.* How is dialogue to take place in *this* context? It is amazing to me that Lindbeck straightaway jumps to the "never heard" scenario without commenting on the often-daily reality of the encounter between Christianity and other religions.

Another attempt to move forward in this area of postliberalism is found in C. C. Pecknold. He sees postliberalism as primarily a program that seeks to remove the obstacles that stand in the way of a broken church.[106] If postliberalism were successful, the church would be able to provide a "more authentic witness to God and neighbor."[107] In his proposal to transform postliberal theology he further adds: "The ambition of postliberalism should be seen as calling for nothing less than another reformation—one that puts a premium on rethinking fractured relationships from the inside-out, both within the church *and beyond its gates.*"[108] The italicized words look promising from the perspective of the type of Christianity

---

[105]Lindbeck, *Nature of Doctrine,* 53-63.
[106]Pecknold, *Transforming Postliberal Theology,* 1-12, 108-12.
[107]Ibid., 1.
[108]Ibid., 108; emphasis added.

described in Acts. But disappointment follows when Pecknold, in the context of the conversation that Christianity ought to have with other religions, adds that the goal should be conversing with those outside the faith so that there would be "deeper participation *in one's own tradition* [in context, Christianity and Judaism], *and so enable that tradition a greater faithfulness, applicability and intelligibility through the transforming presence of God's Word in the communal reading of Scripture.*"[109] I doubt that Paul suffered as he did in his missionary journeys and incarcerations in order that Jews would become more faithful Jews *outside Christ*. Is the missional work of the church to teach Hindus how to be better Hindus, or Muslims how to be better Muslims?

Frankly, what is missing in postliberal engagement with those outside the Christian faith is talk about *conversion*. Not coercion, much less violence; not colonization or acculturation. But conversion that comes as a result of the movement of the Holy Spirit through weak, broken and yet loving and serving vessels. Christians who love even when there is no prospect of conversion but who wisely, patiently "give an account of the hope that is" in them. Anything less than an invitation through words and deeds to follow Christ is foreign to Acts. For in Acts—and the New Testament—Jesus is the Lord who demands the allegiance of all.

A second area where postliberalism is found deficient in light of the way Acts defends evangelistic truth-claims is its use—or nonuse—of the resurrection in a positive apologetic argument.[110] To be sure, postliberals, in line with classic, orthodox Christianity, affirm the bodily resurrection of Jesus. This is not in question. What is in question is why, in contrast to what we have seen in Acts, the resurrection is not appealed to as a positive argument in the context of interreligious dialogue, a situation that is inescapable in our contemporary condition?

---

[109]Ibid., 111; emphasis added.

[110]By a "positive" apologetic argument I mean that the community not only defends its doctrines but also "tries to show that its doctrines are superior, cognitively, epistemically, or ethically, to those of competing religious communities" (Paul J. Griffiths, *An Apology for Apologetics: A Study in the Logic of Interreligious Dialogue* [Maryknoll, NY: Orbis Books, 1991], 60). For a balanced and well-argued account of apologetics see James K. Beilby, *Thinking About Christian Apologetics: What It Is and Why We Do It* (Downers Grove, IL: InterVarsity Press, 2011).

We should recall here that postliberals, when pressed on the question of apologetics (however it be construed), do not deny that it should be done. The key phrase, beginning with Frei, is "ad hoc apologetics." So most postliberals do believe that the church has a duty in this area. As we saw with Frei (and here he has been followed by most of his students), the nonbeliever comes to faith in Jesus by listening to the story of the Gospels. We could perhaps extrapolate from this that the apologetic duty of the Christian community is to tell the story of Jesus, in word and sacrament. In this sense, therefore, postliberals do present the resurrection as reason to believe (and much more), for the resurrection is narrated in the Gospels. Thus the resurrection does figure in, because it is in the Bible. You should believe that Jesus was raised, a postliberal would say, because the Bible says so. I cannot see evangelicals having a problem with this statement!

But what happens when this statement is challenged or flatly contradicted? What happens when the nonbeliever asks: What is it about the Bible that demands my trust? Why should I believe *it* instead of (fill in the blank)? Then the nature of the Bible comes into focus. This is the case when we dialogue with "secular" people who reject on naturalistic grounds and such the possibility of resurrection; or when discussing with other religions that (whether believing in resurrection or not) do not accept the Gospels' account of Jesus' resurrection. At this point, the postliberal tendency for an immanent epistemology and a view of biblical narrative that minimizes its correspondence to the real world (however analogical that correspondence may be) gags the apologetic possibility. For New Testament narratives such as the Gospels and Acts, being historical documents (see chapter two), claim a match between that which is written and the external world written about. As such, when we today appeal to the resurrection of Christ as evidence of our gospel claims, we are saying that one should believe because the resurrection happened and was witnessed by the apostles. We appeal to the Bible because we believe that it is the *inscripturated testimony of the apostles*, a testimony that has been empowered by the Holy Spirit and as such encourages us to give it our full trust.[111]

---

[111]See now also Mats Wahlberg, *Revelation as Testimony: A Philosophical-Theological Study* (Grand Rapids: Eerdmans, 2014), who points out that many contemporary philosophers view testimony as a rational base for belief. I thank Kevin Vanhoozer for pointing me to this recent work.

It is the word of God. McGrath was on target in this criticism of post-liberalism:

> The specific criticism that evangelicalism directs against postliberalism at this point is the following: the prioritization of Scripture is not adequately grounded at the theological level. In effect, the priority of Scripture is defended on grounds that appear to be cultural, historical or contractual. The role of the Qu'ran within Islam could be justified on similar grounds. The normative role of Scripture within the Christian community is unquestionably Christian . . . but is it *right*? For the evangelical, truth claims cannot be evaded at this juncture. Scripture has authority not because of what the Christian community has chosen to make of it, but because of what it *is* and what it conveys.[112]

This does not mean that a nonbeliever, before being presented with the gospel, must first be given a course on the doctrine of the Bible that minutely argues for a high view of Scripture![113] Many come to faith without having worked out a robust doctrine of the Bible (myself included). However, it is the duty of the church, as an instrument of God, to *sustain* the faith of those who have believed; or to guide those who are searching. And here a solid theological account of the divine nature of Scripture is necessary.

Let us now, last, move to an area where postliberalism can help us in understanding how the resurrection can function as a truth-claim. While postliberalism, when put in front of the mirror of the Acts of the Apostles, has failed in the *missional* aspect of theology and in emphasizing the resurrection as an event that serves as apologetic evidence (because it is based on divine, authoritative testimony), it nevertheless can help us understand the, for lack of a better phrase, "transcendent aspect" of the resurrection as found in Acts.

In much traditional evangelical apologetics the resurrection has been presented as an extrascriptural fact for which little or no faith is necessary. Yes, you might doubt the fulfillment of the Scriptures in Christ; yes, you

---

[112]McGrath, "Evangelical Evaluation," 40.

[113]Although it cannot be denied that, for many, coming to faith in Christ is a slow process where numerous, thoughtful discussions about the Bible precede the climactic "moment(s)" of believing in Christ.

might doubt the miracles reported in the New Testament. But the resurrection, it is often said or implied, does not require that much faith. The
women saw him (and who in the ancient world was going to use women
as the first eyewitnesses?)! The apostles ate with him! And look at their
changed lives: they would not have given their lives for Christ had he remained in the tomb after a criminal's death. These arguments (and I believe
that they are indeed powerful arguments) are sometimes presented as
quasi-mathematical equations that one links together in a completely rational way. The resurrection is presented as a proven fact that anyone who
still possesses reason should naturally welcome.

But this is not the way the resurrection is understood in Acts. To be sure,
its facticity is never in question. But facticity, if this implies something that
happens outside revelation and therefore not as God's gracious disclosure,
is not the whole story. Here I think that among postliberals the work of
Frei in particular can help in providing refinement to the understanding of
the resurrection as presented in the Gospels and Acts.

We recall from a previous section that Frei, when questioned by Carl F.
Henry, affirmed the bodily resurrection of Jesus.[114] There is, however, a
nuance in Frei's exposition that I believe guards against the dissolving of
the dialectic of the resurrection present in Acts. I here depend partly on
George Hunsinger's afterword to Frei's *Theology and Narrative*, which I
think is a sound explanation of Frei's sometimes-difficult language about
the resurrection.

Frei notes what I have observed in Acts—namely, that the resurrection
of Christ, while presented as evidence, cannot be apprehended in a positivistic, neutral, independent manner outside the mediation of Scripture.
The resurrection is therefore what he calls a "self-warranting fact." In this
scenario "we have no direct epistemic access apart from the narratives
themselves."[115] While I think that Frei's understanding of the nature of the
narratives is deficient (that is, generically and pneumatologically deficient), his insight is nevertheless instructive. How is it that we have access
to the accounts of the resurrection of Jesus? It is not through "historical

---

[114]He had affirmed this on other occasions as well.
[115]Frei, *Theology and Narrative*, 266.

Jesus" reconstruction; it is not through our own putting together of the resurrection events. Rather, we have access only *through God*. Our only access to the resurrection is pneumatological—that is, through the Scriptures given by the Spirit. For what is Acts and the New Testament if not the Spirit-inspired inscripturation of the apostolic testimony? This means, therefore, that the resurrection of Jesus, although a fact, cannot be properly grasped by us as independent entities outside revelation. The resurrection, in other words, can only be salvifically engaged when we allow *God* to tell us what it means; and here the operative word is faith. And it is only the Holy Spirit, in an act of grace, who can grant us that faith to believe, "lest anyone should boast."

BIBLIOGRAPHY

Adams, Sean A. *The Genre of Acts and Collected Biography.* SNTSMS 156. Cambridge: Cambridge University Press, 2013.

———. "The Genre of Luke and Acts: The State of the Question." In *Issues in Luke-Acts: Selected Essays,* edited by Sean A. Adams and Michael Pahl, 97-120. Piscataway, NJ: Gorgias, 2012.

Ådna, Jostein, and Hans Kvalbein, eds. *The Mission of the Early Church to Jews and Gentiles.* WUNT 1.127. Tübingen: Mohr Siebeck, 2000.

Aletti, Jean-Noël. *Quand Luc Raconte: Le Récit comme Théologie.* Lire la Bible 115. Paris: Les Éditions du Cerf, 1998.

Alexander, Loveday. *Acts in Its Ancient Literary Context: A Classicist Looks at the Acts of the Apostles.* LNTS 289. London: T&T Clark, 2005.

———. "Memory and Tradition in the Hellenistic Schools." In *Jesus in Memory: Traditions in Oral and Scribal Perspectives,* edited by W. H. Kelber and S. Byrskog, 113-53. Waco, TX: Baylor University Press, 2009.

———. *The Preface to Luke's Gospel: Literary Convention and Social Context in Luke 1.1-4 and Acts 1.1.* SNTSMS 78. Cambridge: Cambridge University Press, 1993.

Alston, William. *Beyond "Justification": Dimensions of Epistemic Evaluation.* Ithaca, NY: Cornell University Press, 2005.

Aune, David. *The New Testament in Its Literary Environment.* LEC 8. Philadelphia: Westminster Press, 1987.

Avenarius, Gert. *Lukians Schrift zur Geschichtsschreibung.* Meisenheim/Glan: Hain, 1956.

Barclay, John M. G. *Against Apion: Translation and Commentary.* Vol. 10 of *Flavius Josephus: Translation and Commentary,* edited by S. Mason. Leiden: Brill, 2007.

Barnes, T. D. "An Apostle on Trial." *JTS* 20 (1969): 407-19.

Barrett, C. K. *The Acts of the Apostles.* 2 vols. ICC. London: T&T Clark, 1994–1998.

Barth, Karl. *Protestant Theology in the Nineteenth Century: Its Background and History.* Translated by Brian Cozens and John Bowden. London: SCM Press, 1972.

Bauckham, Richard J. *Jesus and the Eyewitnesses: The Gospels as Eyewitness Testimony.* Grand Rapids: Eerdmans, 2006.

Baur, F. C. *Paul the Apostle of Jesus Christ: His Life and Works, His Epistles and His Teachings.* Translated by A. Menzies. Peabody, MA: Hendrickson, 2003.

Behr, John. *Irenaeus of Lyons: Identifying Christianity.* Oxford: Oxford University Press, 2013.

Beilby, James K. *Thinking About Christian Apologetics: What It Is and Why We Do It.* Downers Grove, IL: InterVarsity Press, 2011.

Bock, Darrell. *A Theology of Luke and Acts: God's Promised Program, Realized for All Nations.* Grand Rapids: Zondervan, 2012.

Bonz, Marianne Palmer. *The Past as Legacy: Luke-Acts and Ancient Epic.* Minneapolis: Fortress, 2000.

Bovon, François. *L'Évangile selon Saint Luc.* 4 vols. CNT IIIa-IIId. Genève: Labor et Fides, 1991–2009.

Bowie, Ewen. "The Ancient Readers of the Greek Novels." In *The Novel in the Ancient World,* edited by Gareth Schmeling, 87-106. Leiden: Brill, 1996.

Bruce, F. F. *Biblical Exegesis in the Qumran Texts.* Grand Rapids: Eerdmans, 1960.

———. *The Book of the Acts.* Rev. ed. NICNT. Grand Rapids: Eerdmans, 1988.

———. *The Speeches in Acts.* London: Tyndale, 1943.

Burke, Peter. "History of Events and the Revival of Narrative." In *New Perspectives on Historical Writing,* edited by Peter Burke, 283-300. University Park: Pennsylvania State University Press, 1992.

———. "Overture: The New History, Its Past and Its Future." In *New Perspectives on Historical Writing,* 1-24.

Burridge, Richard A. *What Are the Gospels? A Comparison with Graeco-Roman Biography.* 2nd ed. Grand Rapids: Eerdmans, 2004.

Byrskog, Samuel. *Story as History—History as Story: The Gospel Tradition in the Context of Ancient Oral Historiography.* WUNT 1.123. Tübingen: Mohr Siebeck, 2000.

Cadbury, Henry Joel. "Commentary on the Preface of Luke." In *BegChr* 2:489-510. London: Macmillan, 1922.

———. "The Identity of the Editor of Luke and Acts: The Tradition." In *BegChr* 2:209-64. London: Macmillan, 1922.

———. *The Making of Luke-Acts.* 2nd ed. London: SPCK, 1968.

Cathey, Robert Andrew. *God in Postliberal Perspective: Between Realism and Non-Realism.* Surrey, UK: Ashgate, 2009.

Clark, Elizabeth. *History, Theory, Text: Historians and the Linguistic Turn.* Cambridge, MA: Harvard University Press, 2004.

Clivaz, Claire. *L'Ange et la Sueur de Sang (Lc 22, 43-44). Ou Comment on Pourrait Bien Encore Écrire l'Histoire.* Biblical Tools and Studies 7. Leuven: Peeters, 2010.

Cohen, Shaye J. D. *The Beginnings of Jewishness: Boundaries, Varieties, Uncertainties.* Berkeley: University of California Press, 1999.

Conzelmann, Hans. *The Theology of St. Luke.* New York: Harper & Row, 1960.

Croce, Benedetto. *Aesthetic as Science of Expression and General Linguistic.* 2nd ed. Translated by Douglas Ainslie. London: Peter Owen, 1953.

Darr, J. A. "Irenic or Ironic? Another Look at Gamaliel." In *Literary Studies in Luke-Acts: Essays in Honor of Joseph B. Tyson,* edited by R. P. Thompson and T. E. Phillips, 121-40. Macon, GA: Mercer University Press, 1998.

Davaney, Sheila. "Mapping Theologies." In *Changing Conversations: Religious Reflection and Cultural Analysis,* edited by Dwight N. Hopkins and Sheila Davaney, 25-58. New York: Routledge, 1996.

DeHart, Paul J. *The Trial of the Witnesses: The Rise and Decline of Postliberal Theology.* Malden, MA: Blackwell, 2006.

Den Boer, Pim. *History as Profession: The Study of History in France, 1818–1914.* Translated by Arnold J. Pomerans. Princeton, NJ: Princeton University Press, 1998.

Dibelius, Martin. *Book of Acts: Form, Style, and Theology.* Minneapolis: Fortress Press, 2004.

———. *Studies in the Acts of the Apostles.* Translated by M. Ling. Edited by H. Greeven. London: SCM Press, 1956.

Dodd, C. H. *The Apostolic Preaching and Its Development.* London: Hodder & Stoughton, 1936.

Dubrow, Heather. *Genre.* London: Methuen, 1982.

Duff, David, ed. *Modern Genre Theory.* London: Longman, 2000.

Dunn, James D. G. *Baptism in the Holy Spirit.* Philadelphia: SCM Press, 1970.

Eckey, Wilfried. *Das Lukasevangelium Unter Berücksichtigung seiner Parallelen. Teilband II: 11,1-24,53.* 2 vols. Neukirchen-Vluyn: Neukirchener, 2004.

Ehrman, Bart. *Lost Christianities: The Battle for Scripture and the Faiths We Never Knew.* Oxford: Oxford University Press, 2003.

Ellis, Earle. "'The End of the Earth' (Acts 1:8)." *BBR* 1 (1991): 123-32.

Feldman, Louis H. *Judean Antiquities 1-4: Translation and Commentary.* Vol. 3 of *Flavius Josephus: Translation and Commentary,* edited by S. Mason. Leiden: Brill, 2000.

Fish, Stanley. *Is There a Text in This Class? The Authority of Interpretive Communities.*
    Cambridge, MA: Harvard University Press, 1982.

Fletcher, J. H. "Rahner and Religious Diversity." In *The Cambridge Companion to Karl
    Rahner,* edited by D. Marmion and M. E. Hines, 235-48. Cambridge: Cambridge
    University Press, 2005.

Fletcher-Louis, C. H. T. "God's Image, His Cosmic Temple and the High Priest: To-
    wards an Historical and Theological Account of the Incarnation." In *Heaven and
    Earth: The Temple in Biblical Theology,* edited by T. D. Alexander and Simon J. Gath-
    ercole, 81-99. Carlisle, UK: Paternoster, 2004.

Fornara, Charles. *The Nature of History in Ancient Greece and Rome.* Berkeley: Uni-
    versity of California Press, 1983.

Fowler, Alastair. *Kinds of Literature: An Introduction to the Theory of Genres and Modes.*
    Oxford: Oxford University Press, 1982.

Franke, John. *The Character of Theology: A Postconservative Evangelical Approach.*
    Grand Rapids: Baker, 2005.

Frei, Hans. *The Eclipse of Biblical Narrative: A Study in Eighteenth and Nineteenth
    Century Hermeneutics.* New Haven, CT: Yale University Press, 1974.

———. *The Identity of Jesus Christ.* Eugene, OR: Wipf & Stock, 1997.

———. *Theology and Narrative: Selected Essays.* Edited by George Hunsinger and
    William Placher. Oxford: Oxford University Press, 1993.

———. *Types of Christian Theology.* Edited by George Hunsinger and William Placher.
    New Haven, CT: Yale University Press, 1992.

Frow, John. *Genre.* London: Routledge, 2005.

Gabba, Emilio. *Dionysius and The History of Archaic Rome.* Berkeley: University of
    California Press, 1991.

Gadamer, Hans-Georg. *Truth and Method.* Translated by Joel Weinsheimer and
    Donald G. Marshall. 2nd ed. New York: Continuum, 2003.

Garrity, Thomas. "Thucydides 1.22.1: Content and Form in the Speeches." *AJP* 119
    (1998): 361-84.

Gärtner, Bertil. *The Areopagus Speech and Natural Revelation.* ASNU 21. Lund: Gleerup, 1955.

Gaventa, Beverly. *The Acts of the Apostles.* ANTC. Nashville: Abingdon, 2003.

Gempf, Conrad. "Historical and Literary Appropriateness in the Mission Speeches of
    Paul in Acts." PhD dissertation. University of Aberdeen, 1988.

———. "Public Speaking and Published Accounts." In *The Book of Acts in Its Ancient
    Literary Setting,* edited by Andrew D. Clarke and Bruce W. Winter, 259-303. Vol. 1
    of *The Book of Acts in Its First Century Setting,* edited by Bruce Winter. Grand
    Rapids: Eerdmans, 1993.

Gill, C., and T. P. Wiseman, eds. *Lies and Fiction in the Ancient World*. Exeter, UK: University of Exeter Press, 1993.

Ginzburg, Carlo. *The Cheese and the Worms: The Cosmos of a Sixteenth-Century Miller*. Translated by John and Anne Tedeschi. Baltimore: Johns Hopkins University Press, 1980.

Goh, Jeffrey C. K. *Christian Tradition Today: A Postliberal Vision of Church and World*. Louvain: Peeters, 2000.

Gomme, A. W. *A Historical Commentary on Thucydides*. Vol. 1. Oxford: Clarendon, 1959.

Goodman, Martin. *The Roman World 44 BC–AD 180*. London: Routledge, 1997.

Green, Garrett, ed. *Scriptural Authority and Narrative Interpretation*. Philadelphia: Fortress, 1987.

Gregory, Andrew. *The Reception of Luke and Acts in the Period Before Irenaeus: Looking for Luke in the Second Century*. WUNT 2.169. Tübingen: Mohr Siebeck, 2003.

Griffiths, Paul J. *An Apology for Apologetics: A Study in the Logic of Interreligious Dialogue*. Maryknoll, NY: Orbis Books, 1991.

Haenchen, Ernst. *The Acts of the Apostles: A Commentary*. Translated by R. M. Wilson. Philadelphia: Westminster Press, 1971.

Hahneman, Geoffrey. *The Muratorian Fragment and the Development of the Canon*. Oxford: Clarendon, 1992.

Harink, Douglas. *Paul Among the Postliberals: Pauline Theology Beyond Christendom and Modernity*. Grand Rapids: Brazos, 2003.

Hays, Richard B. *Reading Backwards: Figural Christology and the Fourfold Gospel Witness*. Waco, TX: Baylor University Press, 2014.

Hemer, Colin. *The Book of Acts in the Setting of Hellenistic History*. WUNT 1.49. Tübingen: Mohr Siebeck, 1989.

Hengel, Martin. *The Four Gospels and the One Gospel of Jesus Christ: An Investigation of the Collection and Origin of the Canonical Gospels*. Translated by John Bowden. Harrisburg, PA: Trinity Press International, 2000.

Higton, Mike. *Christ, Providence & History: Hans W. Frei's Public Theology*. London: T&T Clark, 2004.

Hilgert, Earle. "Speeches in Acts and Hellenistic Canons of Historiography and Rhetoric." In *Good News in History: Essays in Honor of Bo Reicke*, edited by L. Miller, 83–109. Atlanta: Scholars Press, 1993.

Hirsch, E. D. *Validity in Interpretation*. New Haven, CT: Yale University Press, 1967.

Homeyer, Helen. *Lukian, Wie man Geschichte schreiben soll. Herausgegeben, übersetzt und erläutert*. München: W. Fink, 1965.

Hornblower, Simon. *A Commentary on Thucydides*. Vol. 1. Oxford: Clarendon, 1991.

Hubbard, Moyer. "Urban Uprisings in the Roman World: The Social Setting of the Mobbing of Sosthenes." *NTS* 51 (2005): 416-28.

Hunsinger, George. *Disruptive Grace: Studies in the Theology of Karl Barth*. Grand Rapids: Eerdmans, 2000.

———. "Postliberal Theology." In *The Cambridge Companion to Postmodern Theology*, edited by Kevin J. Vanhoozer, 42-57. Cambridge: Cambridge University Press, 2003.

Hurst, André. *Lucien de Samosate: Comment Écrire l'Histoire. Introduction, Traduction et Notes*. Paris: Belles Lettres, 2010.

Iggers, Georg. *Historiography in the Twentieth Century: From Scientific Objectivity to the Postmodern Challenge*. Middletown, CT: Wesleyan University Press, 1997.

———. *New Directions in Historiography*. Rev. ed. Middletown, CT: Wesleyan University Press, 1984.

———, ed. *The Theory and Practice of History*. London: Routledge, 2011.

Insole, Christopher. "The Truth Behind Practices: Wittgenstein, Robinson Crusoe and Ecclesiology." *Studies in Christian Ethics* 20 (2007): 364-82.

Instone-Brewer, David. *Prayer and Agriculture*. Vol. 1 of *Traditions of the Rabbis from the Era of the New Testament*. Grand Rapids: Eerdmans, 2004.

Jervell, Jacob. *Die Apostelgeschichte*. Meyers Kommentar III. Göttingen: Vandenhoeck & Ruprecht, 1988.

———. *The Theology of the Acts of the Apostles*. Cambridge: Cambridge University Press, 1996.

Jipp, Joshua. "Paul's Areopagus Speech of Acts 17:16-34 as *Both* Critique and Propaganda." *JBL* 131 (2012): 567-88.

Kagan, D. "The Speeches in Thucydides and the Mytilene Debate." *Yale Classical Studies* 24 (1975): 71-94.

Kamitsuka, David. *Theology and Contemporary Culture: Liberation, Postliberal and Revisionary Perspectives*. Cambridge: Cambridge University Press, 1999.

Kee, H. C. *Good News to the Ends of the Earth: The Theology of Acts*. London: SCM Press, 1990.

Keener, Craig. *Acts: An Exegetical Commentary*. 3 vols. Grand Rapids: Baker, 2012–2014.

Keylor, William. *Academy and Community: The Foundation of the French Historical Profession*. Cambridge, MA: Harvard University Press, 1975.

Knight, John Allan. *Liberalism Versus Postliberalism: The Great Divide in Twentieth-Century Theology*. Oxford: Oxford University Press, 2013.

Langlois, Charles, and Charles Seignobos. *Introduction aux Études Historiques*. Paris: Hachette, 1926.

Lash, Nicholas. *Theology on the Way to Emmaus.* London: SCM Press, 1986.

Levinskaya, Irina. *The Book of Acts in Its Diaspora Setting.* Vol. 5 of *The Book of Acts in Its First Century Setting,* edited by Bruce W. Winter. Grand Rapids: Eerdmans, 1996.

Lindbeck, George. *The Nature of Doctrine: Religion and Theology in a Postliberal Age.* Philadelphia: Westminster, 1985.

Lowenthal, David. *The Past is a Foreign Country.* Cambridge: Cambridge University Press, 1985.

Lüdemann, G. *Early Christianity According to the Traditions in Acts: A Commentary.* Translated by John Bowden. Minneapolis: Fortress, 1989.

MacDonald, Dennis. *Does the New Testament Imitate Homer? Four Cases from the Acts of the Apostles.* New Haven, CT: Yale University Press, 2003.

MacIntyre, Alasdair. *Whose Justice? Which Rationality?* Notre Dame: University of Notre Dame Press, 1988.

Mainville, O. "De Jésus à l'Église. Étude Rédactionnelle de Luc 24." *NTS* 51 (2005): 192-211.

Mallen, Peter. *The Reading and Transformation of Isaiah in Luke-Acts.* LNTS 367. London: T&T Clark, 2008.

Marguerat, Daniel. *The First Christian Historian: Writing the "Acts of the Apostles."* Translated by Ken McKinney, Gregory J. Laughery and Richard Bauckham. SNTSMS 121. Cambridge: Cambridge University Press, 2002.

———. *Les Actes des Apôtres 1-12.* CNT Va. Genève: Labor et Fides, 2007.

Marincola, John. *Authority and Tradition in Ancient Historiography.* Cambridge: Cambridge University Press, 1997.

———. "Genre, Convention, and Innovation in Greco-Roman Historiography." In *The Limits of Historiography: Genre and Narrative in Ancient Historical Texts,* edited by Christina Shuttleworth Kraus, 281-324. Leiden: Brill, 1999.

Marshall, I. Howard. "Acts and the 'Former Treatise.'" In *The Book of Acts in Its Ancient Literary Setting,* edited by Andrew D. Clarke and Bruce W. Winter, 163-82. Vol. 1 of *The Book of Acts in Its First Century Setting,* edited by Bruce Winter. Grand Rapids: Eerdmans, 1993.

———. *The Gospel of Luke: A Commentary on the Greek Text.* NIGTC. Grand Rapids: Eerdmans, 1978.

———. *Luke: Historian and Theologian.* 3rd ed. Downers Grove, IL: InterVarsity Press, 1998.

Marshall, I. Howard, and David Peterson, eds. *Witness to the Gospel: The Theology of Acts.* Grand Rapids: Eerdmans, 1998.

Martin, Victor, and Rodolphe Kasser, eds. *Papyrus Bodmer XIV-XV: Évangiles de Luc et Jean. Vol. 1, Papyrus Bodmer XIV: Évangile de Luc chap. 3-24*. Cologny-Geneva: Bibliotheca Bodmeriana, 1961.

Matthews, Shelly. *Perfect Martyr: The Stoning of Stephen and the Construction of Christian Identity*. New York: Oxford University Press, 2010.

McCormack, Bruce. *Orthodox and Modern: Studies in the Theology of Karl Barth*. Grand Rapids: Eerdmans, 2008.

McGing, Brian. *Polybius' Histories*. Oxford: Oxford University Press, 2010.

McGrath, Alister. "An Evangelical Evaluation of Postliberalism." In *The Nature of Confession: Evangelicals & Postliberals in Conversation*, edited by Timothy R. Philipps and Dennis L. Ockholm, 23-44. Downers Grove, IL: InterVarsity Press, 1996.

Menzies, R. P. *Empowered for Witness: The Spirit in Luke-Acts*. London: T&T Clark, 2004.

Metzger, Bruce. *The Canon of the New Testament*. Oxford: Clarendon, 1987.

Metzger, Bruce, and Bart Ehrman. *The Text of the New Testament: Its Transmission, Corruption, and Restoration*. 4th ed. Oxford: Oxford University Press, 2005.

Moessner, David P. "'Eyewitnesses,' 'Informed Contemporaries,' and 'Unknowing Inquirers': Josephus' Criteria for Authentic Historiography and the Meaning of ΠΑΡΑΚΟΛΟΥΘΕΩ." *NovT* 37 (1996): 105-22.

Momigliano, Arnaldo. "The Place of Herodotus in the History of Historiography." In *Studies in Historiography*, 127-42. London: Weidenfeld and Nicolson, 1966.

Moore, Stephen D. *Literary Criticism and the Gospels: The Theoretical Challenge*. New Haven, CT: Yale University Press, 1989.

Neagoe, Alexandru. *The Trial of the Gospel: An Apologetic Reading of Luke's Trial Narratives*. SNTSMS 116. Cambridge: Cambridge University Press, 2002.

Novick, Peter. *That Noble Dream: The "Objectivity Question" and the American Historical Profession*. Cambridge: Cambridge University Press, 1988.

O'Brien, Peter. *Gospel and Mission in the Writings of Paul: An Exegetical and Theological Analysis*. Grand Rapids: Baker, 1995.

Ochs, Peter. *Another Reformation: Postliberal Christianity and the Jews*. Grand Rapids: Baker, 2011.

O'Neill, J. C. *The Theology of Acts in its Historical Setting*. 2nd ed. London: SPCK, 1970.

Osborne, Grant. *The Hermeneutical Spiral: A Comprehensive Introduction to Biblical Interpretation*. Downers Grove, IL: InterVarsity Press, 1993.

Padilla, Osvaldo. "Hellenistic παιδεία and Luke's Education: A Critique of Recent Approaches." *NTS* 55 (2009): 416-37.

———. "Postconservative Theologians and the Authority of Scripture." In *"My Words Shall Never Pass Away": The Enduring Authority of the Christian Scriptures*, edited by D. A. Carson. Grand Rapids: Eerdmans, 2016.

———. *The Speeches of Outsiders in Acts: Poetics, Theology and Historiography.* SNTSMS 144. Cambridge: Cambridge University Press, 2008.

Palmer, Darryl. "Acts and the Ancient Historical Monograph." In *The Book of Acts in Its Ancient Literary Setting,* edited by Andrew D. Clarke and Bruce W. Winter, 1-30. Vol. 1 of *The Book of Acts in Its First Century Setting,* edited by Bruce Winter. Grand Rapids: Eerdmans, 1993.

Pao, David. *Acts and the Isaianic New Exodus.* WUNT 2.130. Tübingen: Mohr Siebeck, 2000.

Pearl, Matthew. *The Dante Club.* New York: Random House, 2003.

Pecknold, C. C. *Transforming Postliberal Theology: George Lindbeck, Pragmatism and Scripture.* London: T&T Clark, 2005.

Penner, Todd. *In Praise of Christian Origins: Stephen and the Hellenists in Lukan Apologetic Historiography.* Emory Studies in Early Christianity. New York: T&T Clark, 2004.

Pervo, Richard. *Acts: A Commentary.* Hermeneia. Minneapolis: Fortress, 2009.

———. "Direct Speech in Acts and the Question of Genre." *JSNT* 28 (2006): 285-307.

———. *Profit with Delight: The Literary Genre of the Acts of the Apostles.* Philadelphia: Fortress, 1987.

Peterson, David G. *The Acts of the Apostles.* PNTC. Grand Rapids: Eerdmans, 2009.

Phillips, Thomas E. "The Genre of Acts: Moving Toward a Consensus?" *CBR* 4 (2006): 365-96.

Phillips, Thomas R., and Dennis L. Okholm, eds. *The Nature of Confession: Evangelicals & Postliberals in Conversation.* Downers Grove, IL: InterVarsity Press, 1996.

Pinnock, Clark. *A Wideness in God's Mercy: The Finality of Jesus Christ in a World of Religions.* Grand Rapids: Zondervan, 1992.

Placher, William. *Unapologetic Theology: A Christian Voice in a Pluralistic Conversation.* Louisville, KY: Westminster John Knox, 1989.

Plantinga, Alvin. *Warrant and Proper Function.* Oxford: Oxford University Press, 1993.

Plümacher, Eckhard. "Die Apostelgeschichte als historische Monographie." In *Les Actes des Apôtres. Traditions, Rédaction, Théologie,* edited by J. Kremer, 457-66. BETL 48. Leuven: Leuven University Press, 1979.

Poland, Lynn M. *Literary Criticism and Biblical Hermeneutics: A Critique of Formalist Approaches.* Chico, CA: Scholars Press, 1985.

Porter, Stanley. "Thucydides 1.22.1 and Speeches in Acts: Is There a Thucydidean View?" *NovT* 32 (1990): 121-42.

Powell, Mark Allan. *What Is Narrative Criticism?* Minneapolis: Fortress, 1990.

Praeder, Susan M. "Jesus-Paul, Peter-Paul, and Jesus-Peter Parallelism in Luke-Acts: A

History of Reader Response." In *SBL 1984 Seminar Papers*, edited by Kent Harold Richards, 23-39. Chico, CA: Scholars Press, 1984.

Rahner, Karl. "Anonymous and Explicit Faith." In *Theological Investigations*, 16:52-60. New York: Crossroad, 1979.

Reardon, B. P., ed. *Collected Ancient Novels*. Berkeley: University of California Press, 1989.

Reynolds, J., and R. Tannenbaum, eds. *Jews and Godfearers at Aphrodisias: Greek Inscriptions with Commentary*. Cambridge: Cambridge University Press, 1987.

Ricoeur, Paul. *Time and Narrative*. Translated by Kathleen Blamey and Davie Pellauer. 3 vols. Chicago: University of Chicago Press, 1984–1988.

Ringer, Fritz. *The Decline of the German Mandarins: The German Academic Community, 1890–1933*. Cambridge, MA: Harvard University Press, 1969.

Rosner, Brian. "Acts and Biblical History." In *The Book of Acts in Its Ancient Literary Setting*, edited by Andrew D. Clarke and Bruce W. Winter, 65-82. Vol. 1 of *The Book of Acts in Its First Century Setting*, edited by Bruce Winter. Grand Rapids: Eerdmans, 1993.

Rothschild, Clare K. *Luke-Acts and the Rhetoric of History*. WUNT 2.175. Tübingen: Mohr Siebeck, 2004.

Rowe, C. Kavin. *Early Narrative Christology: The Lord in the Gospel of Luke*. BZNW 139. Berlin: Walter de Gruyter, 2006.

———. "The Grammar of Life: The Areopagus Speech and Pagan Tradition." *NTS* 57 (2011): 31-50.

———. *World Upside Down: Reading Acts in the Graeco-Roman Age*. New York: Oxford University Press, 2009.

Russell, D. A., and M. Winterbottom, eds. *Classical Literary Criticism*. Oxford: Oxford University Press, 1989.

Sanders, John. *No Other Name: An Investigation into the Destiny of the Unevangelized*. Grand Rapids: Eerdmans, 1992.

Sandnes, Karl Olav. "*Imitatio Homeri*? An Appraisal of Dennis R. MacDonald's 'Mimesis Criticism.'" *JBL* 112 (2005): 715-32.

———. "Paul and Socrates: The Aim of Paul's Areopagus Speech." *JSNT* 50 (1993): 13-26.

Scharlemann, Martin H. *Stephen: A Singular Saint*. AnBib 34. Rome: Pontifical Biblical Institute, 1968.

Schmeling, Gareth., ed. *The Novel in the Ancient World*. Leiden: Brill, 1996.

Schnabel, Eckhard J. *Paul the Missionary: Realities, Strategies and Methods*. Downers Grove, IL: InterVarsity Press, 2008.

Schwartz, Daniel R. *2 Maccabees*. Commentaries on Early Jewish Literature. Berlin: Walter de Gruyter, 2008.

Scott, James M. "Acts 2:9-11 as an Anticipation of the Mission to the Nations." In *The Mission of the Early Church to Jews and Gentiles*, edited by Jostein Ådna and Hans Kvalbein, 87-123. WUNT 2.127. Tübingen: Mohr Siebeck, 2000.

Segal, Alan. *Paul the Convert: The Apostolate and Apostasy of Saul the Pharisee*. New Haven, CT: Yale University Press, 1990.

Shauf, Scot. *Theology as History, History as Theology: Paul in Ephesus in Acts 19*. BZNW 133. Berlin: Walter de Gruyter, 2005.

Soards, Marion. *The Speeches in Acts: Their Content, Context, and Concerns*. Louisville, KY: Westminster John Knox, 1994.

Spencer, F. Scott. "Acts and Modern Literary Approaches." In *The Book of Acts in Its Ancient Literary Setting*, edited by Andrew D. Clarke and Bruce W. Winter, 381-414. Vol. 1 of *The Book of Acts in Its First Century Setting*, edited by Bruce Winter. Grand Rapids: Eerdmans, 1993.

Springs, Jason. *Toward a Generous Orthodoxy: Prospects for Hans Frei's Postliberal Theology*. Oxford: Oxford University Press, 2010.

Stanton, Graham. *Jesus and Gospel*. Cambridge: Cambridge University Press, 2004.

————. *Jesus of Nazareth in New Testament Preaching*. SNTSMS 27. Cambridge: Cambridge University Press, 1974.

Sterling, Gregory. *Historiography and Self-Definition: Josephos, Luke-Acts and Apologetic Historiography*. NovTSup 64. Leiden: Brill, 1992.

————. Review of Marianne Palmer Bonz, *The Past as Legacy: Luke-Acts and Ancient Epic*. CBQ 63 (2001): 334-35.

Sternberg, M. *The Poetics of Biblical Narrative: Ideological Reading and the Drama of Literature*. Bloomington: University of Indiana Press, 1985.

Strange, Daniel. *The Possibility of Salvation Among the Unevangelised: An Analysis of Inclusivism in Recent Evangelical Theology*. Paternoster Biblical and Theological Monographs. Carlisle, UK: Paternoster, 2001.

Syme, Ronald. *Sallust*. Berkeley: University of California Press, 1964.

Thiemann, Ronald. *Revelation and Theology: The Gospel as Narrated Promise*. Notre Dame: University of Notre Dame Press, 1985.

Thiselton, Anthony. *New Horizons in Hermeneutics: The Theory and Practice of Transforming Biblical Reading*. Grand Rapids: Zondervan, 1992.

Thompson, Alan J. *The Acts of the Risen Lord Jesus: Luke's Account of God's Unfolding Plan*. NSBT 27. Downers Grove, IL: InterVarsity Press, 2011.

Thornton, Claus-Jürgen. *Der Zeuge des Zeugen: Lukas als Historiker der Paulusreisen*. WUNT 1.56. Tübingen: Mohr Siebeck, 1991.

Toomer, G. J. "Aratus." In *The Oxford Classical Dictionary*, 13-37. 3rd ed. Oxford: Oxford University Press, 2005.

Trites, Allison. *The New Testament Concept of Witness*. SNTSMS 31. Cambridge: Cambridge University Press, 1977.

Tyson, Joseph. *Marcion and Luke-Acts: A Defining Struggle*. Columbia: University of South Carolina Press, 2006.

Van der Horst, P. W. "Drohung und Mord schnaubend (Acts IX 1)." *NovT* 12 (1970): 256-69.

Vanhoozer, Kevin J. *Biblical Narrative and the Philosophy of Paul Ricoeur: A Study in Hermeneutics and Theology*. Cambridge: Cambridge University Press, 1990.

———. "Discourse on Matter: Hermeneutics and the 'Miracle' of Understanding." In *Hermeneutics at the Crossroads*, edited by Kevin Vanhoozer, James K. A. Smith and Bruce Ellis Benson, 3-34. Bloomington: Indiana University Press, 2006.

———. *The Drama of Doctrine: A Canonical-Linguistic Approach to Christian Theology*. Louisville, KY: Westminster John Knox, 2005.

———. *Is There a Meaning in This Text? The Bible, the Reader, and the Morality of Literary Knowledge*. Grand Rapids: Zondervan, 1998.

Veyne, Paul. *Did the Greeks Believe in Their Myths?* Chicago: University of Chicago Press, 1988.

Vielhauer, Philipp. "On the 'Paulinism' of Acts." In *Studies in Luke-Acts*, edited by Leander E. Keck and J. Louis Martyn, 33-50. Nashville: Abingdon, 1966.

Villalba, Pere. *The Historical Method of Flavius Josephus*. ALGHJ 19. Leiden: Brill, 1986.

Volf, Miroslav. "Theology, Meaning & Power: A Conversation with George Lindbeck on Theology and the Nature of Christian Difference." In *The Nature of Confession: Evangelicals & Postliberals in Conversation*, edited by Timothy R. Philipps and Dennis L. Ockholm, 23-66. Downers Grove, IL: InterVarsity Press, 1996.

von Ranke, Leopold. *The Theory and Practice of History*. Edited and with an introduction by Georg Iggers. London: Routledge, 2011.

Wahlberg, Mats. *Revelation as Testimony: A Philosophical-Theological Study*. Grand Rapids: Eerdmans, 2014.

Walbank, F. W. *A Historical Commentary on Polybius*. 3 vols. Oxford: Oxford University Press, 1957–1979.

———. *Polybius, Rome and the Hellenistic World: Essays and Reflections*. Cambridge: Cambridge University Press, 2002.

Walton, Steve. *Leadership and Lifestyle: The Portrait of Paul in the Miletus Speech and 1 Thessalonians*. SNTSMS 108. Cambridge: Cambridge University Press, 2000.

———. "A Tale of Two Perspectives? The Place of the Temple in Acts." In *Heaven and*

Earth: The Temple in Biblical Theology, edited by T. D. Alexander and Simon J. Gathercole, 135-49. Carlisle, UK: Paternoster, 2004.

Watson, Francis. *Text and Truth: Redefining Biblical Theology*. Grand Rapids: Eerdmans, 1997.

———. *Text, Church and World: Biblical Interpretation in Theological Perspective*. Edinburgh: T&T Clark, 1994.

Weaver, J. B. *Plots of Epiphany: Prison-Escape in the Acts of the Apostles*. BZNW 131. Berlin: Walter de Gruyter, 2004.

Webster, John. *Karl Barth*. 2nd. ed. London: Continuum, 2004.

Wellek, René, and Austin Warren. *Theory of Literature*. London: Penguin, 1949.

White, Hayden. *The Content of the Form: Narrative Discourse and Historical Representation*. Baltimore: Johns Hopkins University Press, 1987.

———. *Metahistory: The Historical Imagination in Nineteenth Century Europe*. Baltimore: Johns Hopkins University Press, 1973.

Wolterstorff, Nicholas. "Resuscitating the Author." In *Hermeneutics at the Crossroads*, edited by Kevin Vanhoozer, James K. A. Smith and Bruce Ellis Benson, 35-50. Bloomington: Indiana University Press, 2006.

———. *Thomas Reid and the Story of Epistemology*. Cambridge: Cambridge University Press, 2009.

Yarbrough, Robert W. *The Salvation Historical Fallacy? Reassessing the History of New Testament Theology*. History of Biblical Interpretation Series 2. Leiden: Deo, 2004.

Author Index

Adams, Sean A., 15, 61
Ådna, Jostein, 101, 237
Ainslie, Douglas, 45
Aletti, Jean-Noël, 69
Alexander, Loveday, 36, 60, 65, 70, 77, 79, 82-86, 99, 145-46, 158, 184, 192, 224-26
Alexander, T. Desmond, 167, 183
Alston, William, 215, 217
Avenarius, Gert, 133, 136
Barclay, John M. G., 79, 83
Barnes, Timothy D., 181
Barrett, Charles K., 161-62, 169-70, 181-82
Barth, Karl, 202-4, 211, 219
Bauckham, Richard J., 36, 53, 75, 225
Baur, F. C., 16, 61, 108
Behr, John, 30
Beilby, James K., 239
Benson, Bruce Ellis, 32
Blamey, Kathleen, 118
Bock, Darrell, 151, 196
Boer, Pim den, 112
Bonz, Marianne Palmer, 53-56
Bovon, François, 81, 90
Bowden, John, 26, 116, 202
Bowie, Ewen, 60
Bruce, F. F., 95, 139, 154-55, 162, 182, 189
Bultmann, Rudolf, 120
Burke, Peter, 116-17
Burridge, Richard A., 43, 45, 52, 70
Byrskog, Samuel, 36, 73, 87, 91, 111, 121, 158
Cadbury, Henry Joel, 24-26, 29, 70, 91, 115

Cathey, Robert Andrew, 201
Clark, Elizabeth, 112, 117
Clarke, Andrew D., 34, 61, 65, 139
Clivaz, Claire, 15, 49-51, 110
Cohen, Shaye J. D., 175-76
Conzelmann, Hans, 116, 126, 151
Croce, Benedetto, 45
Darr, John A., 104
Davaney, Sheila, 211
DeHart, Paul J., 201
Dibelius, Martin, 120, 126, 137, 186
Dodd, Charles H., 237
Dubrow, Heather, 40, 43-44, 49
Dunn, James D. G., 231
Eckey, Wilfried, 81
Ehrman, Bart, 21-22
Ellis, Earle, 99
Feldman, Louis H., 134, 141, 144
Fish, Stanley, 49
Fletcher, Joseph H., 174
Fletcher-Louis, Crispin H. T., 183
Fornara, Charles, 136-37
Fowler, Alastair, 40-41, 46
Franke, John, 216-17
Frei, Hans, 32, 151, 202-5, 207-12, 216, 218-23, 237, 240, 242
Frow, John, 40, 43, 45
Gabba, Emilio, 128, 130
Gadamer, Hans-Georg, 32, 51
Garrity, Thomas, 127
Gärtner, Bertil, 177, 188
Gathercole, Simon J., 167, 183
Gaventa, Beverly, 189, 232
Gempf, Conrad, 139
Gill, Christopher, 72
Ginzburg, Carlo, 119-20
Goh, Jeffrey C. K., 201

Gomme, Arnold W., 126-27
Goodman, Martin, 180
Green, Garrett, 207
Gregory, Andrew, 24-26, 28-29
Griffiths, Paul J., 239
Grosskinsky, August, 126
Haenchen, Ernst, 61, 94-95, 108, 115, 137, 162-63
Hahneman, Geoffrey, 24
Harink, Douglas, 237
Hays, Richard B., 166
Hemer, Colin, 122-23, 138
Hengel, Martin, 26-29, 31
Higton, Mike, 201, 205
Hilgert, Earle, 132
Hines, Mary E., 174
Hirsch, Eric D., 40
Homeyer, Helen, 136
Hopkins, Dwight N., 211
Hornblower, Simon, 126
Horst, Pieter W. van der, 105
Hubbard, Moyer, 94
Hunsinger, George, 203-4, 213, 242
Hurst, André, 132, 135
Iggers, Georg, 109, 111
Instone-Brewer, David, 170
Jervell, Jacob, 65, 151, 153, 171, 177-78, 232
Jipp, Joshua, 177, 181, 185
Kagan, Donald, 127
Kamitsuka, David, 201
Kasser, Rodolphe, 22
Keck, Leander E., 21
Kee, Howard C., 151
Keener, Craig, 61, 64, 95, 99, 122-23, 156-57, 161-63, 168, 171, 227

Kelber, Werner H., 158
Keylor, William, 111-12
Kilburn, K., 132
Knight, John Allan, 201
Kraus, Christina Shuttleworth, 47
Kremer, Jacob, 63
Kvalbein, Hans, 101, 237
Langlois, Charles, 112
Lash, Nicholas, 147
Laughery, Gregory J., 53, 75, 225
Levinskaya, Irina, 176
Lindbeck, George, 32, 202-3, 212-14, 220-23, 237-38
Lowenthal, David, 117
Lüdemann, Gerd, 116
MacDonald, Dennis, 56-57
MacIntyre, Alasdair, 221
Mainville, Odette, 90
Mallen, Peter, 193
Marguerat, Daniel, 21, 53, 75, 91, 98, 101, 105, 153, 157, 169, 225, 227
Marincola, John, 47-48, 64-65, 73, 83
Marmion, Declan, 174
Marshall, Donald G., 32
Marshall, I. Howard, 13, 70, 81, 151
Martin, Victor, 22
Martyn, James Louis, 21
Mason, Steve, 79, 134
Matthews, Shelly, 33
McCormack, Bruce, 204
McGing, Brian, 128-29
McGrath, Alister, 220, 241
McKinney, Ken, 53, 75, 225
Menzies, Allan, 108
Menzies, Robert P., 154
Metzger, Bruce, 22, 24
Meyer, Eduard, 126
Miller, Ed L., 132
Moessner, David P., 86
Momigliano, Arnaldo, 73
Moore, Stephen D., 33
Neagoe, Alexandru, 226
Novick, Peter, 113-14
O'Brien, Peter, 237
Ochs, Peter, 201-2
Okholm, Dennis L., 202

O'Neill, John C., 151
Osborne, Grant, 125
Padilla, Osvaldo, 34, 53, 66, 102, 104, 142-43, 201
Pahl, Michael, 61
Palmer, Darryl, 61-64, 66
Pao, David, 81, 96, 99
Pearl, Matthew, 41
Pecknold, Chad C., 201-2, 238-39
Pellauer, David, 118
Penner, Todd, 137, 162, 167
Pervo, Richard, 58-60, 177, 179, 186
Peterson, David G., 151, 231
Phillips, Thomas E., 61
Phillips, Timothy R., 202
Pinnock, Clark, 174-76
Placher, William, 151, 202, 204, 206, 215
Plantinga, Alvin, 216-17
Plümacher, Eckhard, 63, 132
Poland, Lynn M., 32
Pomerans, Arnold J., 112
Porter, Stanley, 127
Powell, Mark Allan, 33
Praeder, Susan M., 101
Rahner, Karl, 174
Ranke, Leopold von, 109-10, 113-14
Reardon, Brian P., 58, 60
Reynolds, Joyce, 176
Richards, Kent Harold, 101
Ricoeur, Paul, 32, 51, 75, 118-20, 219
Ringer, Fritz, 113
Rosner, Brian, 65
Rothschild, Clare K., 92-93, 95
Rowe, Christopher Kavin, 103, 177, 179, 182, 184-85, 188, 190, 194, 225
Russell, Donald A., 43
Sanders, John, 175-76
Sandnes, Karl Olav, 56, 178, 180
Scharlemann, Martin H., 163
Schmeling, Gareth, 58, 60
Schnabel, Eckhard J., 232
Schwartz, Daniel R., 66-67
Scott, James M., 101
Segal, Alan, 115-16
Seignobos, Charles, 112

Shauf, Scot, 116
Smith, Charles F., 126
Smith, James K. A., 32
Soards, Marion, 170, 185
Spencer, F. Scott, 34
Springs, Jason, 201, 207, 211, 222
Stanton, Graham, 29, 172
Sterling, Gregory, 54, 67, 225
Sternberg, Meir, 76
Strange, Daniel, 175
Syme, Ronald, 64
Tannenbaum, Robert, 176
Tedeschi, Anne, 120
Tedeschi, John, 120
Thiemann, Ronald, 200, 202-3, 205-6, 215-16
Thiselton, Anthony, 35
Thompson, Alan J., 170
Thompson, Richard P., 104
Thornton, Claus-Jürgen, 26-27, 29, 74
Toomer, Gerald J., 186
Trites, Allison, 85, 228
Tyson, Joseph B., 51
Usher, Stephen, 130
Vanhoozer, Kevin J., 9, 32, 49, 51, 119, 203, 218-19, 233, 237, 240
Veyne, Paul, 55
Vielhauer, Philipp, 21
Villalba, Pere, 134
Volf, Miroslav, 213
Wahlberg, Mats, 240
Walbank, Frank W., 129
Walton, Steve, 9, 139, 167
Warren, Austin, 44
Watson, Francis, 35, 120, 211-12, 236
Weaver, John B., 104, 106
Webster, John, 203
Weinsheimer, Joel, 32
Wellek, René, 44
White, Hayden, 118
Wilckens, Ulrich, 126, 137
Wilson, Robert M., 94, 162
Winter, Bruce, 34, 61, 65, 139
Winterbottom, Michael, 43
Wiseman, Timothy P., 72
Wolterstorff, Nicholas, 33, 215, 217-18
Yarbrough, Robert W., 76

Subject Index

Acts
 as ancient novel, 58-61
 authorship, 22-31
 date of composition, 51
 as epic, 53-57
 as historical monograph,
  62-74
 and postmodern
  historiography, 116-20
 and professionalization of
  history, 109-16
ancient speech-reporting
 and Dionysius of
  Halicarnassus, 130-32
 and Lucian of Samosata,
  132-35
 and Polybius, 127-29
 and Thucydides, 125-27
"anonymous faith" in Acts, 174-77
apologetics, 235-43
apostolic eyewitness and the
 writing of Acts, 29-31, 35-37
Athens, portrayal of, 177-80
autopsia, 74-88
canon, contribution of Acts to,
 156-59
Christology, 196
emplotment, 57, 76, 118-21
epic. *See* Acts, as epic
epistemology
 and foundationalism, 205-7
 and testimony, 217-18,
  240-41
eyewitnesses, 82-86, 235-42

figural reading in Acts, 165-67
fulfillment of prophecy, 79-82,
 192-93
genre theories, 43-52
 See also Acts, as ancient
  novel; Acts, as epic; Acts,
  as historical monograph
God, doctrine of, in Acts, 195
God-fearers, 174-77
God-fighters, 103-7
Greek philosophy and Acts,
 184-86
historical monograph. *See* Acts,
 as historical monograph
history
 and fiction, 118-20
 postmodern, 116-20
 professionalization of,
  109-16
Jerusalem, 171-72
Luke, identity of, 22-31
narrative techniques in Acts
 dramatic irony, 102-7
 epitomizing, 92-97
 prolepsis, 98-101
 selectivity, 90-92
 syncrisis, 101-2
parallelism between Peter and
 Paul, 173
Paul, speeches of, 177-95, 232-35
Peter, speeches of, 152-61, 168-73,
 227-32
philosophical hermeneutics,
 32-33

pneumatology in Acts, 152-53,
 196-97
politics and Acts, 189-90, 193-95
postliberalism
 and epistemology, 202-7
 history of, 202-10
 and narrative, 207-10
 and the resurrection of
  Jesus, 242-43
 and truth-claims, 210-24
preface of Luke, 77-88
repentance, 187-88
Second Maccabees and Acts,
 65-67
Socrates and Paul, 180-81
Soteriology of Acts, 191-92, 197
speeches in Acts
 and ancient historiography,
  124-38
 as faithful summaries,
  138-46
 and truth, 146-49
Stephen, speech of, 161-68
supernatural interventions in
 Acts, 67-68
temple in Acts, 167-68, 186-87
tongues, 160-61
trinitarian nudges in Acts,
 159-60
truth-claims in Acts, 224-36
Yale school. *See* postliberalism
Zeitgeschichte, 47

Scripture Index

OLD TESTAMENT

GENESIS
1, *183, 185*
1:1, *181*
1:28-30, *182*
17, *176*
22:8, *141*
31:25-38, *143*
39:2, *163*
39:21, *163*
39:23, *163*

EXODUS
3:4-6, *106*
19:16-25, *100*
19:16-19, *152, 160*

DEUTERONOMY
10:17, *170*
11:2, *161*
21:22, *229*
28:49, *99*
32:8, *182*

JOSHUA
24:1-15, *163*

1 SAMUEL
12:1-18, *163*

1 KINGS
8:27, *181*

1 CHRONICLES
25:1, *153*

2 CHRONICLES
19:7, *170*

EZRA
3:1-36, *163*
13:9, *153*

PSALMS
16:8-11, *155*
70:19, *161*
74:17, *182*
104:1, *161*
105:21, *161*
107:20, *170, 229*
110:1, *155*
132:1, *155*
147:18-19, *170*

ISAIAH
2:3, *99*
31:6, *191*
42:5, *181*
44:22, *191*
45:22, *99, 191*
49:6, *99, 191, 193*
51:4, *99*
52:7, *171, 229*
55:4-7, *192*
61:1, *171*
61:1-2, *80*
63:10, *178*
66:1, *181, 187*
66:1-2, *163, 167*

JEREMIAH
16:19, *99*

JOEL
2:28-32, *100, 154*

MICAH
5:11, *153*

ZECHARIAH
10:2, *153*

APOCRYPHA

TOBIT
12:8, *170*
13:13, *99*

JUDITH
5:6-19

WISDOM OF SOLOMON
9:1-9, *181*
15:11, *105*

2 MACCABEES
2:21, *66*
2:22, *66*
2:19-32, *66*
2:32, *66, 70*
3:1-39, *106*
7:19, *103*

NEW TESTAMENT

LUKE
1:1, *77, 79, 80, 81, 82, 87*
1:2, *73, 79, 84, 85*
1:1-2, *86*
1:3, *34, 73, 86*
1:4, *70, 77, 86, 156, 226, 227*
1:1-4, *76*
1:20, *80*
2:15, *81*
3:16, *160*
3:22, *171*
4:18-21, *171*
4:21, *80*
4:43, *102*
8:1, *102*
8:9, *102*
9:47, *180*
21:5-9, *167*
21:5-36, *187*
24, *20, 89, 90, 96*
24:1, *89*
24:1-12, *89*
24:13-29, *102*
24:13-35, *89*
24:13-50, *90*
24:17-18, *102*
24:25, *103*
24:28-49, *230*
24:36, *89*
24:36-41, *230*
24:36-49, *89*
24:37, *236*
24:44, *80, 230*
24:44-48, *158*
24:44-49, *193, 234*
24:44-50, *81, 165*
24:45-49, *81*
24:45, *81, 230, 236*
24:46-48, *81*
24:46-49, *230*
24:47, *99, 160*
24:47-49, *160*
24:48-49, *152*
24:50, *89*
24:50-53, *89*

ACTS
1:1, *225, 231*
1:1-4, *36, 87*
1:1-8, *230*
1:2, *90, 172*

1:2-3, 20
1:3, 90, 102, 172
1:4-8, 152
1:5, 160
1:8, 81, 97, 98, 99, 158,
  160, 193, 195, 231
1:9-11, 67
1:12-26, 90
1:15-26, 56
1:18-19, 171
1:22, 158
1:24-26, 65
2, 19, 101, 107, 188, 196,
  226, 227
2:1-4, 160
2:1-11, 161
2:1-13, 100
2:1-41, 152
2:2, 80
2:2-3, 100
2:2-4, 67
2:3, 160
2:4, 100, 153
2:5, 93
2:5-11, 100, 160
2:6, 161
2:7, 161
2:7-8, 227
2:8, 161
2:9, 98
2:9-11, 101, 161
2:9-12, 93
2:11, 98, 161, 175, 227
2:12, 153
2:13, 19, 100, 153
2:14-20, 100
2:16, 154
2:17, 100
2:17-21, 154, 196
2:19-20, 100
2:21, 100
2:22, 196
2:22-36, 154
2:23, 154, 167, 196
2:24, 155, 171, 228
2:25, 155
2:25-36, 196
2:30-31, 155
2:31, 196
2:32, 155, 188, 227, 228
2:32-33, 228
2:32-34, 97

2:33, 156, 160, 196, 230
2:34, 155
2:36, 97, 156, 196, 227
2:38, 187, 191, 192, 197
2:38-39, 197
2:39, 237
2:40, 197
2:42-47, 93
2:43-44, 93
2:46, 167, 187
2:47, 65, 68, 197
3, 19
3:1, 167
3:1-26, 187
3:11-26, 142
3:15, 171, 188
3:19-20, 187, 191, 197
4:1-22, 98
4:3, 106
4:8, 157
4:10, 171
4:12, 173, 237, 237
4:19, 194
4:21, 106
4:23, 157
4:24-30, 65
4:27, 97
4:29, 237
4:31, 157
4:32-37, 93
4:36-37, 94
5, 56
5:1-11, 93, 98
5:3, 80
5:12, 167
5:13, 187
5:17-41, 98
5:19, 68
5:20, 187
5:28, 80
5:30, 171
5:31, 97, 187, 191, 197
5:35-39, 103
5:40, 106
5:42, 187
6:1-4, 158
6:5, 157, 175
6:11-14, 162
6:13, 162
7, 186
7:1-53, 161
7:2, 163, 167

7:3, 163
7:5, 163
7:6-8, 163
7:9, 163, 167
7:10-11, 163
7:20, 164
7:20-43, 164
7:22, 164
7:23, 80
7:25, 164
7:30-35, 164
7:35, 164
7:36, 164
7:37, 164
7:38, 164
7:39, 164
7:47-50, 195
7:48, 167, 187
7:48-50, 163, 187
7:51-52, 165, 196
7:52, 165, 196
7:54-60, 167
7:54-8:3, 98
7:55, 157
8, 99, 188
8:1, 106, 168
8:4, 106
8:14-25, 173
8:22, 187, 191
8:26-40, 172
8:29, 157
8:39-40, 68
9:1, 105
9:1-2, 98
9:1-29, 105
9:3-18, 68
9:3, 106
9:4, 106
9:15, 92
9:23, 80
9:27, 180
10, 91, 227
10—11, 65, 91, 100, 168
10:1, 176
10:1-11, 56
10:2, 170, 174, 175
10:3, 68
10:4, 175
10:9-15, 173
10:9-16, 68
10:9-48, 197
10:33, 169, 230

10:34, 169
10:34-35, 169, 195
10:34-38, 168
10:36, 170, 196, 229
10:36-43, 169
10:37-39, 171
10:38, 196, 229
10:39, 196
10:39-40, 229
10:40-42, 171
10:41, 158, 172, 188, 230,
  233
10:41-42, 230
10:42, 172, 196, 229
10:43, 172, 192, 197, 229,
  231
10:44, 231
10:44-48, 169, 172
10:45, 168
10:46-47, 169
11, 173
11:14, 230
11:15, 169
11:17, 169, 197
11:17-18, 196, 197
11:18, 169, 187, 191, 197
11:19-21, 100
11:20, 106
11:21, 68
12, 56
12:6-11, 68
12:23, 68
13:2, 68
13:2-4, 65
13:16, 169
13:26, 169
13:31, 188
13:38, 192
13:38-39, 172
13:38-41, 197
13:39, 172, 192
13:43, 175
13:46, 92
13:47, 99, 193
13:48, 233
14:1, 168
14:8-18, 185
14:11, 186
14:15, 185, 188, 192
14:16, 185
14:17, 185
14:19-20, 106

14:22, 189
15, 91, 95, 96, 115
15:1-5, 173
15:1-29, 95, 98
15:4, 95, 96
15:4-6, 95
15:5, 95
15:6, 95, 96
15:7, 95
15:7-11, 91
15:8-11, 197
15:14-18, 92
15:22, 95
15:28, 65
15:36-41, 98
16, 73
16:6, 65
16:7, 65
16:10-16, 22
16:14, 68
16:20-21, 144
16:31, 197
16:37, 145
17, 184, 186, 226, 227
17:1-9, 194
17:5-7, 106
17:6-7, 145
17:12, 168
17:16, 177, 178
17:16-31, 177
17:17, 79, 180
17:18, 179
17:19, 180
17:20, 180
17:21, 179
17:22, 178, 180
17:22-23, 181
17:22-31, 188
17:23, 183
17:24, 181, 185, 187
17:24-25, 181, 195

17:24-28, 184
17:24-29, 181, 232
17:26, 181, 182
17:26-28, 195
17:27, 182
17:29, 184
17:30, 182, 187, 191, 192,
    196, 197, 232
17:30-31, 183
17:31, 183, 187, 195, 232, 233
17:32, 183
18, 189
18:1-3, 91
18:9-10, 65, 68
18:12-13, 106
18:12-15, 190
18:13, 145
18:14-15, 145
19, 99
19:1-7, 197
19:1-41, 94
19:11-12, 69
19:17, 94
19:17-20, 94
19:28-41, 60
20:6, 22
20:7-12, 142
20:18-35, 56, 139
20:21, 192
20:24, 168
21-22, 94
21:22-26, 167, 187
21:27, 94
21:27-36, 94, 106
21:30, 94
22:3-21, 105
22:6, 106
22:7, 106
22:21, 92
23:1, 106
23:6, 106

23:9, 106, 107
23:11, 65, 69, 106
23:12-15, 106
23:19, 180
23:25-30, 190
24, 145, 180
24:2-8, 106
24:10-21, 189, 234
24:24-27, 194
25:6-12, 194
25:11-12, 189
25:19, 190
25:23, 194
25:23–26:1, 60
26, 145, 227, 234
26:1, 189
26:1-32, 189
26:2, 189
26:3, 190
26:5, 190
26:6-8, 190
26:7, 190
26:9-11, 190
26:9-20, 105
26:11, 191
26:13, 106
26:13-18, 191
26:14, 105, 106
26:16, 85, 86
26:17-18, 92
26:18, 172, 191, 197
26:19, 191
26:22-23, 191, 196, 234
26:23, 193, 196
26:24, 189
26:24-29, 191
26:25, 153
26:31-32, 191
28:11-15, 91
28:23-31, 102
28:28, 92

ROMANS
2:4, 182
2:11, 170
10:15, 171

1 CORINTHIANS
15:3-8, 236
15:12-16, 20

2 CORINTHIANS
11:25, 91

GALATIANS
2, 96
2:1-10, 95
2:11-14, 95
3:13, 229
6:6, 224

EPHESIANS
6:9, 170
6:21-22, 71

COLOSSIANS
3:25, 170
4:7-9, 71
4:14, 23
4:16-17, 71

2 TIMOTHY
4:9-10, 23

JAMES
2:1, 170
2:9, 170

1 PETER
5:12, 25

Printed and bound by CPI Group (UK) Ltd, Croydon, CR0 4YY

13/04/2025

14656474-0003